YORK

General

ELIZA

Univers

OCT 14 2003			
NOV 10 2003			

᳀᳀᳀᳀᳀᳀᳀᳀᳀᳀᳀

Piers Plowman

᳀᳀᳀᳀᳀᳀᳀᳀᳀᳀᳀

ELIZABETH SALTER
and DEREK PEARSALL
University of York

EDWARD ARNOLD (Publishers) LTD
41 MADDOX STREET, LONDON, W.1

First published 1967
Reprinted 1968

Boards Edn. SBN: 7131 5323 7
Paper Edn. SBN: 7131 5324 5

PRINTED IN GREAT BRITAIN BY OFFSET LITHOGRAPHY BY
BILLING AND SONS LTD., GUILDFORD AND LONDON

General Preface

The present series of *York Medieval Texts* is designed for undergraduates and, where the text is appropriate, for upper forms of schools. Its aim is to provide editions of major pieces of Middle English writing in a form which will make them accessible without loss of historical authenticity. Texts are chosen because of their importance and artistic merit, and individual volumes may contain a single work, coherent extracts from a longer work, or representative examples of a genre. The principle governing the presentation of the text is to preserve the character of the English while eliminating unnecessary encumbrances such as obsolete letters and manuscript errors. Glossary and explanatory notes operate together to clarify the text; special attention is paid to the interpretation of passages which are syntactically rather than lexically difficult. The Introduction to each volume, like the rest of the apparatus, is designed to set the work in its proper literary context, and to provide the critical guidance most helpful to present-day readers. The intention of the series is exclusively literary: the Editors hope to attract a wider audience not only for works within the accepted literary canon, but also for those which have until now been regarded as 'specialist' in appeal, or which have been presented as if they were.

The offering of the present series of selections from *Piers Plowman* is not difficult to justify in principle. The first part of the poem, the *Vision*, has long been available in the students' editions of Skeat and Davies, but the latter part is known to most readers only by hearsay or in translation. The recent edition of selections by C. H. Wilcockson· (see Bibliography) will do much to remedy this, particularly as regards the great final books, but it still leaves unrepresented the central section of the poem, which, with its intricate allegorical manoeuvring, has claims to be the core of the whole work. The present edition does not aim to offer a skeletal narrative of *Piers Plowman* (the poem is all bone), nor does it offer an anthology of purple passages. Its object is rather to illustrate the major themes of the poem and to indicate its major processes, at the same time giving samples of what is best in Langland's different styles of writing.

Acknowledgements

We are indebted to the Library of University College, London, for making available to us the copy of the rare Huntington Library facsimile of MS HM 143 which belonged to the late Professor R.W. Chambers; and to the British Museum, for providing us with a microfilm of MS Addit. 35157. Our personal thanks are also due to Professor E. Talbot Donaldson for his advice and encouragement in the preparation of this edition, and for the inspiration of his book, which first gave impetus to our study of the C-text.

Contents

Introduction

Piers Plowman, or *The Vision of William concerning Piers the Plowman,* to give
the poem its full title, exists in three recensions, known as A, B, and C, all now
generally attributed to William Langland, and written between about 1360 and
1400. The A-text is 2572 lines long, and is in two parts: the *Vision* proper
(Prologue and Passus I–VIII), an allegorical portrayal of the corruption of the
social estate and of the attempt to remedy this corruption through the agency of
Piers Plowman, representing the life of humble and honest obedience to God's
law; and the *Vita de Dowel, Dobet et Dobest* (Passus IX–XII), a vision of the
poet's search for the good Christian life, conducted in allegorical terms through
a series of interviews with intellectual personifications (Thought, Wit, Study,
etc.). The *Vita* is thus more introspective, seeking a rational basis for individual
faith through intellectual enquiry after the failure of the attempts to reform
community in the *Vision.* The A-text has an ending, but the search is inconclusive. The B-text revises A extensively for as far as it goes, omits Passus XII,
and adds another nine passus (*passus,* pl. *passūs,* is a Latin word meaning 'step' or
'stage'), altogether trebling the length of the poem, to 7241 lines. The quest for
Dowel is continued at length, merging into Dobet, the life of Christ, and Dobest, the life of the Church, both allegorically represented in the person of
Piers Plowman, brilliantly resurrected from the *Vision.* The C-text (7354 lines)
is an extensive revision of the whole of B, with several major additions, though
the last passus are relatively little altered.

The C-text is used as the basis for this edition, not because it is artistically
superior at every point to B—indeed, it is quite possible to show that in vividness, picturesqueness and 'poetic' quality it is sometimes inferior—but because
it clearly represents the author's latest revision of his work, and an author
ought to be allowed his last word. (It is no longer reasonable, since the publica-
tion of Professor Kane's authoritative survey of the question, to presume anything but a single author for the three texts.)[1] Though the excisions from B are
sometimes ruthless in their singleminded concentration on essentials, they are
the work of a man who knows what he is doing, and the additions to C reveal
no waning of poetic power, passion or purpose. The arguments for B as text
are appealing, but the arguments for C are strong. They are reinforced in the
present edition, we believe, by the choice of Huntington MS HM 143 as the
copy-text. Hitherto, C has been available only in Skeat's edition, based on
Phillipps MS 8231 (now Huntington MS HM 137). This was a bad manuscript, a sophisticated recension by an interfering scribe, and the pedantry and

---

[1] G. Kane, *Piers Plowman: the Evidence for Authorship* (London, 1965)

A*

verbosity which have long been laid to the charge of the C-text poet are in fact partly the responsibility of this scribe.[2]

The present selection begins with the setting of the scene, the 'fair feld ful of folk' (Passus I), omitting the fable of the belling of the cat, which is of more topical political interest, and continues with the explanation of the vision by Holy Church (II). This explanation states the question of the poem—'How may I save my soul?'—initiates its movement and establishes its dialectic, as well as offering a preliminary outline of the doctrine of Charity which is its goal. The episode of Lady Meed, which follows (III–V), is more or less self-contained, and is here omitted. Passus VI, after the well-known C-text autobiographical passage, introduces the repentance of the folk, allegorically portrayed through a pageant of the seven deadly sins, represented here in four of the most sharply observed, Anger, Lechery, Avarice and Gluttony (VII). The entry of Piers Plowman, and his allegorical directions to Truth (VIII), mark a positive move in the poem as well as a shift in style. The ploughing of the half-acre (IX), and the episode of the Pardon (X), which is much abbreviated in C, are both omitted, though space has to be found for the C-text interpolation on the salvation of the outcast, where Langland's compassion rubs his conscience characteristically raw. The beginning of the search for Dowel (XI) is represented at length, of necessity, since new procedures are here initiated, and the various stages of the search (XII–XV), with their thickets of theological and intellectual speculation, are sampled in three passages, where major questions concerning the rationale of human existence (XIV) and of human poverty and suffering (XIII) are posed, and major themes, such as the limitations of intellect (XII), announced. The crucial movement from speculation to action, which takes place during the feast with the learned doctor of the Church, Conscience and Patience (XVI), is given in full, but the gathering of humanity into the quest in the person of *Activa Vita*, the common man, is omitted (the episode is much curtailed in C). The comprehensive discourse of Free-Will (XVII–XIX), in which past themes are recapitulated and resolved, and the ground prepared for the search for Dobet, is represented in the two luminous expositions of the doctrine of Charity (XVII) and the Tree of Charity (XIX). The grounding in the Old Law of Abraham (Faith) and Moses (Hope) is omitted, and the theme of Christ taken up again in the skilful transition to the good Samaritan (XX), whose exposition of the doctrine of the Trinity is given in part, and then in the

[2] For a full analysis of the textual situation in relation to C, see Donaldson, *The C-text and its Poet*, pp. 227–47. Those who are interested in comparing the present text with Skeat's might refer specifically to the following readings: 1.2, 49, 72; 2.19, 151; 3.10, 21, 44, 84; 4.16, 189; 5.68, 86; 7. 99; 9.67, 71; 10.20, 33, 44; 11.81, 141; 12.24, 42, 45, 87; 13.38; 15.31–2, 54, 97–9, 213, 404, 418; 16.317. .

majestic account of the Passion and the Harrowing of Hell (XXI), which is given complete. Passus XXII, dealing with the foundation of the Church (Dobest), is omitted, but the latter part of Passus XXIII, Langland's apocalyptic vision of the Church besieged by Antichrist, is fully represented. The sixteen extracts comprise 2685 lines.

ALLEGORY

The Dimensions of the Poem

Langland's dominant concern is to expose and clarify the social and religious issues raised by his conscience: whatever allegorical methods he uses are designed to illustrate and elucidate the great themes of the poem. One of the most important functions of his dreamer-figure is to ensure that we should not find our encounters with allegorical journeys, landscapes and debates riddling or enigmatic, but, if anything, over-directed. It is true, for instance, that we need much less initial equipment for 'interpreting' allegorical actions in this poem than in a secular medieval allegory such as the *Roman de la Rose*: there some preliminary knowledge of the concepts and conventions of medieval love-literature is essential if we are to make proper sense of the fictitious narrative of the dreamer, in his progress through the walled garden, with its pool, rose-bush and tableaux of sensuous delight. Again, no allegorical character in *Piers Plowman* is allowed to remain as mysterious and elusive in nature as the guide-maiden in *Pearl*.[3] Holy Church, Reason, Patience, Clergy, and Wit are self-explanatory, in name, form and function. Even the changing significance of Piers Plowman is deducible from the commentary offered by the poem: the last journey towards Piers—

'By Crist', quod Consience tho, 'I wol bicome a pilgrime,
And wenden as wyde as the world regneth
To seke Peres the Ploghman, that Pruyde myhte destruye'

(16.330–2: C. XXIII. 380–2)

is not a quest into the unknown, but a long-anticipated movement of the conscience towards spiritual well-being and authority.

It would be a pity, when describing the richness of Langland's allegorical invention, to lose sight of this 'openness' of aim and technique, and to risk creating false barriers between the poem and present-day readers. *Piers Plowman* has sometimes been recommended as a work susceptible of many-levelled

[3] The dream-poem probably to be ascribed to the author of *Sir Gawain and the Green Knight*, and contemporary with *Piers Plowman*: ed. E. V. Gordon (Oxford, 1963)

interpretation,[4] as if it could command the same kind of attention from us as the text of the Bible from the medieval scholar—

Blessed are the eyes which see divine spirit through the letter's veil . . . [5]

But its wealth of significance cannot be charted in any very precise and rigorous way. No one would deny that from the moment when the dreamer looks out over his dream province, and recognizes not only the familiar, turbulent scenes of his own day—'al the welthe of the world and the wo bothe'—but also the symbolic tower of Truth and the deep dale of Death (1.14 foll.), *Piers Plowman* engages with some kind of allegorical mode. The rapid and down-to-earth survey of medieval society which follows is broken into by speeches from Conscience and Kind Wit: allegorical characters move easily among the 'bisshopes and bachilers' of fourteenth-century London:

Conscience and the kyng into the court wenten,
Where houede an hondred in houes of silke,
Seriauntes hij semede that seruen atte barre . . .

(C. I. 158–60)

And for all the harsh realism of the closing lines of Passus I, the clamorous invitations of Langland's own world—

. . . Hote pyes, hote!
Goode gees and grys, ga we dyne, ga we!

(1.93–4: C. I. 226–7)

Passus II opens with the dreamer offering us *interpretations* of the scene—

What the montaigne bymeneth and the merke dale
And the feld ful of folk, I shal you fair shewe.

(2.1–2: C. II. 1–2)

'What it all means' will clearly be one of the major preoccupations of the poem. The first words of Holy Church to the dreamer press home the point that most people who 'passeth on this erthe' see only the confused pattern of their own lives:

'Of othere hevene then here thei halde no tale'

(2.9: C. II. 9)

The dreamer's reply is a request for his own—and our—enlightenment: 'what may this be to mene?'

---

[4] In particular, by D. W. Robertson and Bernard F. Huppé, in *Piers Plowman and Scriptural Tradition* (Princeton, 1951)
[5] Quoted from Claudius of Turin by B. Smalley, *The Study of the Bible in the Middle Ages* (Oxford, 1952), p. 1

But if, by the mingling of 'real' and 'allegorical' characters, and by frequent references to the 'meaning' of phenomena, Langland very early on in his poem makes us conscious of appearance and its further significance, he is certainly not laying down or taking for granted specific rules for the realization of that significance. No doubt he was familiar with the time-honoured medieval system of Biblical exegesis, which saw, beneath the literal level of the Scriptures, three separable and gradually deepening kinds of spiritual truth—the allegorical, the tropological and the anagogical.[6] If he had not been formally trained in the use of such a method, he would have seen and heard it in operation in the sermon literature of his time.[7] Although it is true that the popularity of the 'fourfold method' of studying the Bible waned somewhat after the 13th century, treatises outlining it were current in Langland's day, and later. But it is by no means certain that any medieval poet, using an allegorical form, did in fact envisage his work as fourfold of meaning, in just that precise way that the fruitfulness of the Biblical text could be demonstrated by a trained scholar.[8] To be told that there are 'four parallel lines of interpretation . . . sometimes simultaneous, sometimes interlinked', but that 'on all four planes the poem is complete',[9] is a challenging introduction for the new reader of *Piers Plowman* and it is some consolation to know that on good historical grounds such a statement is unlikely to be true. A brief acquaintance with the poem makes clear that it is not 'four layered' in any continuous or consistent way: even a comparison of Passus I with Passus II will display the variation of allegorical texture which is an important feature of the whole work.

On the other hand, a completely literal reading of *Piers Plowman* is liable to be an impoverished one; we can be guilty of dogmatism at either extreme:

---

[6] Langland's contemporary, Walter Hilton, gives a clear definition of these 'kinds' in his *Scale of Perfection*, ed. E. Underhill (London, 1923), Bk. II, Ch. XLIII, p. 445: 'By the letter, that is lightest and most plain, is the bodily kind comforted; by morality of Holy Writ, the soul is informed of vices and virtues . . . by mystihood it is illumined for to . . . apply words of Holy Writ to Christ our head, and to Holy Kirk that is his mystical body. And the fourth, that is heavenly, longeth only to the working of love, and that is when all soothfastness in Holy Writ is applied to love; and for that is most like to heavenly feeling, therefore I call it heavenly.'

[7] See G. R. Owst, *Literature and Pulpit in Mediaeval England* (Cambridge, 1933), Ch. II, 'Scripture and Allegory', pp. 57 foll.

[8] See M. W. Bloomfield, 'Symbolism in Mediaeval Literature', *M.P.*, LVI (1958), 73–81

[9] N. Coghill, Introduction to *The Visions of Piers Plowman*, a verse rendering of the B text of the poem by H. W. Wells (London, 1935), p. xvii

its literal nature renders it an impossible medium for the fourfold method...[10]

For the 'literal nature' of *Piers Plowman* has, first of all, to be defined, and then proved for each part of the poem as we come to it. While it might usefully describe a good deal of Passus I, it would not be helpful, except with changed terms of reference, when applied to Passus II or to Passus XXI.

In the case of Passus XXI, there is a *literal* and agonizing narrative of Christ's passion, just as in Passus I there is a literal narrative of hapenings on the Field Full of Folk. But the narrative flow in Passus XXI is constantly disturbed by depth-charges of significance. Often we might say that the full explosion of sense takes place beneath the *literal* surface of the narrative. If it is unlikely that we shall discover a formally layered, quadruple structure of meaning in Langland's poetry, it is certain that we shall discover a range and allusiveness of meaning not easily covered by the term 'literal'.

There are times in *Piers Plowman* when the rich sense of the poetry can be naturally and continually described by means of the 'fourfold method'. Christ's words at the Harrowing of Hell, for instance, coming at the climax not only of the Passion narrative, but also of the dreamer's long, tortuous search for an understanding of God's intent, are simple, and yet charged with powerful meaning. A 'fourfold' expression of that meaning does not overtax or distort the language:

'That art doctour of deth, drynke that thow madest!
For I that am lord of lyf, love is my drynke,
And for that drynke todaye I deyede, as hit semede.
Ac I wol drynke of no dische, ne of deep clergyse,
Bote of comune coppes, alle Cristene soules;
Ac thy drynke worth deth, and depe helle thy bolle.
I fauht so, me fursteth yut, for mannes soule sake.
    Sicio.
May no pyement ne pomade ne presiouse drynkes
Moiste me to the fulle ne my furste slakke
Til the ventage falle in the vale of Josophat,
And drynke riht rype must, *resurreccio mortuorum.*'

(15.401–11: C. XXI. 405–15)

In these words there is the *literal* drama of Christ poised in triumph, with the gates of hell wide open—a vivid and familiar moment for the artists of the Middle Ages, who recorded it on burnished manuscript pages, and on sculpted

[10] R. W. Frank, 'The Art of Reading Mediaeval Personification Allegory', *ELH*, XX (1953), p. 249

columns and portals. There is the *allegorical* sense of the Harrowing of Hell and
the Resurrection as part of the intimate relationship between Christ and man.
The triumph of love and life over sin and death is the special significance of
Christ for doomed mankind—this thirsting 'lord of life', who will eventually
'have out of hell all men's souls' (C. XXI. 417). Further there is a *tropological*,
or purely moral sense: the speech prescribes as well as exemplifies a proper
way of life. Christ's action holds out hope and establishes a pattern of behaviour:

'And al that men mys-dede, I, man, to amenden hit'

(15.388: C. XXI. 392)

In imitation of the perfect man, mankind can now centre life around selfless-
ness and love, so that

'Adam and alle thorw a tre shal turne to lyve'

(15.397: C. XXI. 401)

Finally, for Langland and some of his readers, there could have been a particular spiritual 'echo' about lines such as

'. . . love is my drynke,
And for that drynke todaye I deyede, as hit semede.'

(15.402-03: C. XXI. 403-07)

The *anagogical* sense would have been appropriate only to the rare and lonely
life of the contemplative, who 'dies' to the world ('as hit semede') for the sake
of the 'drink' of divine love.[11]

At points like these, a fourfold description of what Langland may have
had in mind as he wrote is not extravagant. Other parts of the text do not yield
the same kinds of reward, and our assessment of the depth and the nature of
symbolic meaning in this poetry must depend on close and sympathetic reading. For it may be that we shall find many sorts of meaning knotted into one
crucial passage—as in the Harrowing of Hell speech, above, or in the episode
of the Good Samaritan (see extract 14). At other times, we may find a linear
progression—one 'sense' following and developing out of another. Passus II
of the poem illustrates this exactly: it shifts rapidly among various sorts of significances. The *literal* action—a conversation between Holy Church and the
dreamer about the meaning of the opening panorama—is managed sharply and
humorously:

'Thow dotede daffe', quod she, 'dulle aren thy wittes;
To lyte lernedest thow, I leve, Latyn in thy yowthe.'

(2.139-40: C. II. 139-40)

---

[11] Compare *The Cloud of Unknowing*, ed. P. Hodgson (E.E.T.S., O.S. 218,
1958), pp. 107-8

But the theme of the lady's discourse—the search for, and the means of attaining salvation—is conveyed on different successive levels. Words dealing with salvation in the local and specific context of medieval society—

'Kynges and knyghtes sholde kepen hit by resoun,
Ryden and rappe adoun in reaumes aboute'

(2.90–1: C. II. 90–1)

follow words setting the search on the highest spiritual plane—the man who walks with Truth

'... is a god by the gospel and graunte may hele ...'

(2. 86: C. II. 86)

In turn, the long perspectives of religious history open out: God's plan for man's salvation is evidenced in the solemn narrative of Lucifer's fall, with its eternal consequences of right set against wrong:

'And alle that worchen that wikked is, wenden thei sholle
After here deth-day and dwelle ther Wrong is,
And alle that han wel ywrouhte, wende they sholle
Estward til hevene, evere to abyde
There Treuthe is, ...'

(2.130–4: C. II. 130–4)

Comment on the contemporary scene narrows the field of interpretation:

'Aren none hardere ne hungriere then men of holy chirch,
Averous and evel-willed when thei ben avaunsed'

(2.188–9: C. II. 188–9)

Universal statements expand it again to encompass many kinds of truth—religio-historical, moral, mystical:

'So love is leche of lyf and lysse of alle payne
And the graffe of grace and grathest way to heavene'

(2.200–01: C. II. 200–01)

The real test is not so much the historical probability of 'multiple meaning' in *Piers Plowman*, but our own experience of the work. If Langland did not see the dreamer's quest as an investigation on four separable planes of significance, he did see it as a search for a Truth which was complex, often contradictory, and cumulative.

It need not then surprise us that his methods of charting that search are most various. We should be sceptical of critics who recommend to us one kind of allegorical writing as 'characteristic' of *Piers Plowman*, or who try to convince us that we have a straight choice between 'allegorical' and 'literal' methods of reading it. In fact, a whole spectrum of allegorical modes is characteristic of the poem: it displays almost every type of allegory known to the medieval period. To give a comprehensive account of the sources of Langland's allegory, we should have to range over popular sermon literature, courtly poems in French and English, moral treatises, and, in all probability, illustrations to tracts. Not only can we observe diversity of forms, but also widely differing stages of growth. Moreover, even when Langland appears to dispense, temporarily, with allegory, his 'realism' is by no means as simple to define as our first contact with it might suggest.

Allegorical Categories and Modes

Personification Allegory. A vast number of medieval works are usually described as 'allegorical': 'allegory' has to serve as a portmanteau-word for a range of compositions which require some degree of interpretation from the reader, and invite, through their fictions, an inner commentary on the events narrated. Often those are the only common factors: to see *Piers Plowman* and the *Divina Commedia* as allegories, a very flexible frame of reference indeed has to be allowed. Within such a frame, various attempts have been made to sort and regroup allegorical writings. For instance, one of the major methods of procedure in allegory is that of personification, and Langland's poem has been called, in company with other English and French poems, 'personification allegory'.[12] In this, abstract qualities or faculties are given human form, and display their natures or re-enact some experience by means of a typical human activity— a debate, a fight, a feast, a trial, a journey. So, in the *Roman de la Rose*, the experience of falling in love is first abstracted from a particular human situation, and reshaped in terms of personified faculties—Reason, Shame, Jealousy, Idleness, Welcome—who meet, hinder and help the lover in his search for the rose of love. And in the English alliterative poem *Winner and Waster*,[13] man's natural and opposed tendencies to extravagance and miserliness are set before the reader as two figures in debate about their ways of life.

But difficulties arise when we associate them with each other, and *Piers Plowman* with them, as 'personification allegories'. It is true that all three poems 'personify': Langland breaks down the lesson of preserving humility in the face of great provocation into its component parts of patience, reason, anger, and sets them up as characters at a feast (see extract 11). But more important is a comparison of how each poet *used* the device of personification: Guillaume de Lorris's poem is a formal tableau of characters in an enclosed garden: *Winner*

---

[12] R. W. Frank, op. cit., pp. 238 foll.
[13] Ed. Sir I. Gollancz (London, 1930)

and Waster is a ceremonious encounter on a tournament field: Langland's Feast episode is a dynamic, wry scene of mounting tensions, insults, and reconciliations, which materializes and disintegrates before our very eyes. Not that this is always the case with *Piers Plowman*: Langland has static debates as well as bustling feasts—between Reason and the dreamer, Holy Church and the dreamer. The point to make is that the category 'personification allegory' is only of limited help in placing *Piers Plowman*, as, indeed, it may be in placing other medieval works. Personification is a weapon for many allegorists, but they can only be properly distinguished by their ability and inclination to handle it. And, as we shall see, personification is not the whole story: allegory has many faces.

The same difficulty arises when we try to assign *Piers Plowman* to any particular allegorical class or category, and it seems more useful to begin by recognizing its comprehensive allegorical span. This involves not only recognition of the variety of traditional methods Langland draws upon, but also his unique use and combination of those methods.

Dramatic Allegory. Usually—and rightly—singled out for attention is the kind of allegory we find in the Lady Meed episodes of *Piers Plowman* (C. III–V) or in the Feast of Patience (extract 11: C. XVI). Here a central subject is investigated by means of an actively developing allegorical narrative, with conceptional and fictional elements in perfect, continuous adjustment. The whole sequence of events involving Lady Meed—the arranging of the marriage, the journey to Westminster, the arraignment at the king's court—is dramatically convincing, as well as deeply meaningful. No detail is imprecise in significance, or flat in design. Liar, for instance, evading the King's summons to judgment, is accurately analysed for us, but he leaps into the poetry with the sure energy of an English medieval line-drawing:[14]

> Lyghtliche Lyere lep away thennes,
> Lorkynge thorw lanes, tologged of menye.
> He was nawher welcome for hus meny tales,
> Oueral houted out and yhote trusse,
> Til pardoners hadden pitte and pullede hym to house.
> Thei woshe hym and wypede hym and wonde hym in cloutes,
> And sente hym on Sonnedayes with seeles to churches . . .

> (C. III. 225–31)

[14] Some of the crude but vigorous scenes from the *Holkham Bible Picture Book* come to mind: produced in the earlier 14th century, it represents a kind of illustrative art with which Langland might easily have been familiar. See the facsimile edition by W. O. Hassall (London, 1954) and plate 134 in M. Rickert, *Painting in Britain: the Middle Ages*, Pelican History of Art (London, 1954)

It is visually satisfying as well as morally instructive that Lady Meed—the essence of material reward—should be fêted by a 14th-century court, and presented to society by 'a clerk—ich can nouht his name':

> Cortesliche the clerk thenne, as the kynge hyghte,
> Toke Mede by the myddel, and myldeliche here broughte
> Into boure with blysse and by hure gan sitte,
> Ther was myrthe and mynstralcy Mede to plesen . . .
>
> (C. IV. 9–12)

All gestures are vividly realized, yet full of 'sentence'—Meed, hard pressed, looks to the lawyers to save her from Reason's logic:

> Mede in the mote-halle tho on men of lawe gan wynke,
> In sygne that thei sholde with som sotel speche
> Reherce tho anon ryght that myghte Reson stoppe.
>
> (C. V. 148–50)

But her faded glamour comes under harsh scrutiny:

> And alle ryghtful recordeden that Reson treuthe seyde . . .
> Loue let lyght of Mede and Leaute ȝut lasse . . .
> Mede mornede tho, and made heuy cheere,
> For the comune called hure queynte comune hore.
>
> (C. V. 151, 156, 160–1)

Similarly, the description of the Feast of Reason, to which the dreamer goes with Conscience, Clergy and Patience, proceeds as a continuous and highly amusing narrative, but skilfully utilizes every property or speech to convey a bitter lesson of endurance. While the learned and pompous friar is fed on delicacies, 'mortrews and poddynges/Braun and blod of the goos, bacon and colhoppes . . .', Patience and the impatient dreamer are more straitly and healthily served by Scripture:

> He sette a sour lof, and saide, '*Agite penitentiam,*'
> And sethe he drow us drynke, *diu-perseverans*:
> 'As longe,' quod he, 'as lyfe and lycame may duyre.'
> "This is a semely servyce!' saide Pacience.
>
> (11.56–9: C. XVI. 56–9)

We should not pass too quickly over the outraged astonishment of the dreamer as Patience accepts his fare *with gratitude*:

> Pacience was wel apayed of this propre service,
> . . . ac I mournede evere.
>
> (11.64–5: C. XVI. 63–4)

It is a master stroke of dramatic writing, but it is also a highly appropriate witness to the dreamer's unreformed, and therefore rebellious, state of mind.

In both of these sequences—and in others like them—Langland mingles personifications with 'real' figures: Meed, Falsehood, Liar, Conscience, Peace, and Wrong thread their way through undefined crowds of the medieval world—pardoners, lawyers, soldiers. The words spoken by personifications give glimpses of rough, authentic life; Peace describes Wrong at work, and there behind the personified figure, with his formal Bill of Complaint, is a whole landscape overrun by men on aggressive, everyday business:

> 'He menteyneth hus men to morthre myn hewes,
> And forstalleth myn faires and fyghteth in my chepynges,
> And breketh up my bernes dore and bereth away my whete'
>
> (C. V. 58–60)

This mixture of personification and vivid local reportage is not new; Langland would have known of it from many earlier poems, in which Truth or Covetousness travel the English countryside:

> Coveytise upon his hors he wole be sone there,
> And bringe the bishop silver, and rounen in his ere.[15]

Winner and Waster do not manage their debate in generalities, but by reference to the stuff of fourteenth-century living:

> '... thy wyde howses full of wolle sakkes,
> The bemys benden at the rofe, siche bakone there hynges,
> Stuffed are sterlynges undere stelen bowndes ...'
>
> (El. 250–2)

But such episodes in *Piers Plowman* modulate the 'real' and the personified in an especially delicate and powerful way; the details of the landscape behind Peace illustrate but do not dominate the central moral theme of the passage—the tyranny of violence. In the Feast scene, the particular references to the friar preaching at St. Paul's lead the eye out through an open window to the contemporary scene:

> Hit is nat thre daies don, this doctour that he prechede
> At Poules byfore the peple what penaunce they soffrede ...
>
> (11.70–1: C. XVI. 69–70)

Nothing outside, however, distracts attention from the essential moral drama indoors: the discovery of the very basis of patience in willingness to listen to half-truths delivered by a corrupt man (see 11.113n).

[15] *The Simonie*, Auchinleck MS., f.328ᵇ, ed. T. Wright, *The Political Songs of England* (Camden Society, VI, 1839)

This is allegory at its most expansive—richly conceived, precisely executed. But there are growing-points for such writing all the way through the poem—embryonic allegory. Langland frequently rests on the very brink of 'realizing' an allegorical sequence. A quotation may suggest to him a theme for development, and he makes a brief, telling sketch for a larger design. The words 'Multi enim sunt vocati, pauci vero electi' (*Matthew* 22: 14) are rapidly set as an allegorical feast-scene:

> *Multi* to a mangerie and to the mete were sompned,
> And whan the peuple was plener come, the porter unpynnede the gate,
> And plyghte in *pauci* pryueliche and leet the remenant go rome.
>
> (C. XIII. 46–8)

'Iustus vix salvabitur' (*I. Pet.* 4: 18) is dramatized, in simple but striking terms, as a court scene, with 'vix' personified, and interceding for 'justus':

> . . . how Ymaginatyf saide
> That *justus* bifore Jesu *in die judicii*
> *Non salvabitur* bote if *vix* helpe . . .
>
> (11.21–3: C. XVI. 21–3)

These little episodes, arrested between concept and allegorical action, and rich in potential, show how Langland was constantly drawn to allegory (cf. 16.84–5). But the fact that they remain undeveloped is interesting too: if Langland's movement towards allegory was instinctive, it was also controlled. For him, allegory vivified and clarified doctrine; its form and scope depended intimately upon the needs of the sense at any given moment. We can compare his compact treatment of these quotations with his elaborate drawing-out of a Biblical quotation in the 'Four Daughters of God' debate which prefaces the Harrowing of Hell (15.116 foll.) Here *Psalm* 85, verse 10, 'Misericordia et veritas obviaverunt sibi: iusticia et pax osculate sunt', is expanded into a full-scale encounter and debate on the reasons for man's salvation.[16] The positioning of this debate is all-important: the length and detail of the allegory are closely related to Langland's concern for absolute clarity on the subject of atonement and salvation. Differences between such passages are those of extent rather than of nature: the minuscule sketches are capable of expansion into robust allegorical scenes—they cry out for lively development.

Diagrammatic Allegory. But there are forms of allegory in *Piers Plowman* which make no such claims upon us. By comparison, they are flat and unspec-

---

[16] He had many precedents for this in art and literature: the verse had been dramatized and illustrated from the 9th century onwards. See A. Katzenellenbogen, *Allegories of the Vices and Virtues in Mediaeval Art* (New York, 1964), pp. 40–1 and plate xxv, fig. 44: see also 15.117n.

tacular, and it is all the more important for us to understand their nature and function. Very frequently Langland uses an allegorical mode which is closely connected with a particular kind of medieval art: in fact, 'diagrammatic' is the best descriptive term to use of it. Although no exact sources have been identified, it seems possible that Langland was influenced by schematized drawings when he devised his allegory of the Tree of True-Love, growing in man's heart (13.6 foll.: C. XIX. 6 foll.). Medieval moral treatises constantly used the image of the tree, formally divided into branches, leaves and fruit, as a way of expressing man's life, and his relationships to God.[17] And Langland could easily have been familiar with some of the more popular handbooks of the Middle Ages, made probably for the clergy, which gave 'clear visual representation, that the reader, in the midst of a complicated world of abstractions, might see and grasp the essentials'[18]. The description of the Court of Truth (5.86 foll.: C. VIII. 232 foll.) and the Barn of Unity (C. XXII. 320 foll.) which Piers Plowman builds for his spiritual harvest recall many manuscript drawings of allegorical buildings, quite as stiffly constructed and carefully labelled as Langland's:[19]

> He made a maner morter and Mercy hit hihte.
> And therwith Grace bygan to make a good foundement,
> And watelide hit and wallyde hit with hus peynes and hus passion,
> And of alle holy writt he made a roof after . . .
>
> (C. XXII. 326–9)

It may be that Langland worked from purely literary materials, and not from the visual arts: allegorical buildings were favourite 'exempla' with medieval preachers,[20] and a well-known 14th-century text such as the *Abbey of the Holy*

---

[17] The origins of the tree image are various, but *Matthew* 7: 17 must have been a central text: 'Every sound tree bears good fruit, but the bad tree bears evil fruit. . . . Thus you will know them by their fruits.' See Katzenellenbogen, op. cit., pp. 63–8. M. W. Bloomfield, in *'Piers Plowman* and the Three Grades of Chastity', *Anglia*, LXXVI (1958), 245–53, makes suggestions about the particular sources of Langland's tree.

[18] Katzenellenbogen, p. 63. British Museum Additional MS 37049 is a fine example of such a book: its allegorical trees range over the vices and virtues, religion, love, etc. It may be significant for Langland's tree of 'cor-hominis' that many of them are rooted in man's heart.

[19] The 'turris sapientiae', for instance, on f.20b of British Museum MS Arundel 507, a 14th-century collection of texts and drawings, owned by a monk of Durham.

[20] Owst, *Literature and Pulpit*, pp. 77 foll.

Ghost,[21] with its meticulous architectural symbolism, might very well have been read and used by Langland. Its stone walls are 'festenande togedir with the lufe of gode', its 'syment or morter' is the 'qwykelyme of lufe and stedfaste byleve . . .' (p. 323), its foundations are laid by Meekness and Poverty, its walls raised by Buxomness and Misericord (pp. 322–3). Or, again, his debt may be double: he may have gone to illustrated texts which provided him with both 'mental images and actual forms'[22]. His phasing occasionally suggests direct debts to visual allegory; to a Tree of the Vices, for instance—

'Ac whiche be the braunches that bryngeth men to sleuthe?'

(C. VIII. 70)

and to a Tree of the Vices compounded with a Tree of Life—

. . . Pruyde hit aspide,
. . . greuen he thenketh
Conscience, and alle Cristene and cardinale uertues,
To blowen hem doun and breken hem and bite atwo the rotes . . .

(C. XXII. 337–40)

Here Langland draws upon two iconographical features—Pride, traditionally at the base of the Tree of Vice, and animals (usually identified as Day and Night) gnawing at the roots of the Tree of life.[23] The total image, built up from simple parts, is unusually complex.

But if our knowledge of particular sources must remain incomplete, we can still use art to help us define the character of Langland's diagrammatic allegory. For like the didactic illustrations of the period, it is static, precise, and formalized: what it lacks in evocative power it makes up in faithful accuracy of communication. The description of the way to St. Truth, offered by Piers Plowman (5.87: C. VIII. 157 foll.), illustrates this well. It is a route plan, laid before the 'thousand of men' who have been stirred by Repentance to 'go to Treuthe'. The passage has often been dismissed as dull and wooden. But like the maps and diagrams of medieval religious art, it is not meant to be visualized *in depth*. It is a blue-print for action, not a picture or a full description of the action itself. Similarly, the meticulous setting-out of the tree of 'Trewe-love', planted by the Trinity in man's heart, with its flowers of 'benygne-speche', and its fruits of 'caritas', does not amount to a picture of a tree: it is nearer to an anatomical or botanical abstract of those physical entities, in which our obser-

[21] Ed. C. Horstmann, *Yorkshire Writers: Richard Rolle of Hampole* (London, 1895), I. 321–37

[22] Katzenellenbogen, p. 73

[23] British Museum MS Additional 37049 has examples of both kinds of trees, on f.48[a] and f.19[b] respectively.

vation is guided to general structural truths, rather than to variations within the species.

The same comment can be made about the final ploughing scene of the poem (C. XXII. 262 foll.). Piers 'tilling truth', with a team of the four Evangelists, and sowing in man's soul four seeds of the cardinal virtues, only barely achieves any sort of dramatic presence—in contrast to an earlier ploughing scene (C. IX. 112 foll.) when 'Perkyn with the pilgrimes to the plouh is faren' and we feel his sturdy personality directing the familiar activities of the land:

> Dykers and deluers diggeden up the balkes; ...
> And somme to plese Perkyn pykede aweye the wedes ...
>
> (C. IX. 114, 118)

In the later passage, what matters above all is that each component part of the allegory should be accurately labelled and understood. For this vital account of the establishing of spiritual authority on earth, the fictional element is firmly disciplined. The idea that 'Grace gaf to Peers greynes, cardinales vertues/And sewe hit in mannes soule ...' (C. XXII. 274–5) has visual and dramatic potential, but the poet is primarily concerned that we should understand what those grains were called, and what were their properties. Such allegory, in which nothing is left to chance, or to the reader's imagination, must be seen as the verbal equivalent of the elaborately inscribed and glossed art of medieval tract illustrations. In fact, it could be said that in its simple, linear quality it bears the same relationship to fully active and rounded allegory (the Meed episodes of C. III–V, for instance) as the diagram does to the picture, with its deep perspective and its more complex media of communication.

Non-visual Allegory. But Langland can, on occasion, deal even more severely with our visual expectations. The way to Truth may have to be 'realized' as a map, and not as a picture, but there are times when his allegorical writing is clearly not meant to be visualized in any form whatsoever. We should be mistaken in trying to make ordinary visual sense out of the descriptions of Book, Wit and Anima:

> Thenne was ther a wihte with two brode yes,
> Boke hihte that beau-pere, a bolde man of speche.
>
> (15.239–40: C. XXI. 240–1)

> He was long and lene, ylyk to noon other.
>
> (7.115: C. XI. 114)

> Tyl I seigh, as it sorcerye were, a sotyl thinge withal,
> One withouten tonge and teeth ...
>
> (B. XV. 12–13)

In these, the eye is refused any help: the details do not build up into a logically and visually acceptable whole, but are isolated symbolic features. Thus the protean shape of Anima—by turns Love, Conscience, Memory, Spirit, Reason—is properly denied a physical identity because this would limit and confine it: it is 'spirit specheles' (B. XV. 36) and only assumes bodily form to operate God's will in man. The staring eyes of Book refer us directly to the double authority of the opened Gospel pages—an immediate confrontation with the revealed word of authority, rather than with 'a bold man' *representing* authority. Wit is a particularly interesting example; the blocking of a visual response in the second half of the line ensures that the details 'long and lene' are rapidly related to the judicious and sober nature of the faculty of Wit, and not allowed any physical reality.

If, to us, this seems a somewhat cold and intellectualized allegorical mode,[24] we may be taking for granted that visual clarity and forcefulness are always the most effective means of communication for poet or artist. Langland's readers—many of whom were by no means unsophisticated—may have found the very impossibility of visualizing Book a short-cut to grasping its full significance. Clearly Langland could count upon a sensitive response to widely differing allegorical methods, and it is not surprising if, with his comprehensive and complex subject matter, he availed himself of all known devices to capture the understanding.

Allegory through Exempla. Somewhere between the full-scale allegorical sequence and the formal allegorical design lie numerous passages of illustrative material, presented very much like parables or 'exempla' in the sermon literature of Langland's time. They do not make use of personification, and they are not diagrammatic: occurring mostly within the speeches of allegorical characters, they are short narratives within narratives. Their function is essentially allegorical; the events they describe are meant to be translated into more significant conceptual terms—and, in fact, are often translated on the spot. But their most distinctive feature is their positioning, for they are experienced by the dreamer at one remove. They are reported allegory. And, like their counterparts in the sermon literature of the Middle Ages, they are vivid and authoritative. Their message is trenchant, but it is also limited: because of their special, circumscribed position in the poem, they can only be developed to a certain extent. Sometimes Langland uses them to make a moral point more tellingly

[24] Such non-visual allegorical 'picturing' is to be found in some of the Latin literature of the earlier 14th-century; see B. Smalley, commenting upon the work of the Franciscan John Ridevall: '. . . all this fancy is verbal, not visual; the "pictures" will serve as aural aids to preaching' (*English Friars and Antiquity*, Oxford, 1960, p. 118).

than subtly: the rough effectiveness of the friar's 'forbisene' (in 7.32: C. XI. 32 foll.) is deliberate. Here sinful man is likened to a man in a boat in peril of the waves and the wind, and 'waggynge of the bote', but saved by the very condition of his humanity, which is set in faith and love. Man falls, but not into the sea; he only stumbles within the boat, and is saved: he sins, but only within the body, which, in its frailty, draws God's compassion to it:

'So hit fareth', quod the frere, 'by the ryhtful mannes fallynge;
Thogh he thorw fondynges falle, he falleth nat out of charite . . .'

(7.41-2: C. XI. 41-2)

It is immediately obvious that the 'equivalences' will not stand up to rigorous analysis—the boat as the body is a tricky concept and, indeed, Langland's purpose in the whole episode is to show us a spiritual teacher who is only superficially clever. The friars are a constant butt of his irony and anger for their glib, popular methods and their presumption. But Langland will also use the 'forbisene' in a favourable context, as a swift means of clinching a protracted argument, or as a sudden—but not necessarily final—simplification of a complex debate. So Ymaginatif (in C. XV. 103 foll.) offers the puzzled dreamer a chance to resolve, temporarily, some of the long-worked-over problems of the debate on salvation by faith, good works, or learning. The man with learning, he says, can be compared to a man in the water who knows how to swim—he is more likely to be able to save himself from sinking, because of his knowledge:

'Ryght so,' quath that renke, 'reson hit sheweth,
That he that knoweth cleregie can sonnere aryse
Out of synne, and be saf, thow he synegy ofte.'

(C. XV. 110-12)

The sense of relief, shared by dreamer and reader, when they come upon what seems to be a neat and apt analogy, is short-lived. It soon becomes clear that there is much more to say about 'cleregie', and that Ymaginatif is certainly not envisaging it simply as a useful sort of expertise. Neither is he convinced that it is always as efficacious as his parable would have; his last words dwell upon truth, hope, and love, not upon learning:

'And where hit worth other nat worth, the byleyue is gret of treuthe,
And hope hongeth ay theron to haue that treuthe deserueth;
Quia super pauca fidelis fuisti, supra multa te constituam:
And that is loue and large huyre yf the lord be trewe,
And cortesie more than couenant was, what so clerkes carpen.'

(C. XV. 213-16)

But as an interim comment, the parable had value: it helped to concentrate the dreamer's diffuse thoughts, and it encouraged him to use his reason as well as his feelings when tackling the thorny problem of salvation for the simple and the learned.

But if we can distinguish four or five allegorical methods at Langland's easy command, we should not think of them as operating independently of each other. Whatever approach is made—diagrammatic, exemplary, active—it is chosen to display or to investigate subject matter most effectively at that particular point, and may be preceded or superseded by an entirely different kind of approach. The merging of one type of allegory into another is a characteristic of *Piers Plowman*, not shared by many other poems of its time, though frequent enough in some types of devotional prose writing.[25] The most striking example of this comes in extract 13 (C. XIX. 106 foll.) when the static allegory of the Tree of Trewe-love quickens, and in the presence of the dreamer becomes an active allegorical drama of man's subjection to the devil—

> For evere as Elde hadde eny down, the devel was redy,
> And gadered hem alle togyderes, bothe grete and smale,
> Adam and Abraham and Ysaye, the prophete . . .
>
> (13.111–13: C. XIX. 111–13)

and of the decision to save him—

> Thenne moved hym mod *in majestate dei*,
> That *Libera-Voluntas-Dei* lauhte the myddel shoriar
> And hit aftur the fende . . .
>
> (13.118–20: C. XIX. 118–20)

The passage from this to the actual historical moment of the Annunciation—

> And thenne spak *Spiritus Sanctus* in Gabrieles mouthe
> To a mayde that hihte Marie . . .
>
> (13.124–5: C. XIX. 124–5)

is, in one sense, a startling and brilliant move by Langland, but in another sense it is quite natural—a stage in a continuous process of evolution, from design to life, which in its turn is drawn back again to attitude and gesture.

Nor should we think that all in *Piers Plowman* which cannot be categorized as one or other type of allegory is therefore the very reverse of allegory, with only literal or realistic force. In the passages discussed so far, realism has been

---

[25] See, for instance, the section on Love in the 13th-century spiritual guide, the *Ancrene Wisse*, ed. G. Shepherd (Nelson's Medieval and Renaissance Library, 1959), pp. 21–3. This work was highly influential in the 14th and 15th centuries.

either subtly adjusted or subordinated to conceptual truth: no problem has
arisen. But there are many parts of *Piers Plowman* in which Langland does not
appear to be working in any allegorical mode at all. Moreover, it will be obvious that some very important characters in *Piers Plowman*—Piers himself,
Abraham, Trajan, the Good Samaritan—are not easily accounted for 'allegorically'. And yet they are hardly to be described as 'real', or 'historical':
Trajan is accepted by the poet as 'real', but also as 'symbolic' of salvation by
works (C. XIII, 74 foll.): Abraham, is double-named "Faith" (C. XIX, 186,
200, 275, etc.)

REALISM AND THE FIGURAL APPROACH TO REALITY

Realism

It is here that we might try to consider more precisely the nature and the context of what often strikes the new reader as the distinctive *realism* of *Piers Plowman*: it is the realism of a good deal of later medieval literature and art. The
Tavern scene of extract 4 springs to mind; Gluttony is diminished to the status
of a real-life gluttonous 'cherl', weak-minded, unable to hold his drink, offen-
sive to his fellow revellers. The stale and raucous atmosphere of the ale-house
is perfectly captured by the poetry:

> There was leyhing and louryng and 'lat go the coppe!'
> Bargaynes and bevereges bygan tho to awake,
> And seten so til evensong, and songen umbywhile,
> Til Glotoun hade yglobbed a galoun and a gylle.
> His guttes gan to gothly as two grydy sowes . . .
>
> (4.181–5: C. VII. 349–53)

And so, too, is the easy corrupt life of worthless beggars:

> In hope to sitte at even by the hote coles,
> Unlouke his legges abrood or ligge at his ese,
> Reste hym and roste and his rug turne,
> Drynke druie and depe and drawe hym thenne to bedde . . .
>
> (6.82–5: C. X. 142–5)

No other medieval poet writes with such relish of the simple pleasures of a

> loof or half-loof other a lompe of chese . . .
>
> (6.90: C. X. 150)

There is realism, too, in Langland's opening presentation of his focal character, Piers—a man who, whatever his high destiny, comes bursting into the poem

full of ardent certainties, quick to anger and to pity, and humbly reconciled to the hard life of the land he tills:

'And a cow with a calf and a cart-mare,
To drawe afeld my donge the whyle drouth lasteth.
By this lyflode we mote lyue tyl Lammasse tyme.'

(C. IX. 312–14)

The imaginative realism which makes his account of the Good Samaritan episode in extract 14 so much more than Biblical paraphrase, also enables him to write of the Virgin as

'a pure, pore mayde, and to a pore man wedded...'

Both historical personage and parable figure come to life as we read; the Samaritan, with his practical charity:

And to this wey he wente, his woundes to byholde.
He perseyvede by his pous he was in perel to deye,
And bote if he hadde recover the rather that ryse sholde he nevere,
And unbokelede his boteles and bothe he atamede;
With wyn and with oyle his woundes he can lithe ...

(14.20–4: C. XX. 65–9)

and his brisk instructions to the innkeeper:

'And that more goth for his medicyne I make the good ageynward,
For I may nat lette', quod that lede, and lyard he bystrideth.

(14.30–1: C. XXI. 51–2)

Most affecting in its simple brevity is Langland's moment of Christ's crucifixion:

And nayled hym with thre nayles, naked upon a rode
And, with a pole, poysen putten up to his lippes ...

(15.51–2: C. XXI. 51–2)

and of the moment of death:

'*Consummatum est*', quod Crist, and comsed for to swone,
Pitousliche and pale, as prisoun that deyeth.

(15.58–9: C. XXI. 58–9)

It would be easy to conclude, from material such as this, drawn from contemporary life, past history, and sacred fiction, that whatever the range and subtlety of his allegorical usages, Langland works most powerfully in literal, realistic modes of expression. In this, he could be associated with many others of his age—artists of all kinds. The increasing regard of the 14th and 15th centuries for familiar and recognizable fact provided the atmosphere in which Chaucer could begin to envisage the Canterbury pilgrims: in which Italian and Flemish painters could visualize Christ, the Virgin and Joseph as a sentient human family. Paintings such as Bellini's *Madonna of the Meadows*, with its pensive woman in an autumn landscape, or Campin's *Merode Altarpiece*, with its town vistas, and the Virgin receiving the angel in a spotless parlour, adjoining Joseph's workshop —these belong to a noonday world, where light falls simply and directly, recording shapes and surfaces without a shadow of implication.

But painting can often signal to us more urgently than poetry that it is dangerous to take an easy view of later medieval realism. The harrowing Crucifixion pictures of the time, the sculpted plague crosses of Germany and Scandinavia, score deep gashes in Christ's body not simply as a reminder of 'man's inhumanity to man' but as a symbol, in all the 'reality' of their depth and width, of the extent of divine compassion for fallen man. The quiet domesticity of Campin's altarpiece is 'real', indeed, but is also richly symbolic. Joseph, in his crowded carpentry shop, refers precisely (and, from the *literal* point of view, quite inappropriately) to the brutal death of the unborn child: he is boring holes in a spike-block, similar to those dragged by Christ in Flemish pictures of the *Road to Calvary*. Many of the tidy 'realistic' objects in Mary's parlour are meant to symbolize the power and innocence of the woman as a receptacle of the divine—the lily in a jug of Delft ware, the shining bronze laver, the candle and candlestick, and the window through which light streams, unimpeded.[26] This double use of realism is something we should entertain for *Piers Plowman* too, even when Langland is not committed to allegory.

Moreover, we should be wise to attend to the larger contexts of realism: here again the painters can achieve at a glance what the poet, with his more complex spatial problems, must take time to establish. But there are strong similarities, for instance, between Langland's use of realism in his tavern scene (4.148: C. VII. 353 foll.) and that of Hieronymus Bosch, in the Hell volet of his *Garden of Delights*.[27]

Bosch, a painter of almost photographic accuracy, but of deeply symbolic import, sets a perfect miniature study of tavern debauchery within a broken egg-shell. The egg-shell is the body of a despairing monster, who is rooted in the murky waters of hell, by two decaying tree stumps of legs. The further implications of *realism* are sharply brought to our attention by the strange,

[26] See the article in the *Metropolitan Bulletin of Art*, XVI, No. 4 (December, 1957), by M. B. Freeman, 'The Iconography of the Merode Altarpiece'.

[27] In the Prado, Madrid: painted before 1516. See *Hieronymous Bosch, The Garden of Delights*, ed. W. Hirsch (Amsterdam, 1954), which reproduces the tavern scene in Hell with excellent detail.

horrifying, and patently *unreal* nature of its setting. Langland's version of the same sort of material, with Glutton superbly rounding out the definition of excess, is not an isolable dramatic episode, but is set into a total vision of sin and redemption, as the words of Repentance, which close the confessions, make absolutely clear:

'God, that of thi goodnesse gonne the world make
And madest of nauhte auhte and man liche thysulve,
And sethe soffredeste hym to synege, a sykenesse to us alle,
And for oure beste, as I beleve, what-so the book telle.
O felix culpa, O necessarium peccatum Ade!'

(5.4–8: C. VIII. 123–6)

The same could be said of Langland's picture of the honest poor—

The wo of this wommen that wonyeth in cotes;   (6.23: C. X. 83)

it is a picture bordered by a larger discussion of divine justice and mercy. Truth's 'perpetual pardon' to Piers and his heirs on earth (C. X. 3 foll.) is itself a truth which modifies or gives a new perspective upon the terrible social injustices of the medieval peasant's lot.

The Figural Approach

This easy commerce between a vivid sense of the real, the actual, and an equally vivid sense of spiritual implication is as characteristic of *Piers Plowman* as it is of the whole outlook of the Middle Ages. And when we have finally distinguished and categorized all types of allegory in the poem, we are left with many vigorous creations which, without any loss of their 'reality', may still be intended as 'figures and foreshadowings of great things'.[28] For an understanding of these, we must look not to allegorical processes of thought and composition, but to *figural*.[29] The difference is important: in terms of biblical study, for instance, the allegorical method uses the literal, historical narrative merely as

[28] Quoted and translated from Lactantius, *Divinae Institutiones*, by E. Auerbach, in his essay 'Figura', *Scenes from the Drama of European Literature* (New York, 1959), p. 35
[29] The best short exposition of the figural outlook is by Auerbach, in the essay noted above. But see also C. Donahue, 'Patristic Exegesis: Summation', in *Critical Approaches to Mediaeval Literature*, ed. D. Bethurum (Columbia University Press, 1960), p. 81, who comments perceptively that the figural or typological approach 'might turn imaginative writers towards realism rather than towards allegory'.

point of departure for various kinds of spiritual interpretation—the figural
method maintains the historical truth of Biblical events, while seeing in them,
simultaneously, a 'foreshadowing of greater things'. So the Old Testament is
'real', but is also a 'figure' of the New Testament: in its turn, the New Testament, fulfilling the Old, is an incarnation not quite complete. It is itself a
promise or augury of the ultimate truth which will be revealed after the Last
Judgment. It was an attitude which had far-reaching consequences, in art and
literature: 'No student of the Middle Ages can fail to see how it provides the
medieval interpretation of history with its general foundation and often enters
into the medieval view of everyday reality' (Auerbach, p. 61). It is this which
underwrites not only Langland's acceptance of the concrete, historical actuality
of the life of Christ ('Jesus Christ on a Jews douhter alight'), of Abraham, or of
the life of the patient poor in the 14th century, but also his ability to place them
in a 'perspective of eternity' (ibid., p. 42). *Piers Plowman* bases itself firmly on a
figural interpretation of reality,[30] upon 'the idea that earthly life is thoroughly
real, with the reality of the flesh into which the Logos entered, but that with all
its reality it is only *umbra* and *figura* of the authentic, future, ultimate truth,
the real reality that will unveil and preserve the *figura*'.[31]

Such a statement makes it easier to understand the whole complex relationship between the real, the literal, the dramatic and the spiritual in *Piers Plowman*.
It is easier, in particular, to understand 'characters' such as Abraham, the Good
Samaritan, and Piers Plowman himself. For they are not presented as 'allegorical' in the same way as the personified abstractions Clergy, Study, Reason, are
presented. On the other hand, they are not dealt with in terms of unequivocal
realism. They shift easily between literal and symbolic modes. The simplest
example is that of Abraham. He is movingly 'real' as the dreamer meets him—

And thanne mette ich with a man on Mydlentens Soneday,
As hor as an hawethorn and Abraam he hihte.

(C. XIX. 183–4)

and hears him describe, almost conversationally, as an old man might, his
vision of the Trinity:

[30] See the clear 'figural' statement about Christ at C. XV. 38–9:

Lawe of loue oure lorde wrot, longe er Crist were.
And Crist cam *and confermede*, and holy kirke made . . .

[31] Auerbach, p. 72. The figural or typological view of history is especially
clear in the double row of personages and events from the Old and the New
Testaments in medieval choir stall carvings, for instance, and in the series of
Old Testament episodes chosen for the Miracle Play Cycles.

'Hauest thow seyen this?' ich seide, 'alle thre, and o god?'
'In a somer ich seyh hym,' quath he, 'as ich sat in my porche,
Where god cam goynge a-thre, ryght by my gate;
Tres uidit et unum adorauit.
Ich ros up and reuerencede god and ryght fayre hym grette,
Wesh here feet, and wypede hem, and after thei eten . . .'

(C. XIX. 241 foll.)

The 'reality of the flesh' is here—the accepted historical truth of the wife, the 'faire sone Ysaac', the sacrifice, the blood shed for God:

'Myself and my meyne . . .
Bledden blod for that lordes loue . . .'

(C. XIX. 254-5)

But equally present is the concept of Abraham as a 'type' of faith. Born in the Old Law, he looks towards, and is fulfilled by the New: he counsels the questioning dreamer in the name of Faith—

'Muse not to muche ther-on,' quath Faith, 'tyl thow more knowe,'

(C. XIX. 200)

and he is explicit about the fact that his worship of God 'wyth wyn' and wyth bred bothe/At ones on an auter' is a symbolic reference forwards to the sacrament instituted by Christ:

'And make sacrifice so, somwhat hit bytokneth:
Ich leyue that thilke lorde thenke a newe lawe to make;'

(C. XIX. 265-6)

The phrase 'somwhat hit bytokneth' ('signifies or symbolizes something') is a pointer to the double aspect of most of Abraham's speech: the father's sacrifice of the son, the blood shed for love, remind us of the event which the dreamer and Abraham are waiting to see completed—the sacrifice of Christ:

'. . . . Crist is hus name,
That shal delyuery ous som day out of the deueles powere . . .'

(C. XIX. 283-4)

Similarly, Langland presents his Good Samaritan in a manner not totally realistic, but certainly not allegorical. Accepting Christ's parable as virtual sacred history, he develops the man warmly and vividly—but we are not allowed to forget that the action of the Good Samaritan is a 'figure' of Christ's rescue of wounded mankind. The Samaritan's words make this quite clear:

B

'Have hem excused,' quod he, the Samaritan, 'here helpe may nat availe,
Ne no medicyne under molde the man to hele brynge,
Nother Faith ne fyn Hope, so festred aren his woundes.
Withoute the blod of a barn he beth nat ysaved ...'

(14.36–9: C. XX. 81–4)

The curiously 'echoic' quality of the language at times springs from the assumption that any 'real' event or action can be deepened and extended in significance by later happenings. Thus the Good Samaritan echoes or anticipates Christ's words when he speaks of the protective power of his doctrine of charity:

'For wente nevere man this way that he ne was here yryfled,
Save mysulve sothly, and suche as I lovede.'

(14.45–6: C. XX. 90–1)

The 'character' of Piers Plowman might also be regarded as a natural product of figurative thinking. This highly complex creation of Langland's cannot be dealt with in terms of allegory or social realism. Piers comes before us with particular historical and dramatic force: he is rooted in the life of the 14th-century peasant—

'Bothe to sowe and to sette, the while I swynke myhte'

(5.67: C. VIII. 186)

He provides all classes of men with the very stuff of their earthly lives—grain *is* life. But from the beginning, we are made conscious that he 'figures' much more than this; he is in touch with mysteries, and it is instantly clear that he has it in his power to provide spiritual sustenance, as well as material. He expounds, to the crowd of waiting pilgrims, not only the Ten Commandments of the Way to God, but also the miraculous heart of the matter—the ultimate recognition of God, dwelling in man:

'And yf Grace graunte the to go in in this wyse,
Thow shalt se Treuthe sitte in thy sulve herte,
And solace thy soule, and save the fram payne ....'

(5.135–7: C. VIII. 254–6)

Here he hints at his own 'fulfilment', as incarnate spiritual wisdom and love: at the height of the poem, he comes before the dreamer's astounded gaze as the human 'form' of Christ (15.8: C. XXI. 8, and C. XXII. 6 foll.). His constant function—for dreamer and mankind—is that of guide to salvation and to the knowledge of God. In fact, when Christ says (in C. XXII. 260–1)

'My prower and my plouhman Peers shall beo on erthe;
And for to tulye treuthe, a teome shall he haue.'

we accept his words as a confirmation of what has already been understood: Piers is 'incarnate revelation, that part of the divine plan of salvation which ... is the miracle whereby men are raised above other earthly creatures ...'[32] But, as is proper and natural to the figurative view, the 'man Piers' is never lost to our sight: indeed, for his complete spiritual fulfilment to take place, he must remain recognizable. What Langland shows us in Piers the Plowman is the operation of God through a man in a state of grace; he is not propounding, by personification, a theological concept of grace in humanity. Consequently, Piers is always familiar, always sought-for, acclaimed by the dreamer and other characters—'the historical reality is not annulled, but confirmed and fulfilled by the deeper meaning' (Auerbach p. 73).

The most dramatic visual illustration of this comes late in the poem, when the dreamer sees a figure who resembles both Piers and Christ:

> ... and sodeynliche me mette,
> That Peers the Plouhman was peynted al blody,
> And cam yn with a croys byfore the comune peuple,
> And ryght like in alle lymes to oure lord Iesu.

(C. XXII. 5–8)

Here, coalesced, in one staggering moment of revelation, is the man and the power working through him—

'the reality of the flesh into which the Logos entered ...'

What then, seems to be true is that some of the most significant parts of *Piers Plowman* cannot be dealt with in terms of allegory: neither can they be satisfactorily dealt with as areas of dramatic or social realism. Allegory provides Langland with a wide variety of literary methods for examining and displaying his wealth of material: it allows him freedom of play in many poetic styles and genres, ranging from fictions of strong visual content to designs of flat diagrammatic clarity. But allegory is no help to us when we come to consider how Langland 'built' his central character, Piers, nor is it helpful to our understanding of Langland's basic attitude to historical and spiritual truth—to his concept of 'reality'.

The essential structure of his thought is figural, with all that this implies about the co-ordination of the real and the spiritual. No-one could have felt more intensely and described more vividly the often claustrophobic 'reality' of later 14th-century England: this did not prevent Langland from 'interpreting' it in a perspective of eternity, both in the first disturbing long shots, and in the last terrifying close-ups of the poem—

[32] Auerbach, op. cit., p. 75, writing of Beatrice, in the *Divine Comedy*

'the figural structure preserves the historical event while interpreting it as revelation, and must preserve it, in order to interpret it' (Auerbach, p. 68).

Form

Piers Plowman is related to numerous kinds of medieval literature, but cannot be exactly matched with any one. The most recent long study of the poem proposes 'six forms—three literary and three religious' as the 'genres in which Langland chose to work, and with which he attempted to give structure to his poem'.[33] Those poems range widely: the allegorical dream narrative, the dialogue or debate, the encyclopaedic satire, the complaint, the commentary and the sermon. Elements of all can be recognized—although, according to our own particular reading of the poem, we may differ in judging which genre was most significant. But when we have set out all the possible literary relationships of *Piers Plowman*, we are left with a problem: how can such varied allegiances encourage a poem of structural coherence, much less structural excellence? Critics have written of the 'confusion and even clash of genres'[34] in *Piers Plowman*: they have said that Langland 'hardly makes his poetry into a poem'.[35] It could easily be said that, in encompassing or in sampling from so many medieval genres, Langland abandoned hope of formal success from the very start. It is highly significant that the only writers prepared to describe *Piers Plowman* as no less perfect structurally than the *Divine Comedy* had to base their proof upon improbable theories of the poem's allegorical nature.[36]

Structure

The manuscripts of the poem tell us that *Piers Plowman* is divided into four large sections: in the C text, they consist of Passus I–X, Passus XI–XVII headed '. . . de Dowel', Passus XVIII–XXI, '. . . de Dobet', and Passus XXII–XXIII, '. . . de Dobest'. It is not, of course, certain that Langland himself was responsible for such rubrics, but they do provide a sensible comment on certain important developments of subject matter and theme. To some extent, therefore, they ask us to consider a fourfold structural pattern in *Piers Plowman*. Passus I–X are mainly introductory—opening up the problems of remedial action, and

[33] M. Bloomfield, *Piers Plowman as a Fourteenth Century Apocalypse* (Rutgers University Press, 1963), p. 34
[34] Bloomfield, op. cit., p. 8
[35] C. S. Lewis, *The Allegory of Love* (Oxford, 1936), p. 161
[36] *Piers Plowman and Scriptural Tradition*, p. 247

generally indicating, to the reader as well as to the dreamer, that the road to salvation invites man urgently, but that the journey is painful, dangerous, and difficult. Passus XI–XVII investigate, under the heading of 'Dowel', the immensely complex business of 'doing well', as a guarantee of ultimate salvation: it is a section which probes deeply, often savagely, and it ranges, sometimes confusedly, over a whole area of thought and personal experience, weighing learning against faith, love and patience against knowledge, grace against good works. Passus XVIII–XXI, '. . . de Dobet', is a splendidly clear and positive vision of God's love, centred in the Crucifixion and Harrowing of Hell. 'Dobet' is far removed from the agonized self-searchings and castigation of 'Dowel'. The dreamer has passed beyond doubt and protest to a wondering acceptance of the rightness of God's purpose. Passus XXII–XXIII, '. . . de Dobest', both concludes and restarts the dreamer's search for salvation. The problem he first had stated for him, in the opening Passus, is restated, in grim terms, but 'Dobest' is now clear: the dreamer has his help, in God's Church, and in her ministers, symbolized ideally by Piers the Plowman. Such a summary does rough justice to the poem. The four headings correspond to well-defined stages in the growth of themes: however we may wish to define the central activity of the poem, Passus I–X introduce, Passus XI–XVII explore, Passus XVIII–XXI confirm, and Passus XXII–XXIII both conclude and initiate a fresh beginning.

Problems

But it would not be sensible to try to make a very precise scheme of those headings—'Dowel, Dobet, and Dobest'. Langland, for instance, discusses all three concepts in the section named 'Dowel': the boundaries are not fixed, and material overlaps from one section into another. As we are told in the A text, Dobet and Dobest are natural growths out of Dowel:

> Riht as the rose that red is and swote,
> Out of a ragged roote and of rouwe breres
> Springeth and spredeth that spicers desyreth.
> Or as whete out of a weed waxeth uppon eorthe,
> So Dobest out of Dowel and Dobet doth springe
>
> (A. X. 119–23)

This the poem illustrates perfectly.

Nor are the definitions of those headings or concepts absolute: Langland uses 'Dowel, Dobet and Dobest' to express a number of connected ideas and states. The triple formulation itself would have been attractive and familiar to medieval readers, who would have kept in mind, as Langland developed and reworked his sections, many 'triads': the three 'estates' of labourer, knight and clergy: the three kinds of life—active, contemplative, and the mixed life of the administrative church, part thought, part action: the special categories within the enclosed religious life—the triple division of the contemplative way into active prayer and repentance, illumination, and meditation on the fruits of visionary experience. 'Dowel, Dobet, Dobest' could serve as useful summaries for any or all of these patterns of life and experience: indeed, over the length of the poem, Langland gives us good grounds for believing that this is exactly what he intended we should discover.[37]

It would not be honest, therefore, to base theories of the structure and organization of the poem on 'Dowel, Dobet and Dobest' except in a rather general way.[38] The same could be said of Piers Plowman himself as a structural device: his appearances are most important, his function essential, but he alone is not sufficient to pull together the diverse materials of the poem. It is true that he serves to point the major preoccupations of the four main sections: he is, among other things, successively 'Dowel', the obedient son of the Church, 'Dobet', the man of perfect love, and 'Dobest', the representative of God in his Church on earth. He often acts as a focus of attention, a clearing-house of themes. But he cannot be made to assume heavy responsibility for the ordering and unifying of the poem.[39]

Faced with these problems, some critics have preferred to shift their ground entirely, feeling that the poem's coherence lies in its 'perception of moral values and social principles, and . . . preoccupation with human material'[40] or, simply, in its 'truly imaginative' rather than 'formal . . . unity'.[41]

And yet there is something very compelling about Piers Plowman, which makes one dissatisfied with a wholesale contracting out of the matter, or any simple explanation of its structural defects. It is interesting to see how various are the theories put forward to justify what might—on a quick reading—be thought clear faults of construction.

[37] See S. Hussey, "Langland, Hilton and the Three Lives', R.E.S., N.S. VII (1956), for an enlightened discussion of Langland's intentions: '. . . the various definitions (of Dowel, Dobet and Dobest) are not mutually exclusive, but complementary . . .' (p. 148).

[38] H. W. Wells, in 'The Construction of Piers Plowman', P.M.L.A., XLIV (1929), proposed Dowel, Dobet and Dobest as dominant organizing factors in the poem.

[39] N. Coghill's article, 'The Character of Piers Plowman considered from the B Text', M. Aev., II (1933), encouraged this idea.

[40] A. H. Smith, Piers Plowman and the Pursuit of Poetry (London, 1950), p. 19

[41] J. Lawlor, 'The Imaginative Unity of Piers Plowman', R.E.S., N.S. VIII 1957), p. 126

The abruptness of the transitions, for instance, which could be due to Langland's carelessness or ineptitude, has been given much critical attention. There are the sudden switches of scene and subject: in Passus I, when, with a single word of introduction, the 'route of ratones' displace the crowd of lawyers and courtiers surrounding the King and Conscience; in Passus XIX, when Liberum Arbitrium hits out at the devil with the second 'plank' of the Trinity, and the Incarnation begins—

> And thenne spak *Spiritus Sanctus* in Gabrieles mouthe
> To a mayde that hihte Marie ...',
>
> (13.124–5: C. XIX. 124–5)

the frequent vanishings and appearances—in Passus XVI, when Piers Plowman speaks, unexpectedly, at the Feast of Patience:

> Quod Peres the Ploghman: '*Pacientes vincunt.*'
>
> (11.138: C. XVI. 138)

These 'phenomena' have been variously explained—as a very deliberate imitation of the irrationality of dream experience,[42] as a literary method akin to photographic or cinematographic technique, with strong dramatic intent,[43] and, most recently, as the result of the influence of the Biblical commentary— 'it is like reading a commentary on an unknown text'[44]. In the case of the rapid comings and goings of Piers Plowman himself, another idea can be put forward. He operates more and more certainly, as the poem progresses, in a revelatory capacity: his 'materializations' will therefore be incalculable, since they are divinely controlled and only *intimations* of truth to the struggling dreamer. The transitory and sudden arrivals of Piers Plowman, in the 'Dowel' section of the poem, are directly related to the muddied state of the dreamer's comprehension: he has not yet won through to a steady vision of the Truth, but is allowed glimpses. Langland's contemporary, Walter Hilton, explains the situation in a different, but parallel, spiritual context—that of the contemplative 'touched' but not stabilized by divine favour:

> ... all such feelings come to them in that state *as it were unwarily*, for they come or they wit it, and go from them or they wit it, and they cannot come thereto again nor wit not where they should seek it ... for they have not yet no homeliness with them, *but suddenly go and suddenly come* ...[45]

There is the same sense of loss and fear in the poem when:

[42] R. Woolf, 'Some Non-Mediaeval Qualities of *Piers Plowman*', *Essays in Criticism*, XII (1962), p. 118

[43] J. Lawlor, *Piers Plowman: An Essay in Criticism* (London, 1962), p. 263

[44] Bloomfield, op. cit., p. 32

[45] *Scale of Perfection*, Bk. II, Ch. XXIX, p. 355

... wiste no man after

Where Peres the Ploghman bycam, so priveliche he wente.

And Resoun ran after and riht with hym yede;

Save Concience and Clergie I couthe no mo aspye.

(11.149–52: C. XVI. 149–52)

On this one point of structure alone, Langland has been both defended and condemned; the same holds for most of the larger structural features of the poem. Perhaps it is true that 'he could not properly solve his formal problem',[46] but the fact that *Piers Plowman* constantly tempts us to reconsider that 'formal problem' is some testimony to its holding power. It may be that we should regard Langland's loose-woven fabric of procedures not so much as a failure to achieve structural tautness, as a way of capturing something of a kaleidoscopic vision of truth. In this sense, indeed, the substance of the poem *is* the form, and the reader of *Piers Plowman* must agree to be 'carried forward not merely or chiefly by the mechanical impulse of curiosity, nor by a restless desire to arrive at the final solution, but by the pleasurable activity of mind excited by the attractions of the journey'.[47]

Thematic versus Narrative Unity

In the first place, unless we accept that the poem has no proper narrative structure, we are still liable to make unjustifiable demands of Langland's handling of his material. Narrative as a form is utilized in the poem—often for long stretches as in the allegorical narrative of Lady Meed's marriage and trial—but Langland is not committed to a narrative structure in any continuous way. Here the poem differs from many other allegorical works of the period: a knowledge of the *Roman de la Rose* or of religious allegories such as the *Voie de Paradis* could not prepare us for its interrupted and suspended narratives. Langland *is* committed, however, to a continuous development of themes, which may be served, as needed, by various narratives. Thus the narratives of Holy Church and the dreamer (extract 2, C. II), of the Meed trial (C. III–V), of the Confessions of the Seven Deadly Sins (extract 4, C. VII–VIII), of the ploughing of the half-acre (C. IX), of the Feast of Patience (extract 11, C. XVI. 26 foll.), are all, to some extent, isolable. They are illustrative of great moral themes which build up, irresistibly, while characters and *mise-en-scène* change and shift. Holy Church, Meed, Gluttony, Waster, Patience and the doctor of divinity do not reappear outside their own sections as 'characters in a narrative': they do reappear, however, as concepts. The themes of spiritual authority, reward, reformation of sin,

---

[46] Bloomfield, op. cit., p. 34

[47] Coleridge, *Biographia Literaria*, Ch. XIV

patience and love, are constantly developed and enriched, but their narrative exposition frequently alters.

This explains, in part, the long delays and interruptions to which narratives as vital as that of the life of Christ are subjected. Passus XIX–XXI (extracts 13–15) of the C text cover events from the Annunciation to the Harrowing of Hell, but Langland's eye is as much upon the spiritual hinterlands of that story as it is upon its agonizing and triumphant sequence of events. It is significant that the story is introduced (at 13.121) almost as an illustration of the allegory of the Tree of Charity and life, whose apples are menaced by the devil: the moral allegory precedes and is confirmed by the historical narrative. As the narrative develops, we are taken through Christ's life to the point when he is led before the Justices—

Thus Iewes to the Iustices Iesus thei ladden . . .   (C. XIX. 179)

but then the dreamer wakes, 'ner frentik' at the loss of his vision. He engages in a series of meetings and conversations with Abraham, Spes, and the Good Samaritan,[48] and during this time, when he is being taught various important truths about faith, love, the Trinity, temptation, amendment of life, the narrative of the Passion is suspended. There is a sense that something is waiting to be completed, just beyond the dreamer's grasp. All those he meets are on their way to Jerusalem—the Samaritan

. . . rapede hym to ryde the rihte way to Jerusalem.
Bothe Faythe and his felawe *Spes* folewede faste aftur . . .
                    (14.32–3: C. XX. 77–8)

but as the dreamer follows after, and interrogates the Samaritan, there is time for lengthy discussion about the nature of the Trinity. Nothing that is said in this discussion is irrelevant to the coming events of the Passion. It is of prime importance that the dreamer should understand the *total* significance of the Crucifixion: what will happen to Christ is an offence (although divinely accepted) against the Father and the Spirit. God is to be crucified for the sins of man:

'Ryȝt so, faillede the sone, the syre be ne myghte,
Ne holde, ne helpe, ne hente that he louede.'
                    (C. XX. 138–9)

When the dreamer next sleeps (15.4: C. XXI. 4), he still does not resume contact with the Passion narrative. His first vision is of Christ, 'semblable to the Samaritan, and somdeel to Peers the Plouhman', on his triumphal entry into

---

[48] Although these apparently begin in a waking interval, Langland infers, at C. XX. 332 ('and therwith ich awakede'), that they are part of the dreamer's sleeping experience.

B*

Jerusalem. The sight is a confirmation of the preceding discussion of the Trinity; this knight, 'that cometh to be doubed/To geten his gilte spores ...' and who is to joust with Death in Jerusalem, is backed by the power of God:

'For no dynt shal hym dere as *in deitate patris.*'

(15.25: C. XXI. 25)

Before the dreamer rejoins the crowd at the trial of Christ, Faith puts him in possession of all the salient facts about the scenes he is to witness: nothing is left to chance—'O mors, ero mors tua'. And at last (at 15.35: C. XXI. 35) the story is taken up again; it continues to the death of Christ, and there (at 15.115) it again halts. The dreamer is poised on the very brink of the Harrowing of Hell and Resurrection episodes, and then, suddenly,

... I saw sothly, *secundum scripturas,*
Out of the west, as it were, a wenche, as me thouhte.

(15.116–17: C. XXI. 117–18)

What follows is the well-loved, medieval allegorical debate of the Four Daughters of God. Before Langland will relate the Harrowing of Hell, he insists on making quite sure that his dreamer—and his readers—understand the terms and premises of the redemption of mankind. Before the event, the theory of the event. The debate of Truth, Righteousness, Mercy and Peace ranges over the whole course of sacred history, from the fall of Lucifer to the present moment of Christ's death. Consequently, when the Passion narrative is resumed—

'Soffre we', sayde Treuthe, 'I here and se bothe
A spirit speketh to helle and bit to unspere the gates'—

(15.268–9: C. XXI. 271–2)

not only does it come with fresh dramatic force, but it can be seen as part of a vast historico-religious plan, which will not be completely fulfilled until Judgment Day.

This is a particular instance of a general characteristic of the poem; Langland is always willing to abandon narrative continuity for the sake of greater richness of significance. Narratives for him are illustrative of themes. And if in one important way this reminds us of medieval sermon structure and technique— moral lessons enforced by short narratives, or 'exempla'—in another way it can be seen as the structural consequence of the figural approach to reality, discussed in the last section. For the assumption underlying it is that sequences of events are not laws unto themselves, but are connected, at every point, with other events, past and future, and with an all-embracing divine plan, in which they have always had a timeless existence. So narrative Truth must always be fulfilled by thematic; the narrative of the Passion

> is not regarded as a definitive self-sufficient reality, nor as a link in a chain of development in which single events . . . perpetually give rise to new events, but *viewed primarily in immediate vertical connection* with a divine order which encompasses it.[49]

This 'vertical connection' is made explicit in Langland's handling of the Passion episodes: the 'horizontal' or sequential flow is constantly interrupted to point 'vertical' significances. It may even be that here we touch upon another reason for abruptness of movement in the poem: the ordinary causal sequences can, at any time, be violated or at least modified, in the interests of a higher order of truth.

The effects of such an attitude are very clear in medieval art of Langland's own period; the relationship of narrative to theme is particularly well illustrated in the drawings accompanying semi-popular devotional texts of the time. British Museum Additional MS 37049, which is a collection of diagrams, drawings and religious pieces in prose and verse, was probably intended to help less learned clergy in their tasks of instruction; its public may well have overlapped with the lower strata of Langland's clerkly readers. The manuscript has already been mentioned in this Introduction for its allegorical tree diagrams (see pp. 14–15 above): some of its miniatures range more widely. A double-page miniature, with the Seven Sacraments as its subject,[50] takes various narratives to implement that subject—the Fall of the Angels, the Fall of Man, the Crucifixion, sinners entering Hell and the saved entering Purgatory. But it is not primarily a narrative picture, and the narrative episodes remain isolable, even strangely dislocated, until the eye registers the thematic centre of the whole design: the Seven Sacraments, raying out from the crucified body of Christ. The *theme* of the picture is the salvation of man through Christ's death and the sacraments of the Church: its unity, even its sense, cannot be properly argued on any other formal grounds.

Such parallels can help us to understand Langland's 'shifting organization' of his poem, and the 'paradoxical space'[51] inhabited by the dreamer and his visions. As in the picture, we must not hope for continuous narrative structure:

[49] Auerbach, 'Figura', p. 72

[50] Ff. 72b–73a. Reproduced by F. Wormald, 'Some Popular Miniatures and their Rich Relations', *Miscellanea Pro Arte, Festschrift für H. Schnitzler* (Düsseldorf, 1965), Pls. CLVI and CLVII

[51] Charles Muscatine, 'Locus of Action in Mediaeval Narrative', *Romance Philology*, XVII (1963), p. 122

as in the picture, we should envisage space as a concept of timelessness, in which past, present and future coexist, and are equally powerful: 'in transcendence the revealed and true reality is present at all times, or timelessly'.[52] This is as much the 'context' of the sequence of events leading from the discovery of the Tree of True-love to the morning of Resurrection as it is of Holy Church's discourse to the dreamer in Passus II (extract 2). For that discourse ranges restlessly over the Creation, the Incarnation and Passion: it sees man's present and future in immediate and vital relationship with Lucifer's pride, Adam's disobedience, and Christ's suffering:

'... the fader that formede us alle,
Lokede on us with love, let his sone deye
Mekeliche for oure mysdedes, to amende us alle.'

(2.163–5: C. II. 163–5)

Cohesive Elements

The Dreamer. But there are certain formal binding elements in *Piers Plowman*. The constant presence of the dreamer should not be undervalued: it has dramatic, didactic and structural significance. In one sense, the dreamer acts as a compass needle held before us as we make our way into the poem: it is not so much that he leads us on a straight course as that he plots and defines for us the inevitable curves and detours of this most elaborate search for truth. Convinced, early on, by his earnest and pressing desire to *arrive* at truth,

'Teche me to no tresor, but telle me this ilke,
How I may save my soule ...'

(2.79–80: C. II. 79–80)

we are the more likely to endure the trials of the journey with some measure of good-humour and fortitude. Travelling with the dreamer is a consistent, though not a direct path: incentives and impetus remain constant, while the terrain may change rapidly. It is not simply a dramatic but a structural device to have the dreamer always inquiring for us, pushing ahead for us, taking the weight of our own ignorance and impatience upon himself, and ensuring that our confusion never goes unrecognized, or unattended. Whether we hear him asking our simple questions—

'Charite,' quod I tho, 'That is a thyng forsothe
That maistres comenden moche; where may hit be yfounde?'

(12.1–2: C. XVII. 284–5)

'Wher Sarrasyns,' ich seyde, 'seo nat what is charite?'

(C. XVIII. 150)

[52] Auerbach, loc. cit.

protesting our fatigue with lengthy lectures, or brashly revealing our Faustus-like ambition—

'Alle the science under sonne and alle sotile craftes
Ich wolde ich knewe and couthe kyndeliche in myn herte,'

(C. XVII. 210–11)

he represents our own unbroken relationship with the poem—a predictable (though often fallible) commentator, who never ceases to work for us towards mastering and unifying the diverse materials of the visions.

The Dream-Vision. Then there is the dream-vision itself. Langland adopts this well-known and well-used medieval literary form, but adapts it for his own more complex purposes. The poem spans a whole series of dreams, and the rhythm of sleeping and waking becomes a familiar part of the process of reading. Both dreamer and reader learn and fall back, despair and understand, in great waves of waking and sleeping experience.

Structurally, the 'dream-device' is both vital and problematic. It serves, in the first place, to give some definition to the poem as a whole: the dreamer falls asleep in the first ten lines of the poem, and wakes in the last. And between those points, the acts and thoughts of one man's life-time are exposed—used as a centre for the widest survey of man and his destiny. This outer demarcation is important: it is not only a formal method of enclosing a vast amount of subject-matter, nor is it only a means of indicating to the reader that his close attention is required. We should give Langland full credit for the words used by the dreamer to describe his first encounter with the dream:

And merveylousliche me mette, as I may telle.   (1.9)

The 'miraculous' element in Langland's dreaming is very early stressed: like the contemporary dream poem, *Pearl, Piers Plowman* is concerned with revelation, as well as with action and discussion:

My goste is gon in Godes grace
In auenture ther meruayles meuen ...   (*Pearl*, ll.63–4)

Backing Langland's dreams are statements like that of *Job* 33: 15–17:

In a dream, in a vision of the night, when deep sleep falleth upon men, in slumbering upon the bed; then he openeth the ears of men, and sealeth them in slumber ...

And, from his own period, the words of Walter Hilton:

Ego dormio, et cor meum vigilat. I sleep and my heart waketh . . . The more I sleep from outward things, the more wakeful I am in knowing of Jhesu and of inward things. I may not wake to Jhesu, but if I sleep to the world . . .[53]

For the dream in *Piers Plowman* can indicate status as well as map out areas in the poem: to sleep may not only be a means of attaining a special vantage-point from which to view great expanses of man's past, present and future, but also a means of attaining a special position of privilege for the interpretation of that view. Though it often takes the dreamer a long time to benefit from what he sees and is told, he is, in sleep, receptive and open to whatever influences may be exerted upon him:

a reasonable instrument wherein that he (Christ) worketh.[54]

The great dream-boundary of *Piers Plowman* marks out a potential field of revelation: it could be said, at its most significant, to define an area within which grace can freely operate. The last line of the poem:

And sethe he gradde aftur grace tyl I gan awake

(16.336: C. XXIII. 386)

is therefore particularly meaningful. And this is the general sense in which the dream-device unifies and reconciles all the multifarious events, speeches and transformations in *Piers Plowman*. Langland is not likely to have been concerned with the irrationality of dream experience as a phenomenon, although the poem does appear, at times, to be counterfeiting it. But he did want to establish, within the dream, the possibility (and the acceptability) of a different order of naturalness in a world directly, and miraculously, subject to the workings of the divine will. The mysterious comings and going of Piers Plowman are as unexpected, and yet as 'natural', as the workings of grace: the final search of the poem is for Piers and for grace in a world which has temporarily lost sight of both. It is 'natural', in this context, that the dreamer only comprehends within the dream, through grace, and often loses all sense of contact with truth and reality when awake:

. . . 'Slepynge, hadde I grace
To wyte what Dowel is, ac wakynge nevere!'

(10.89–90: C. XIV. 218–19)

The mounting urgency of the call towards sleep is a striking dramatic—and thematic—feature of the poem. Leisurely introductions to the dreams, with

[53] *Scale of Perfection*, Bk. II, Ch. XL, p. 424. See also *The Book of Privy Counselling*, ed. P. Hodgson, op. cit., pp. 151–2
[54] Ibid., Ch. XXIV, p. 318

some concessions to the medieval literary morning of sun, birdsong and running water, give way to brief peremptory references:

... me lust to slepe ... *   (11.25: C. XVI. 25)

And if sleep, with its invitation to knowledge and understanding, becomes, at certain times, an almost compulsive force, the turning towards sleep is usually a signal of heightened awareness, a directive which *may* be momentous, for dreamer and reader. This, as it occurs over the length of the poem, like a warning-light, switched on and off, has obvious structural importance.

Waking episodes are often simply reflective pauses in the development of the poem: brief, slightly dazed recollections of the crowded and exciting events of the dream. So (in 11.1–25: C. XVI. 1–25) the dreamer muses over the long speech of Ymaginatyf, which has revealed to him how learning and humility and grace can be reconciled—'al worth as god wole'. He picks up a few points made by Ymaginatyf—'of Kynde and his connynge ... how lovyng he is to uch a lyf ... for alle he wisseth and yeveth wit ...'—but his overriding desire is to sleep and learn more: 'me lust to slepe ...' What follows, in sleep, is a particularly subtle and valuable lesson on how to put Ymaginatyf's *dicta* into practical use: the Feast of Patience, in which the dreamer is directly confronted with learning devoid of humility and grace, and is asked to make the most of the teaching offered by the doctor of divinity. 'Al worth as god wole' is not a sentiment that comes easily to the dreamer's lips as he sits next to placid Patience, and watches the display of hypocrisy at the high feasting table—'this goddes gloton, ... with his gret chekes ...'

But there are many examples of Langland's use of sleep as an index of change and significance. At one point (C. XII. 167) the dreamer sleeps again, within his dream:

And in a wynkynge ich worth and wonderliche ich mette.

This second falling asleep is an unmistakable sign of a new direction in argument and procedure. The dreamer is in need of new direction: he has been receiving a substantial amount of teaching on the subject of Dowel, from such 'characters' as Wit, Studye, and Clergye. Dame Studye's scepticism about his fitness to receive such teaching—expressed with the tartness Langland usually reserves for his allegorical and academic ladies—

... 'Nolite mittere, ye men, margerie-perles
Among hogges that han hawes at wille'

                                                (8.7–8: C. XII. 7–8)

has been counterbalanced by Clergye's willingness to be constructive about Dowel, and to give sensible—if not very original—definitions of the three 'states'. But this in its turn is followed by an unexpectedly savage attack upon the dreamer by Clergye's wife, Scripture, who scorns him, for no apparent reason, only throwing out the phrase 'seipsos nesciunt' as a positive clue (C. XII. 166). The new dream begins, and it comes in immediate response to the accusation of Scripture that the dreamer is very ill-informed about his inner self. His ability to receive and deal with such information as Wit, Studye, Clergye have to offer depends upon a better state of self-knowledge. The dream-within-a-dream marks an attempt by the dreamer to come to closer grips with this problem: it is not a solution of the problem, but it meaningfully shifts the basis of the inquiry on to a deeper, more personal and private plane.

Within this dream, the wilful errors of the dreamer's life are brought under closer scrutiny: he is led by Fortune, seduced by the flesh, comforted by Recklessness:

> 'Ye, recche the neuere', quath Rechelesnes, stod forth in raggede clothes,
> 'Folwe forth that Fortune wol, thou hast ful fer to elde.'
>
> (C. XII. 195-6)

The very serious limitations of his power to understand and reform are displayed, as he repents and corrects his way of life, only to fall into the error of rebuking Reason for apparent lack of attention to human affairs—

> 'I have wonder in my wit, so wys as thow art holden, ...
> That thow ne reuledest rather renkes then other bestes?'
>
> (10.56, 58: C. XIV. 185, 187)

As a result of his rebuke, he is thrown out of the dream: wilfulness is with him to the end! But all is not on the debit side: if Recklessness speaks, initially, for the dreamer's *selfish* carelessness, he comes to express, in warmest terms, a doctrine of *spiritual* carelessness, or reliance upon God's provision for the dedicated Christian (see 9.1n.):

> 'For-sak al and sue me and so is thi beste.'   (9.27: C. XIII. 166)

The long and moving speech of Recklessness 'in a rage' against Clergye argues the sufficiency of grace, and the superior strength of patience, poverty and love: when he comes to an end (at C. XIV. 128), it is clear that he stands for a double-sided tendency in the dreamer. The same swift extravagance of feeling that leads him to a life of heedless rebellion, to anger and frustration when encountering the 'academic' personnel of his religion—Clergye, Scripture, and Study—leads him also to identify in sympathy with those who will risk everything for God.

Recklessness speaks for the good and the bad in his nature, and the inner-dream episode takes a close-up view of his chances of success in the search for truth. It magnifies—even distorts, by magnifying—a small area of the human organism, and shows us how the instincts may often lead astray, but how some intuitions may be confirmed as sound, and channelled, under guidance, into good.

In such cases, and many others, the dream operates in a clearly defined way. But we should not press its structural importance too far. It is not always true that Langland uses the dream meaningfully. On one occasion at least the dreamer wakes, without ever having slept (C. XX. 332). There are times when it is difficult to see how Langland distinguished—and expected his readers to distinguish—the different quality of experience received in waking and sleeping states. This would not matter if we could always bring to Langland's defence the idea that he might have deliberately blurred or removed those boundaries in keeping with some concept of psychological or spiritual truth. There is some point, for instance, in thinking that the very easy movement between sleeping and waking in 15.468 foll., C. XXI. 471 foll. is significant: the church-bells in the vision of the Resurrection set the dreamer awake, direct him (and his family) to church, and thence back to sleep (C. XXII. 5). At this stage the dreamer has reached some firm understanding of God's purposes: he is *at one* with his visions, and can sum up their meaning:

'. . . crepe to the cros on knees and kusse hit for a jewel . . .
And hit a-fereth the fende, for such is the myhte . . .'
(15.472, 475: C. XXI. 475, 478)

The flight to sleep as a desperate attempt to draw order out of living chaos is no longer a dramatic necessity, and the dreamer slips again, almost peacefully, into his next vision:

In myddes of the masse, tho men yeden to offrynge'
(C. XXII. 4)

Examples such as this should not blind us to the fact that Langland's handling of dream-procedures in some parts of the poem is arbitrary. As a structural device it has a variable role, and he seems to have been capable of using it in a purely mechanical as well as a richly significant way. His interest and attention fluctuate.

The Search. But this could not be said of another feature of the poem—the search or quest. The basic and recurrent pattern of *Piers Plowman* is that of a journey or a series of journeys—interrupted frequently by static debates, and often halted by allegorical incidents,[55] but always resumed in one form or another. Thus the dreamer—like many of the characters in the poem—is either

[55] So the ploughing of the half-acre 'delays' the first search for Truth (C. IX. 2 foll.).

on the move, or on the brink of movement. He meets others, who sometimes overtake him and pass on, sometimes persuade him to go with them. He sees journeys begun by others, arrested, fulfilled. The last thing he reports from his dream is the resolution of Conscience to 'go on pilgrimage' to find Piers Plowman: the first real advancement of the poem is his own resolution to pursue the goal of Truth.

Between those two moments, the dominant theme and design of the poem is the search: it is no light comment when Ymaginatyf addresses the dreamer as one '... that sekest after weyes' (C. XV. 157). For 'seeking after ways' is the most characteristic and continuous form of action in *Piers Plowman*, and, perhaps, its most positive structural asset. Once the reader has accepted the fact that he, with the dreamer, is not merely a witness to dramas involving others, nor a passive recipient of information, but is expected to engage directly in the gradual discovery of truth for himself, he can be more easily reconciled to the apparent inconclusiveness and deviousness of the poem's movement. That is, once he has accepted and therefore undertaken the journey, he has accepted the conditions of journeying—exhilaration mingled with frustration, a sense of purpose, an apprehension of the unknown shot through with misgiving as the landscape widens and changes unexpectedly.

For Langland, as indeed for the whole medieval world, the metaphor of the journey was both commonplace and extraordinary. It is drawn readily from the everyday business of travelling in the 14th century as an illustration of the different ways of rich and poor towards God (C. XIV. 33 foll.). Merchant and messenger, we see them dealing with their papers, paying tolls, taking short-cuts through the wheatfields, on their way to Winchester fair. But it is used most seriously in pilgrimage form: the whole of life, from birth to death, was regarded as a pilgrimage, equally beset by perils as by aids to salvation. Christ's life, the pattern for mankind, had been essentially one of wayfaring, and medieval man never forgot that on both the dedicated pilgrimage and on the everyday journey Christ's presence might again, as to the disciples on the road to Emmaus, be revealed:

> 'Witnesse in the Paske-woke when he yeode to Emaus,
> Cleophas ne knew hym nat, that he Crist were,
> For hus poure aparail, and pilgrimes clothes ...'   (C. XIII. 122–4)

Nor is it surprising that a poem which so much concerns itself with the problem of salvation should take as its dominant structural device that very metaphor of the 'via' used by Christ of himself: 'I am the way, the truth, and the life: no man cometh unto the Father, but by me'(*John* 14: 6).[56]

[56] Quoted by Langland at C. XI. 255: 'For ich am *uia et ueritas*, and may auaunce hem alle.'

The dreamer either sees or takes part in many journeys, as the poem opens out: some can be seen as sections of longer routes, some are tangential: some overlap others. But there is no doubt that they are Langland's happiest solution of the formal problems his vast collection of materials set him. At least six important searches are undertaken in the poem—for St. Truth, for Dowel, for Clergye, for Parfitnesse, for Charity, and for Piers Plowman. But it would be wrong to suggest that these are in any way disconnected, or in simple sequence. Although they seem, when baldly defined, to be so disparate in aim, they are closely linked. In fact, the greatest advantage of the search or journey form for Langland is that multifarious paths, involving a variety of travellers, stopping-places and incidents, and setting out, apparently, in different ways, can be gradually or dramatically revealed as similar, even identical in direction and end-point. Thus a vast area of material can be traversed and explored, but a final unified perspective of the whole can be achieved. Many of the searches upon which the dreamer embarks bring him to the same resting place—and in one vital sense all searches in the poem, whether his or not, are variations of the one great search for St. Truth, recommended by Holy Church at the very beginning of the poem (2.203: C. II. 203, etc.), again by Reason (C. VI. 199), and first turned into a practical proposition by Piers himself (5.63 foll.; C. VIII. 182 foll.).

Although the pilgrimage to St. Truth, as it is envisaged by repentant mankind—

A thousend of men tho throngen togyderes,
Criede upward to Crist and to his clene moder
To have grace to go to Treuthe—god leve that they mote!

(5.36–8: C. VIII. 155–7)

—is never literally completed, all the searches which succeed it are, essentially, for St. Truth or Truth. They unfold out of the first search in a way which is more like a process of organic growth than deliberate literary design. So the search for Dowel is initiated by the words of the Pardon, sent by St. Truth to Piers Plowman and the hopeful pilgrims, encouraging them to abandon pilgrimage and stay at home (C. X. 1–8). The injunction 'Dowel . . . and god shall haue thy saule' (C. X. 289) formulates, in a different way, the dreamer's first request for help—'how I may save my soul'—and Holy Church's advice—'Truth is the best'. Dowel replaces Truth as the dreamer's immediate goal, but as a warning that this is no side-tracking or diminution of great issues, the search for Dowel is almost immediately rephrased in triple terms—Dowel, Dobet and Dobest: Thought replies to the dreamer

'Dowel and Dobet,' quod he, and Dobest the thridde
Aren thre fayre vertues and ben nat fer to fynde.'

(7.76–7: C. XI. 76–7)

The dreamer is, in fact, still pursuing Truth, but in its component parts—three 'true' ways of life, states of grace, grades of charity. The problem of 'seeking truth' has been broken down into smaller, more manageable units for investigation. And the various journeys which are recommended and undertaken while the search for 'Dowel, Dobet and Dobest' is still under way—the journeys to Clergye, to Parfitnesse, to Charite—are all exploratory within the terms of that search. Clergye is consulted as the voice of authority on Dowel, and the road to salvation—

'To Clergie shult thow neuere come, ne knowe what ys Dowel . . .'

(C. XII. 113 foll.)

Parfitnesse is sought as an alternative route towards Dowel: the dreamer follows Conscience 'with gret wil', who has already turned against Clergye, and decided

'With Pacience wol I passe, parfitnesse to fynde.'

(11.184: C. XVI. 184)

But it is Dowel they speak of, as they travel: the search has changed course, but not ultimate direction:

And as thei wente by the wey, of Dowel gan their carpe.

(C. XVI. 190)

And when the dreamer asks for help in his search for Charite—

'Leve *Liberum Arbitrium*,' quod I, 'I leve, as I hope,
Thow couthest telle and teche me to Charite, as I leve?'

(13.1–2: C. XIX. 1–2)

it comes not only as the climax to numerous affirmations of love as the underlying principle of Dowel, Dobet and Dobest, but is specifically called up by the statement that salvation can only be achieved through belief in Holy Church, which *is* belief in Charity. The dreamer asks

'What is holychurche, frend?' quoth ich; 'Charite,' he seyde . . .

(C. XVIII. 125)

And the way to heaven is once more opened out:

'And that is Charite, my leue childe . . .
Contrarie hure nauht, as in conscience, yf thou wolt come to heuene.'

(C. XVIII. 148–9)

Such words make it clear that the nature of the quest has not really changed since the dreamer first asked Holy Church 'how I may save my soul'. And, indeed, from this point forward, the quest is seen less in triple than in unified concepts, as if the time for diversified exploration is past, and the time for re-joining main routes is near. Although the last two sections of the poem are labelled 'Dobet' and 'Dobest', the activity of the poem from Passus XVIII on-wards is increasingly centred upon Charity and upon Piers the Plowman, who exemplifies and encloses within himself the trilogy, Dowel, Dobet and Dobest, and who finally reveals Truth in human form.[57] There is no contradiction in the fact that the poem starts out to seek Truth, and ends by seeking Piers Plow-man: Langland is as much concerned to provide means as he is to provide goals. The perplexity of the dreamer, when he is told by Holy Church in Passus II to seek Truth, is gradually replaced by a sense of relief as he realizes he can seek Piers Plowman to reveal that Truth: this is as fine a witness to Langland's penetrating knowledge of the human predicament as it is to his dramatic inventiveness.

Finally, it is important to see that the directions given by Piers for the arrested pilgrimage to Truth (5.86 foll.: C. VIII. 204 foll.) are not wasted. They lay down general guiding lines for all later quests. We are meant to find that the dreamer, asking for help as he seeks a variety of goals, receives familiar answers and recognizes old familiar routes. So the journey to Clergye (itself a part of the search for Dowel) proceeds, as Piers had forecast, through humility and patience and avoidance of sin. The dreamer appeals for 'som tokne, for tyme is that I wende', and gets from Dame Studye brief confirmation of what Piers has said—that obedience and active virtue are prime requisites for the pilgrim:

'Aske the heye wey,' quath hue, 'hennes to Suffre—
Bothe-wele-and-moche-wo yf thow wolt lerne . . .
Bothe wommen and wyn, wratthe, yre, and slewthe,
Yf thow hem vse other haunte, haue god my treuthe!
To Clergie shult thow neuere come, ne knowe what ys Dowel.'[58]

(C. XII. 107–8, 111–13)

And when Clergye is found, his advice about how to reach and recognize Dowel confirms once more Piers' doctrine of obedience to the ten command-ments,[59] and belief in the miraculous atoning power of the Incarnation:[60]

[57] In Passus XXII, when Christ assumes a form acclaimed by the dreamer as that of Piers (ll. 6–8) and when he delegates his power on earth to Piers (ll. 182 foll.).
[58] Compare, specifically, 5.142 foll.; C. VIII. 261 foll.: 'Be war thenne of Wrath, that wikkede shrewe . . .'
[59] Compare 5.94 foll.; C. VIII. 213 foll.
[60] Compare 5.132–3: C. VIII, 251–2:
'A ful leel lady unlek hit of grace,
And she hath the keye and a clycat, thogh the kynge slepe.'

'By Cryst,' quath Clergie, 'yf thow coueyte Dowel,
Kep the ten commaundemens and kep the fro synne;
And by-leyf leelly how godes sone a-lyghte
On the mayde Marie . . .'

(C. XII. 142-5)

Perhaps the most significant fact to observe is that whatever the nature of the
search, and whoever the guide, whoever the seeker, Langland never allows
dreamer or reader to forget the emphatic statements made by Piers, so early on,
about love. Love 'roofs over' the court of Truth (5.118-9: C. VIII. 237-8) and
the travellers to that court are urged to discover in their own hearts Truth
enshrined in love (5.136-7: C. VIII. 257-8).

The austere Dame Studye recommends love as the 'clue' to Dowel, Dobet
and Dobest:

'Lerne for to louye, yf the lyke Dowel,
For of Dobet and of Dobest here doctor is dere Loue.'

(C. XII. 135-6)

Clergye reinforces this in his discussion of Dowel, seeing love as the crown of
faith:

'Thus Byleyue and Leaute and Loue is the thridde,
That maketh men to Dowel, Dobet, and Dobest.'

(C. XII. 161-2)

The essence of the search for Parfitnesse is sacrifice of all for love: pilgrims
moving on this lonely path must travel by love:

'And for goddes loue leueth al and lyueth as a beggere.'

(C. XVII. 105)

It comes as a natural conclusion that when the dreamer asks to be directed to
'charite' (13.1 foll: C. XIX. 1 foll.), he is led to a country called 'cor-hominis',
in which the tree 'true-love' grows. Piers' original assurance that the questing
for Truth will end in love, in man's own heart—'. . . charge Charite a churche
to make/In thyne hole herte, to herborwe alle trewe'[61]—is here confirmed.
The dreamer has now, in fact, advanced along that road to Truth sketched out
by Piers: he stands in the land of the 'hole herte', 'cor-hominis', and sees Truth
and Love face to face—

'The tree hatte Trewe-love,' quod he, 'the trinite hit sette'.

(13.9: C. XIX. 9)

[61] 5.138-9: C. VIII. 257-8

But confirmation is also given by the very last search of the poem, announced by Conscience, and set towards Piers Plowman (16.330 foll.: C. XXIII. 380 foll.). In a strange and powerful way, the directions first given by Piers are proved not only upon the dreamer's experience, but upon that of Piers also. For in the centre of Piers, as 'Dowel', lie also 'Dobet', love, and 'Dobest', spiritual authority. Piers tells us, and the poem then reveals to us, by his successive appearances and transformations, how Truth and Love live in the heart of man:

'For Peres love the palmare, that impugnede ones
Alle kyne konnynges and alle kyne craftes ...
And preveth by puyre skyle inparfyt alle thynges,
Bote lele love and treuthe. . . .'

(11.131-3, 136-7: C. XVI. 131-3, 136-7)

The stirring of Conscience towards Piers Plowman is, in its deepest sense, the stirring of man's desire for regenerative growth: to seek Piers Plowman is not only to seek spiritual authority, the ideal Pope, but to seek the inner sources of good, the materials and energy for reform, the prerequisite for life's journeying.

It has been possible to distinguish for *Piers Plowman* a four-part structure, enclosed and subdivided again by dream-boundaries, threaded through by the constant presence of the dreamer-figure, punctuated by significant appearances of Piers Plowman, and patterned by recurrent forms of search or pilgrimage. Even this complex statement does not give an entirely accurate impression of the experience of reading the poem: an experience we may find both richer and, at times, more confusing than any analysis or abstract can suggest.

Procedures

For Langland's procedures, his manipulative habits, can strike the reader as strange. We may be able to accept the need to look for thematic and not for narrative continuity in the poem, but the building of themes does not go forward in a direct and obvious manner. So many subjects seem to be held under consideration at the same time: Langland's attention is frequently diverted by fresh objects and ideas. We can often detect a leaning to the impromptu in his dealings with chosen material. It is not always clear on what principles he becomes expansive or economical: on the one hand, he shows himself fond of insistent, repetitious treatment of themes; on the other, only too willing to abandon or curtail or interrupt a sequence of thought. Evidence of planning we can discern, but it is clear that Langland had no intention of being constrained by plan. To put this down simply to his unpredictable or idiosyncratic nature would not be just, however. Difficult as he may sometimes be to follow, he had good precedent for the more unfamiliar of his movements—the techniques and procedures of the looser medieval sermon, constructed 'd'après un plan dont la logique nous échappe, nourris d'associations, d'idées qui ne nous semblent ni naturelles ni surtout nécessaires'.[62] Étienne Gilson's analysis of this elusive sermon logic is useful and appropriate to a reading of *Piers Plowman*: Langland often preaches—either openly or through his characters:[63]

   ... prechours of godes wordes
Sauen thorgh here sermons mannes soule fro helle.

                                    (C. VIII. 88–9)

It is natural that we should find strong similarities between his poem and the literature of the medieval pulpit, not only in basic material, but also in techniques of exposition.[64]

Sermon Techniques

Digressive and Diffuse Procedures. For our present purposes, it is important that the accepted theory of medieval sermon composition, aiming at the fullest possible 'drawing-out' of its themes, allowed and even encouraged sudden departures from plan, and maintained loose-knit unity by a linking system of repetitions, correspondences, and cross-references. The frequent twists and abrupt changes of direction in *Piers Plowman* can be quite easily explained in terms of the 'logique interne' of the pulpit, whose theorists were eager to claim freedom from the tyranny of form, when moral fruitfulness was an issue: 'edification of souls is more to be prized than continuity of discourse'.[65] Langland often demonstrates the 'déplacements brusques des prédicateurs', the unannounced flight from a subject in hand 'chaque fois que son zèle pour les âmes propose à son imagination quelque nouvel objet'.[66] What may sometimes look like a wilful disregard for orderly procedure or an inability to control the flow of thought may be based upon a conviction that the impulse to teach must not, on any purely formal or artistic grounds, be resisted. The priorities are spiritual.

---

[62] E. Gilson, *Les Idées et les Lettres* (Paris, 1932), p. 95
[63] See, for instance, C. VI. 114 foll., C. XIII. 40 foll.
[64] See Owst, *Literature and Pulpit*, Ch. IX; E. Salter, *Piers Plowman: An Introduction* (Oxford, 1962), Ch. II; and A. C. Spearing, *Criticism and Mediaeva, Poetry* (London, 1964), Ch. IV
[65] 'Magis enim amanda est animarum aedificatio quam sermonis continuatio', quoted by Gilson, op. cit., p. 143
[66] Ibid., p. 144

On one occasion, at 15.356–7: C. XXI. 360–1, Langland admits that he has digressed from his main theme for the sake of such 'edification'.

(A litel I over-leep for lesygnes sake,
That I ne sygge as I saw, syunde my teme!)

The example is a decisive one: Langland has apparently been struck by Satan's use of the word 'lesynges' to Lucifer (15.346, 347: C. XXI. 350, 351) and has interrupted the account of the Harrowing of Hell to enlarge on the significance of 'lying' for his own age:

Beth ywar, ye wyse clerkes and witty men of lawe.
(15.353: C. XXI. 357)

It is, on a first reading, surprising that Langland should have been willing to delay that magnificent exchange between Lucifer and Christ—

'What lord artow?' quod Lucifer. A voys aloud saide:

—for such a comparatively minor piece of teaching: on reflection, it seems entirely characteristic, and, within its own terms of reference, quite logical —'magis ... aedificatio quam ... continuatio ...'

But it is not only dislocation of flow which can be better understood by reference to sermon theory. One of the most characteristic and, to the new reader, most frustrating, features of *Piers Plowman* is Langland's circuitous method of dealing with themes. The long speech by Wit, for instance (beginning at C. XI. 127), is, to us, a very diffuse answer to the dreamer's desire to know 'wher Dowel and Dobet and Dobest ben in londe .../And what lyues they lyuen, and what lawe they usen ...' (ll. 123, 125). An illustrative allegory of the castle of Sir Dowel, man's soul, is interrupted by a description of Kynde, the creator of the castle, and succeeded by a special examination of Inwit, guard of the castle, and rational power of the soul. Those who misused this faculty are reviewed—Lot, Noah, Herod: the attack then widens to take in man's deficiencies in virtuous living and in charity, and the Church's responsibility for failure to enforce the lessons of Christ. By the time Wit returns to this original theme, and gives the dreamer a compact definition of Dowel, Dobet and Dobest, the Fall, the Flood and contemporary marriage-broking have all been dealt with. While nothing in the speech is irrelevant to the three states or lives, it can hardly be called a systematic treatment of the subject.[67]

[67] See the long speech by Ymaginatyf, C. XV. I foll., which attempts to expose the folly of the dreamer's presumptuous behaviour to Reason, and, appropriately though discursively, winds through magisterial statements about salvation to a thoughtful and inconclusive end—'al worth as god wole'. And see also the whole of extract 6.

Langland would probably have offered no defence of this. For a good part of medieval sermon theory and practice would have encouraged him to feel that a theme might be developed quite as usefully and pleasurably in a woven fabric of statement and variation as it might be in simple sequence. If repetition were involved, it served to enforce the message of the theme: if the poet—or the preacher—elected to traverse his material much in the way that the weaver's shuttle traversed the web, he could at least guarantee that his meaning would be covered thoroughly and closely. To accept this is not necessarily to find passages such as those cited above any more attractive to modern taste: they do, however, become more intelligible and seem more responsible in their approach.

Repetitive Devices. But pulpit theory encouraged Langland in other methods of work which actively contributed to the overall unity of the poem. *Piers Plowman* makes full use of those repetitive devices, recommended by sermon manuals as teaching aids—not only within individual passages, as 'word-play', but as 'foretastes and echoes'[68] running the whole length of the poem.

The subject of the Seven Deadly Sins is an obvious example. Lightly touched upon in the first passus,

... this wastors with glotony destrueth.	(1.24: C. I. 24)
... summe putte hem to pruyde ...	(1.25: C. I. 25)
Slep and also slewthe sueth suche ever.	(1.46: C. I. 46)
And leneth it lorelles that lecherye haunten.	(1.75: C. I. 75)

it is written in more deliberately in Passus III (ll. 79 foll.) where Lady Meed's marriage charter describes a whole world of evil feature and attribute—'the erldom of enuye and yre', 'the lordshep of lecherye ... '. So far, the sins have been viewed objectively, as abstract qualities: in Passus VII (extract 4), through their confessions, they are personalized, in horrifying detail. This thorough scrutiny of sin, its various faces and its subtle operation, confirms what has gone before, and, for the future, makes it impossible for us to accept even the briefest mention of sin without bringing to it the fearsome associations of Passus VII.

Thus, when Patience sketches the seven deadly sins (in C. XVII. 44 foll.), proving that they have no strength against poverty, we are able to provide the passage with a deep hinterland of evil and suffering. And, when the poem begins to come full circle, and Antichrist attacks (16.3 foll.: C. XXIII. 69 foll.), the fact that many of his officers are deadly sins is grimly familiar. Their re-entry into the poem is dramatically effective—

[68] The phrase is that of Professor Nevill Coghill, who used it in 'The Pardon of Piers Plowman', *Proceedings of the British Academy*, XXX (1944), p. 312, without relating it to sermon practice.

And Pryde hit bar baldly aboute   (16.20: C. XXIII. 70)

This Lecherye leyde on with lauhyng chere   (16.64: C. XXIII. 114)

Thenne cam Covetyse ...
And armed hym in avarice and hungriliche lyvede.

(16.71, 73: C. XXIII. 121, 123)

But there is, by now, cause for hope as well as for despair: we have already seen them rendered powerless—once by Repentance (Passus VIII) and once by Poverty (Passus XVIII). Their antics can now be more soberly judged than when they first erupted into Langland's vision, on the Field full of Folk.

The presence of these 'foretastes and echoes'—so reminiscent of the verbal correspondences used by preachers to link the various parts of their sermons together—means that Langland's poetry often makes its mark cumulatively. The speech of Christ, after the Harrowing of Hell (15.270 foll.: C. XXI. 404 foll.), has been singled out for its great wealth of significance: more precisely, every phrase in it reverberates, drawing verbal and conceptual powers from close surroundings and distant regions of the poem.[69]

A passage such as this, in its relationship to the rest of the work, points to one very characteristic way in which *Piers Plowman* operates upon us. For Langland, like many medieval preachers, allowed main themes to act as magnets, attracting to themselves a rich abundance of expressive associations. The central themes of sin and love are 'expressed' throughout the poem in innumerable variations and transpositions; though the method may be repetitive, it does ensure that when the dreamer asks one of his last questions—

'Consaileth me, Kynde', quod I, 'what craft be beste to lere?'

(16.157: C. XXIII. 207)

the answer not only rings with immediate authority, but echoes back through the poem, harmonizing and unifying it:

'Lerne to love', quod Kynde, 'and leef alle othere'.

(16.158: C. XXIII. 208)

THE POETRY OF PIERS PLOWMAN

Over the last few years, increased attention has been paid to Langland as a poet:[70] this means that it is no longer necessary to set out all the old charges

[69] See the detailed exposition of this, using the B text, in E. Salter, *Piers Plowman*, pp. 49–52
[70] See E. T. Donaldson, *Piers Plowman: the C Text and its Poet* (New Haven, 1949), Ch. III, 'The Art of the C Reviser'; Salter, *Piers Plowman*, Ch. II, 'The

against him, or to proceed entirely on the defensive. It is now possible to claim recognition for the amount of fine poetry which exists in a work of this size before offering apologies for the inferior writing. Langland's status is secure enough for us to bring comments from the *Biographia Literaria* to bear upon our judgment of *Piers Plowman*:

> . . . a poem of any length neither can be, nor ought to be, all poetry. Yet, if a harmonious whole is to be produced, the remaining parts must be preserved in keeping with the poetry.[71]

A case can here be made for Langland, as it can be for Wordsworth in *The Prelude*, or for Milton in *Paradise Lost*.

It is also possible to recommend Langland's poetry to the modern reader as the most accessible of medieval verse: lacking the sumptuous vocabulary, the contorted syntax of many other alliterative poems, and the often elaborate metrical patterning of the Chaucerian 'school', it comes closer than anything else in its period to modern accentual verse. The approximation of its grammar to that of ordinary speech, the simple vividness of its language, give us a direct line of approach to *Piers Plowman*:

> Adam, the whiles he spak nat, hadde paradys at wille,
> Ac when he mamelede aboute mete and musede for to knowe
> The wisdom and the wit of god, he was put out of blisse.
>
> (10.98–100: C. XIV. 227–29)

It is easy for us to understand and appreciate the flexibility of Langland's line: it is the most versatile of all medieval forms—able to encompass the free conversational rhythms of

> 'What manere mynstralcie, my dere frend,' quath Conscience,
> 'Hast thou used other haunted al thy lyf-tyme?'
>
> (C. XVI. 196–7)

as well as the formal, processional movement of Christ's speech at the Harrowing of Hell.

And it is no longer necessary to spend much time proving Langland's poetic ability: when he wished, he could polish and perfect a line—compare his last version of Christ's words to Lucifer

---

Art of *Piers Plowman*'; Lawlor, *Piers Plowman: An Essay in Criticism*, Part II, 'The Poetic Techniques'; and Spearing, *Criticism and Mediaeval Poetry*, Ch. III, 'The Art of Preaching and *Piers Plowman*'
[71] *Biographia Literaria*, Ch. XIV

'May no pyement ne pomade, ne presiouse drynkes
Moiste me to the fulle, ne my furste slakke . . .'

(15.408–9: C. XXI. 412–13)

with his earlier version

'May no drynke me moiste, ne my thruste slake . . .'

(B. XVIII. 366)

And when he wished, he could avail himself of verbal devices:

'At churche in the charnel, cheorles aren uvel to knowe,
Other a knyght fro a knaue, other a queyne fro a queene.'

(C. IX. 45–6)

'And riht as the gylour thorw gyle bygiled man formest . . .'

(15.163: C. XXI. 164)

More generally, it is now possible to demand a sympathetic hearing for a
poet whose attitude to his art is above all honest, whose principles may not
always be conducive to 'fine writing', but will always discourage empty showi-
ness of style. Langland's poetry is at its best when his religion and his imagination are in perfect accord, and direct, jointly, his verbal skills. If his faith had
the right to set 'imprimatur' to his poetry, it had also absolute right to inspire
and sustain it. In this context, rapid fluctuations of poetic quality from a work
which has been justly called 'at once magnificent and impoverished'[72] are to
be expected. The great Christian themes of suffering, patience and love, the
great Christian mysteries of incarnation and resurrection, constantly fire Langland's verse:

For the hye holygost shall heuene to-cleue,
And loue shal leepe out after into this lowe earthe.

(C. XV. 84–5)

But his dedication to a primarily religious purpose—'how I may save my
soul'—may, at times, command from him verse in which everything has been
reduced to the bare bone of sense. Piers Plowman's directions for the pilgrims
to Truth, or Wit's discourse to the dreamer on Dowel, and Kynde and Inwit
(C. XI. 127 foll.), consist of nothing but information to be absorbed by the
reader and dreamer. On such occasions—and there are many similar—we are
not called upon to be moved or exhilarated, but only edified. We cannot commend the *poet*, but we can, still, respect the man of religion. Whether we like
it or not, it is as a man of religion that Langland would have expected his age
and succeeding centuries to remember him. It would probably be more re-

[72] Spearing, op. cit., p. 87

warding for us to admire the ways in which his devotion so often inspired and nourished his poetry than to regret the ways in which it diminished it.

We should remind ourselves that, in the medieval period, the use of verse did not necessarily commit the writer to 'high art'. For an age in which literature still performed many of its traditional oral functions, verse, rather than prose, was the more usual, the more normal medium of expression. The really complex and difficult works of the period, written for highly specialized groups of readers, were written in prose: The *Cloud of Unknowing*, for instance. Verse covers the whole spectrum of medieval taste. As well as the 'court' poets, such as Chaucer and his equally sophisticated contemporaries, the alliterative poets of English provincial centres, whose work was backed by an expert knowledge of rhetorical techniques, there were many fourteenth-century English writers who used verse only because it was a popular and convenient means of communication. The lesser romance writers, the compilers of verse treatments of sacred history, of saints' lives, the chroniclers, the complaint writers, and many of the so-called 'lyric' writers, do not use verse in preference to prose because of its stronger imaginative and decorative potential: they use it because it is easier to recite and to memorize.

Our expectations of what kind of poetry we are to find in *Piers Plowman* would be more realistic if we associated it less with *The Canterbury Tales*, *Pearl*, or *Winner and Waster*, and more with verse histories of the world, such as the *Cursor Mundi*, treatise poems, such as Robert Mannyng's *Handlyng Synne*, religious allegories, such as Guillame de Deguilleville's *Pèlerinage* poems, or satirical complaints in verse, such as the earlier fourteenth-century *Simonie*. For although *Piers Plowman* was probably designed for a rather more learned public than theirs, and although Langland shows himself capable of, and interested in, a range of poetry quite outside their reach, he shares with them—as he does not share with Chaucer—a basically utilitarian attitude to his art. Verse, for him, is to be used, not specially revered or respected for its own sake.

The famous defence of his position as a poet (B. XII. 20 foll.) refers to his pleasure in 'makynges', but rests ultimately upon practical considerations: through writing poetry he is searching for spiritual understanding. Of course prayer is of a higher order than writing verse: only the extreme form of his moral dilemma justifies his pursuit of the truth in poetry, or, indeed, in any other way but in total dedication to God:

> 'Ac if there were any wight that wolde me telle
> What were Dowel and Dobet and Dobest atte laste,
> Wolde I neuere do werke, but wende to holicherche.'   (B. XII. 26–8)

Here the logic of the major changes Langland made in his last version of the poem, the C text, becomes understandable. The C text embodies, in the quality of its verse, the spirit of the principles outlined above. When we compare its opening twenty lines with those of the B text, we may at first only notice Langland's rejection of the drowsy felicities of medieval dream poetry: the hint of enchantment, the hillside, the stream and its chattering waters have disappeared. But in their place we have a poetry of grave and disciplined beauty in which meaning and form are quintessential. It is Langland's peculiar achievement that out of commitments and materials which appear daunting, even prohibitive, and which *proved* to be for many medieval poets, he so often managed to create a poetry finely adjusted to satisfy the moral senses as well as the imagination:

> And seith, 'lo, briddes and bestes that no blisse knoweth,
> And wilde wormes in wodes, thorw wynter thow hem greuest,
> And makest hem wel ney meek and mylde for defaute;
> After than thow sendest hem somere, that is here souereyn Ioye,
> And blisse to alle that been bothe wilde and tame.
> Then may beggers, as bestes, after blysse asken,
> That al here lif hauen lyued in langour and defaute.'
>
> (C. XVI. 292–8)

But this should not blind us to the fact that there are many stretches of *Piers Plowman* in which Langland is unlikely to be doing more than communicating plain sense as plainly as possible in verse form. This, to him and to his age, would have been permissible and comprehensible. The 'harmonious whole', demanded by Coleridge of the long poem, can be seen in *Piers Plowman* if we are not prejudiced against the groundbass of verse statement and exhortation from which Langland's imaginative poetry takes flight. It is, indeed, 'in keeping' with the finest poetry that it should exist in juxtaposition with the prosaic: it is all in keeping with Langland's honesty about the relationship of his art to his religion.

Significant here is the passage (6.47 foll.: C. X. 107 foll.) in which Langland speaks of 'God's minstrels' as distinct from 'alle manere mynstrales' of the secular world. It looks very much as if he may be giving us his own concept of the poet in his highest function—a prophet figure, who speaks to man as inspired by God:

> Ne none muracles maken—ac many tymes hem happeth
> To prophecye of the peple, pleyinge, as hit were, . . .
> For hit aren merye-mouthed men, munstrals of hevene,
> And godes boys, bordyors, as the book telleth.
>
> (6.53–4, 66–7: C. X. 113–14, 126–7)

Much that is initially puzzling about the matter and the art of *Piers Plowman* becomes clear if we accept Langland's view of himself as one of 'godes myn-stralles and hus messagers'.

With such an outlook, and such allegiances, it should not surprise us that when Langland mentions 'rhetoric', he does not mean poetic rhetoric but that of the pulpit:

> 'Thinge that al the worlde wote wherfore shuldestow spare
> To reden it in retoryke, to arate dedly synne?'
>
> (B. XI. 97–8)

Many of the devices prescribed by such sermon 'retoryke' are prescribed by the manuals of poetic theory too: Chaucer, like Langland, was interested in various forms of verbal repetition, and both poets use them with skill and assurance. The difference lies in the reason for their use: Langland and the preachers view repetition primarily as a teaching aid, a method of underlining or summing up an important idea.[73] In particular instances, it is true, Langland transforms a teaching device into an illuminative feature: the use of the word 'guile' in the Harrowing of Hell debate (15.311–98: C. XXI. 315–402) is an obvious example. Musical analogies are not out of place here: the whole episode, from the beginning of the defiant speeches of Satan and Lucifer to the last triumphant words of Christ at their fall, uses language as music uses chords, to transpose from one key into another. 'Guile', first played upon as a single note, is gradually combined with 'life' and 'grace', in different variations, and resolved into the major mode of 'life' and 'love':

> '. . . The olde lawe techeth
> That gylours be bigiled and in here gyle falle'
>
> (15.380–1: C. XXI. 385)

> 'So that with gyle was gete, thorw grace is now ywonne.
> And as Adam and alle thorwe a tre deyede,
> Adam and alle thorw a tre shal turne to lyve'
>
> (15.395–7: C. XXI. 399–401)

> 'For I that am lord of lyf, love is my drynke.'
>
> (15.402: C. XXI. 406)

Langland is, by general definition, an 'alliterative poet'; his line is, basically, the four-stress accentual measure of *Sir Gawain*, *Winner and Waster* or the *Parliament of the Three Ages*. Yet many have been impelled to comment upon, and to suggest reasons for, the unique qualities of his verse. So, one of the most recent writers on the poem sums up the situation:

[73] For further comment on sermon and poetic rhetoric, see Salter, op. cit., pp. 26–40, and Spearing, op. cit., pp. 88–92

. . . the impression one receives from reading the other alliterative poems enforces the difference between them and *Piers Plowman* . . .[74]

A far less specialized poetic vocabulary and a far freer rhythmical range distinguish *Piers Plowman* immediately from much of the poetry of the 'alliterative revival', which so often gives the impression of having been wrought in stiff brocade, or in glittering cloisonné. It had, of course, a more ordinary style at its command: there are poems and parts of poems from the 14th-century alliterative 'school' which are nearer to *Piers Plowman* than *Pearl* or *Sir Gawain*. *Richard the Redeless*,[75] for instance, has something of its toughness and forth-rightness:

A! Hicke Heuyheed! hard is thi nolle
To cacche ony kunnnge but cautell bigynne!
Herdist thou not with eeris how that I er tellde. . . . .

(Passus III, ll. 66–8)

But no single alliterative poem, in its entirety, reminds us of *Piers Plowman*. It is as if Langland accepted certain basic structural features, and certain stylistic traits of the alliterative poetry he must have known from his youth in the west of England, but totally rejected other features, shaping a verse medium more properly suited to his diverse materials and purposes. Many factors must have operated upon him. Writing in London, for an amorphous clerkly public, and not in a provincial castle, for a particular baronial audience, he would hardly have been tempted to experiment with the encrusted alliterative styles which were so much to the taste of western poets and their patrons. And it is probable, too, that the wide range of his reading—wider, certainly, than that of any other alliterative poet of his time—would have affected his style. In London he must have come into contact with many different kinds of English verse, rhymed, semi-alliterative, popular and instructive, satirical and serious.[76] It is more than likely that the looser, more various rhythmic nature of his verse is in part the result of this contact: it could also have shown him how to utilize alliteration as an index of sense, rather than as an insistent pattern of sound. Few full-scale alliterative poems can offer lines so similar to *Piers Plowman* as this from *The Simonie*, a semi-alliterative poem of London provenance:

[74] S. Hussey, 'Langland's Reading of Alliterative Poetry', *M.L.R.*, LX (1965), p. 170

[75] Ed. W. W. Skeat, *Piers the Plowman in Three Parallel Texts and Richard the Redeless* (Oxford, 1954), pp. 603–28

[76] See E. Salter, '*Piers Plowman* and *The Simonie*', *Archiv*, CCIII (1967), pp. 241–54

C

And there they clateren cumpelin, whan the candel is oute. (l. 120).[77]

Ultimately, we must restate the singularity of Langland's most impressive verse. Admirable for its dramatic verve, and for its descriptive pungency, it is remarkable—almost inimitable—for the way in which it charges the simplest language with imaginative energy:

Deth cam dryvyng aftur and al to duste paschte
Kynges and knyhtes, caysers and popes.

(16.50–1: CXXIII. 100–01)

[77] 'And there they gabble compline, when they've put out the light'—a reference to the idle priest and his mistress. Compare Langland's

'And gnawen god with the gorge, whan her gutte is fulle'

(B. X. 57: 8.41).

NOTE TO THE TEXT

This edition of selections from *Piers Plowman* is based on MS HM 143 (X) of the C-text. Capitals and punctuation are modern, and contractions have been silently expanded; ȝ is replaced by *gh* or *y* as appropriate, þ by *th*, and *u/v*, *i/j* are distinguished as vowel and consonant according to modern practice. Certain eccentricities in the spelling of X have been eliminated, particularly the scribe's use of *o* in unstressed syllables (e.g. *-ore* for *-ere*) and his use of *ae, oe* for *a, o*, respectively. Other departures from X are indicated in the Textual foot-notes. Errors are corrected, and omissions supplied, from British Museum Additional MS 35157 (U), another manuscript of good descent, not used by Skeat. Where both X and U agree in an obviously inferior reading, we have had recourse to Skeat's text (P, i.e. MS HM 137, or S, where Skeat indicates he is not following his copy-text).

B text
looks in the
waters.

a reflection
because later look in your hear

Piers Plowman

1. The Fair Field full of Folk (Passus I, lines 1–84, 218–31)

In a somer sesoun, whan softe was the sonne,
I shope me into shroudes, as I a shep were,
In abite as an heremite, unholy of werkes,
Wente forth in the world wondres to here,
And saw many selles and selcouthe thynges.   5
Ac on a May mornyng on Malverne hulles
Me biful for to slepe, for werynesse of walkyng;
And yn a launde as I lay, lened I and slepte,
And merveylousliche me mette, as I may telle.
Al the welthe of the world and the wo bothe   10
Wynkyng, as hit were, witterliche I saw hit,
Of treuthe and tricherye, tresoun and gyle,
Al I saw slepynge, as I shal telle.
    Estward I beheld aftir the sonne
And saw a tour—as I trowe, Treuthe was there-ynne.   15

---

7. walkyng : X walked   **15.** I *supplied from* U

1–9. The spring-setting is conventional as a prelude to the dream. It makes
a familiar entry into the audience's attention, tells them that they are listening
to a particular kind of poem, and orientates them in relation to the 'I' of the
poem. The dream, too, works as a conventional technique to direct the expectations of the audience towards non-realistic allegory.

2–3. 'I dressed myself in rough clothes, like a shepherd, in the garb of a
hermit of secular life.' Such easy-going hermits, dedicated to no strict rule but
that of not working, are severely criticised by Langland himself later on
(C. X. 188–212; cf. 28–9, below)—but then, he had no illusions about how his
own life looked to the world (see extract 3). The literary purpose is clear: to
establish the dreamer-narrator, as Chaucer does, as an outsider, a spectator,
and one who has no pretensions to superiority over the reader (the 'low-
mimetic' mode of Frye).

5. 'And saw many marvels and strange things'. *Selles* could mean 'hermits'
cells', but the sense is poor.

6. There is evidence that Langland as a boy was put to school at Great
Malvern priory, at the foot of the Malvern hills in Worcestershire (see 3.36n).

10–13. These lines in C replace further scenic description and dream-setting
in B, and are an example of C's ruthless exclusion of non-functional 'poetic'
ornament. See Donaldson, *The C-Text and its Poet*, pp. 48–50.

Westward I waytede in a while aftir
And saw a depe dale—Deth, as I leve,
Woned in tho wones, and wikkede spiritus.
A fair feld, ful of folk, fond I there bytwene,
Of alle manere of men, the mene and the pore,   *good or bad* **20**
Worchyng and wandryng as this world asketh.   *as you understand*
    Somme putte hem to the plogh, playde ful selde,
In settynge and in sowynge swonken ful harde,
And wonne that this wastors with glotony destrueth.   *bad*
And summe putte hem to pruyde and parayled hem ther-after,   25
In continance and clothyng in many kyne gyse.   *disguise*
In preiers and penaunces putten hem mony,
Al for love of oure lord lyveden swythe harde,
In hope to have a good ende and heven-riche blisse:
As ankeres and eremites, that holdeth hem in here selles,   30
Coveyten noght in contreys to cayren aboute
For no likerous liflode here lycame to plese.

21.   wandryng *U* : *X* wondryng

14–18. B has the tower and the dale, too, but does not explain them specifically. C rejects the vaguely ominous in favour of the didactically explicit, and tells us the significance of the two places straight away, as well as assigning them their symbolic directions. (Eastward is toward the sun and God, westward away from God; in churches, the West window would often contain a representation of the Judgment, dominated by Hell-mouth.) The setting of the vision owes nothing to the Malvern hills, but something probably to techniques of staging morality plays, such as the *Castle of Perseverance*, in which the World, the Flesh, the Devil and God are located on scaffolds or platforms at symbolic points on the circumference of a central audience-area. See R. Southern, *The Medieval Theatre in the Round* (London, 1957).

24. The contrast here recalls a poem of the early alliterative revival, *Winner and Waster* (1352–3), an allegory of the social-economic state of England in the years after the Black Death. It may have influenced the original conception of *Piers Plowman*, though it has a more sophisticated view of the usefulness of 'wasters' (conspicuous consumers) in an expanding economy.

25–6. 'Some abandoned themselves to vanity, and arrayed themselves accordingly, both as regards appearance and dress, in various ways.'

30. 'Stability' of life is a crucial moral issue for Langland. Compare Chaucer's Monk and his contempt for such 'old rules' (*CT* I. 177–81).

31–2. 'Are not over-anxious to wander about the countryside, nor to indulge their flesh in luxurious living.'

And summe chesen chaffare—thei cheveth the bettre,
As it semeth to oure sighte that suche men thryveth;   *complications*
And summe merthes to make, as mynstrels conneth,   35 *begin*
Wolleth neyther swynke ne swete, bote sweren grete othes,
Fyndeth out foule fantasyes and foles hem maketh
And hath wytt at wille to worche yf thei wolde.
That Poule prechede of hem preve hit I myhte;
Qui turpiloquium loquitur is Luciferes knave.   40

Bidders and beggers faste aboute yede   *Bad Guys*
Til here bagge and here bely was bretful ycrammed,
Fayteden for here fode and foughten at the ale.
In glotony tho gomes goth thei to bedde
And riseth with rybaudrye tho Robardus knaves;   45
Slep and also slewthe sueth suche ever.

Pilgrymes and palmers plighten hem togyderes
To seke seynt James and seyntes of Rome,

44. tho *U* : *X* the

33-4. 'And some chose trade—they get on better, for it seems to us (in our limited way) that such men do well.'

37-8. 'And invent filthy stories and make fools of themselves, and (yet) have it in their power to do something useful, if they wanted to.' Minstrels, true and false, figure large in Langland's view of society (cf. 6.68–73), partly through personal pressures, for in his more comfortable moments he must have regarded himself as a minstrel of God and therefore wished to defend his profession against those who misused it, and partly through an image he has of the minstrel as the man who, granted his gift, sins against grace if he misuses it. See Donaldson, pp. 136–55.

39-40. The text of Paul referred to (not quoted) is 'If any would not work, neither should he eat' (*2 Thess.* 3: 10). *Qui turpiloquium loquitur* ('He who speaks filth') is an *ad hoc* invention, reminiscent of *Eph.* 5: 4 and *Col.* 3: 8. There are, it will be seen, plenty of sharp moral judgments in this vision of the world at work, but it is a fundamentally disordered, uninitiated vision (hence the bewildering kaleidoscope of trades and professions). The dreamer does not like what he sees, but cannot isolate what is wrong.

45. *Robardus knaves:* the phrase 'Robert's men' was proverbial for lawless vagabonds, perhaps from an association with Robin Hood (to whom *Piers Plowman* has the first reference in literature, C. VIII. 11), perhaps from *robber*.

48. *seynt James:* the shrine of St. James of Compostella, in Galicia, N. Spain, a famous place of pilgrimage.

Wenten forth on here way with many wyse tales
And hadden leve to lye aftir, al here lyf-tyme.   50
Eremites on an hep with hokede staves   *bad.*
Wenten to Walsyngham, and here wenches aftir;
Grete lobies and longe, that loth wer to swynke,
Clothed hem in copis to be knowe fram othere
And made hemself heremites, here ese to have.   55
   I fonde there of freris alle the foure ordres,   *B*
Prechyng the peple for profyt of the wombe,   *of himselven*
And glosede the gospel as hem good likede;
For coveytise of copis contraryed somme doctours.
Mony of thise maistres of mendenant freres   60
Here moneye and marchandise marchen togyderes;
Ac sith charite hath be chapman and chief to shryve lordes,
Mony ferlyes han falle in a fewe yeres,
And but holi chirche and charite choppe adoun suche shryvars
The moste meschief on molde mounteth up faste.   65
   There prechede a pardoner as he a prest were

61. marchen *P* : *X* maken

---

49. *wyse:* the text of C in Skeat's edition, based on *P* (MS HM 137), reads *unwyse.* It is not surprising that this kind of pedantic scribal interference has given the C-poet a bad name.

52. The shrine of Our Lady of Walsingham, in Norfolk, was second only to Canterbury as a place of pilgrimage in England.

54. They used the hermit's cloak not as a sign that they were different, but to disguise the fact that they were really the same.

56. Dominicans, Franciscans, Austin friars and Carmelites.

58–9. A familiar complaint against the friars was that they twisted the interpretation of the Scriptures, and contradicted established authority, for their own ends. See Chaucer's *Summoner's Tale, CT* III. 1793.

61. 'Their love of money and their trade (in souls) go hand in hand.'

62. 'But ever since friars made a merchant of charity [by using confession to make money] and became confessors-in-chief to lords . . .' Friars were accused of making confession easy to win money—Chaucer's portrait of the Friar in the *General Prologue* is an anthology of such grievances—and of cultivating the favour of high-ranking nobles in the same way (the royal confessors were always friars, and nearly always Dominicans, in the 14th and 15th centuries).

64. The violence of expression in C (cf. B: 'But holychirche and hii holde better togideres') anticipates the final vision, where friars form a kind of fifth column of Antichrist.

And brouht forth a bulle with bischopis selys,
Sayde that hymself myhte assoylen hem alle
Of falsnesses and fastynges, of vowes ybrokene.
Lewed men leved hym wel and lykede his wordes   70
And comen and knelede to kyssen his bulles;
He bounchede hem with his brevet and blered here yes
And raughte with his rageman rynges and broches.
Thus ye gyve youre gold, glotons to helpe,
And leneth it lorelles that lecherye haunten.   75
Were the bischop yblessed and worth bothe his eres,
His seel sholde nought be ysent in deseyte of the people.
Ac it is nought by the bischop, I leve, that the boy precheth,
For the parsche-prest and the pardoner parten the selver
That the peple in parsches sholde have, yf thei ne were.   80
    Persones and parsche-prestis pleyned to the bischop
That here parsches were pore sithe this pestelence tyme,
To have a licence and a leve in London to dwelle
And synge ther for symonye, while selver is so swete.

The original vision is here expanded in the B and C texts with a further
exposure of corruption in ecclesiastical high places, an allegorical account

72. brevet *S* : *X* bulles

68–9. This is the false claim. Pardons and indulgences offered remission of
penance (such as *fastynges*), here and hereafter, but not absolution from sin.
   72–3. 'He tapped them on the head (in token of forgiveness) with his letter
of authority, and, having properly pulled the wool over their eyes, raked in
their rings and brooches with his roll of papal parchment.'
   74. The directness and vehemence of Langland's condemnation of the false
pardoner is in striking contrast with Chaucer's dramatic indirection in the
Pardoner's Prologue and Tale.
   75. 'And give it to worthless wretches who habitually indulge in lechery.'
   76. 'If the bishop were truly saintly and worthy of his office . . .'
   78. 'But it is not for the bishop's benefit, I admit, that the rogue preaches.'
   80. '. . . if it were not for them.'
   82. *pestelence tyme:* the Black Death of 1348–9. There were further severe
outbreaks of plague in 1361–2, 1369, and 1375–6.
   83. '(And petitioned) to have . . .' Priests could earn an easy living saying
masses for the souls of the dead (i.e. as chantry-priests) in a wealthy city like
London. The practice was common enough for Chaucer to use his Parson's
repudiation of it (*CT* I. 507–11) as a technique of moral idealization.
   c*

of the monarchic political contract, and the topical fable of the belling of
the cat, designed to show the ineffectuality of 'democratic' movements
(the mice) against tyrannical authority (the cat, John of Gaunt).

Yut mette me more, of mene and of riche,   85
As barones and burgeys and bonde-men of thorpes,
Al I saw slepynge, as ye shal here herafter,
Bothe bakeres and breweres, bochers and other,
Webbesteres and walkeres and wynners with handes,
As taylers and tanners and tulyers of erthe,   90
As dykers and delvers, that doth here dedis ylle,
And driveth forth here days with 'Dew vous save, dame Emme!'
Cokes and here knaves cryede 'Hote pyes, hote!
Goode gees and grys, ga we dyne, ga we!'
Taverners til hem tolde the same: 95
'Whit wyn of Oseye and wyn of Gascoyne,
Of the Reule and of the Rochele, the roost to defy!'
Al this I saw sleping, and sevyn sythes more.

2. *The Vision of Holy Church* (Passus II, complete)

What the montaigne bymeneth and the merke dale
And the feld ful of folk I shal you fair shewe.
  A lovely lady of lere, in lynnene yclothed,
Cam doun fro the castel and calde me by name
And sayde, 'Wille, slepestou? Seestow this peple,   5

90. of *P* : *X* the   98. *Line supplied from UP*
3. lere *P* : *X illegible over erasure*; yclothed *P* : *X* in clothed

85-98. The picture becomes crowded and blurred, and the vision dissolves
in a chorus of street-cries, rather like the end of the second section of Eliot's
Waste Land. The blurring of vision and the dominant images of gluttony are
all part of the allegorical meaning.
  92. A line from a popular song, 'God help you, Dame Emma.'
  95-7. 'Innkeepers cried their wares to them in the same way: "White wine
of Alsace and wine of Gascony, wine from La Reole and Rochelle to wash
down your roast meat".'
  5. *Wille* (*Sone* in A and B) is a convenient as well as an actual name for the
dreamer, since it associates him with the abstraction *Will* (self-will, wilfulness,
unredeemed self), conventionally set against *Wit* (Reason, Wisdom).

Hou bisy thei ben aboute the mase?
The moste party of this peple that passeth on this erthe,
Hadde thei worschip in this world, thei wilneth no better;
Of othere hevene then here thei halde no tale.'

    I was afeered of here face, thogh she fayre were,   10
And sayde, 'Mercy, ma dame, what may this be to mene?'

    'The tour uppon the tofte,' quod she, 'Treuthe is there-ynne,
And wolde that ye wroughten as his word techeth.
For he is fader of fayth and formor of alle;
To be faythful to hym yaf yow fyve wittes   15
For to worschipe hym ther-with the whiles ye lyven here.
Wherfore he hette the elementis to helpe yow alle tymes
And brynge forth youre bilyve, bothe lynnen and wollene,
And in mesure how muche were to make yow attese;
And comaundede of his cortesye in comune thre thynges—   20
Aren non nideful but tho thre, and nemne hem I thenke
And rekene hem by rewe—reherse hem where the liketh.

    The firste is fode, and vesture the seconde,
And drynke—that doth the good, ac drynke nat out of tyme.
Loot in his lyve thorw likerous drynke   25
Wykkede wroghte and wrathed god almyhty.
In his dronkenesse a day his doughteres he dighte
And lay by hem bothe, as the boke telleth,
In his glotonye bygat gurles that were cherles,
And al he witte the wyn his wikkede dede.   30

---

19. how *U* : *X* thow   **24.** ac *P* : *X* and

8–9. 'If they had honour and success in this world, they want nothing better; they take no account of any other heaven than the one here.'

18–19. 'And to produce food and clothing—both linen and wool—and however much was needed to make you reasonably comfortable.'

25. The story of Lot would spring unbidden to the mind of the preacher denouncing drunkenness, as it did to the mind of Chaucer's Pardoner (*CT* VI. 485). The use of *exempla*, short illustrative stories of Biblical or other origin, is one of the main techniques of persuasion in sermons, and Langland and his characters frequently slip into homiletic modes of address. Indeed, of all forms of discourse, *Piers Plowman* is perhaps closest to the sermon. G. R. Owst, *Literature and Pulpit in Medieval England* (Oxford, 1933, rev. ed., 1961), provides the essential background material. With the Bible and the Roman Missal, this book is the best companion to *Piers Plowman* studies.

Inebriamus eum vino et dormiamus cum eo, ut servare
possimus de patre nostro semen. Genesis.

Thorw wyn and thorw woman there was Loot acombred;
Forthy drede delitable drynk bothe day and nyghtes.
  Mesure is medecyne, thogh thow muche yerne;
Al is nat good to the gost that the gutt asketh,
Ne liflode to the lycame that lef is the soule.   35
Leef nat thy lycame, for a lyare hym techeth,
Which is the wrecchede world, wolde the bigyle;
For the fend and thy flesch folewen togederes,
And that seeth the soule and sayth hit the in herte
And wysseth the to ben ywar what wolde the desseyve.'   40
  'A ma dame, mercy, me lyketh wel youre wordes;
Ac the moneye of this molde, that men so faste kepen,
Telleth me to wham that tresour bylongeth?'
  'Go to the gospel,' quod she, 'and se what god sayde,

39. seeth *S* : *X* sche(ne)th (*for* schendeth?)

30f. 'Come, let us make our father drink wine, and we will lie with him,
that we may preserve seed of our father' (*Gen*. 19: 32). This Biblical quotation,
and all subsequent quotations, are given in the English of the King James Bible.
In the original they are of course in the Latin of the Vulgate Bible, translated
from the Hebrew and Greek by St. Jerome in the 4th century, and universal
in the Western world until the beginning of vernacular translation in the
14th century. The function of such quotations in a literary work is fundamentally
homiletic—this is the 'text' of the discourse. The text is also a touchstone of
truth (Langland tends to use them most when dealing with complex theological
matters), as well as liturgically evocative in a way not easy to appreciate
nowadays.
  33–5. 'Moderation is the source of health, even though you do want a lot;
what the stomach craves is not always good for the spirit, nor is what is dear
to the soul always food for the body.'
  37–8. The World, the Flesh and the Devil are the enemies of the soul in
numerous allegories (e.g. Chaucer's *Tale of Melibeus*, *CT* VII. 970, 1421). The
triad was developed from Scriptural passages such as *Ephes*. 6: 11–12 to
correspond to the Trinity in medieval numerical schemes. See 13. 19–52.
  39–40. 'And the soul sees that and tells you of it in your heart and advises
you to be wary of what would deceive you.'
  42–3. This question introduces the theme of the right use of worldly goods,
which dominates succeeding passus and indeed the whole of the *Vision*.

Whenne the peple aposed hym of a peny in the temple, 45
And god askede at hem whos was the koyne.
"Cesares", thei sayde, "sothliche we knoweth".
"*Reddite Cesari*", sayde god, "that Cesar byfalleth,
Et que sunt dei, deo, or ye don ylle".
For rightfulliche resoun sholde reule yow alle 50
And kynde witte be wardeyn, youre welthe to kepe,
And tutor of youre tresor, and take hit yow at nede;
For hosbondrye and he holdeth togederes.'

    I fraynede her fayr tho, for hym that here made,
'The dep dale and the derke, so unsemely to se to, 55
What may hit bymene, madame, I byseche?'

    'That is the castel of care—whoso cometh ther-ynne
May banne that he born was in body and in soule.
Ther-ynne wonyeth a wyghte that Wrong is his name,
Fader of falshede, fond hit firste of alle; 60
Adam and Eve he eggede to ylle
And conseylede Caym to cullen his brother.
Judas he byjapede thorw Jewene sulver
And afterward anhengede hym hey uppon an ellerne.
He is lettere of love and lyeth alle tymes; 65
That tristeth in tresor of erthe he bytrayeth sonest;
To combre men with coveytise, that is his kynde and his lore.'

    Thenne hadde I wonder in my wit what woman she were
That suche wyse wordes of holy writ shewede,
And I halsed here on the hey name or she thennes wente 70
What she were wytterly that wissede me so and tauhte.
'Holy churche I am', quod she, 'thou oughtest me to knowe;

---

46. whos *U* : *X* hoes   **70.** halsed *U* : *X* hanslede

48–9. 'Render therefore unto Caesar (the things which are Caesar's); and unto God the things that are God's' (*Matt.* 22: 21).
    51. *kynde witte*: natural wisdom, or, one might say, common sense.
    54. '. . . for the sake of Him that made her.'
    55–6. The question follows from the answer begun at line 12.
    59. 'Therein dwells a creature whose name is Wrong.'
    65–7. "He is the hinderer of Love and tells lies always; those that trust in earthly treasure he betrays soonest; his nature and method is to blind and destroy men with avarice.'

I undirfenge the formeste and fre man the made.
Thow broughtest me borewes my biddyng to fulfille,
Leve on me and love me al thy lyf-tyme.'   75
   Thenne I knelede on my knees and kried here of grace
And prayede here pitously to praye for me to amende
And also to kenne me kyndly on Crist to bileve:
'Teche me to no tresor, but telle me this ilke,
How I may save my soule, that saynt art yholde.'   80
   'When alle tresores ben tried, Treuthe is the beste—
I do hit uppon *Deus caritas*, to deme the sothe.
Hit is as derworthe a druerie as dere god hymselven,
For who is trewe of his tonge and of his two handes
And doth the werkes therwith and wilneth no man ylle,   85
He is a god by the gospel and graunte may hele
And also lyk oure lord, by saynt Lukes wordes.
Clerkes that knowen hit is thus sholde kenne it aboute,
For cristene and uncristene claymeth it ech-one.
   Kynges and knyghtes sholde kepen hit by resoun,   90

___

79. no *omitted in* X

___

73. 'I first received you and made you free of sin' (at baptism).
80. '. . . (tell me, you) who are counted blessed.' The question initiates the movement of the whole poem, which can be seen, in its simplest terms, as a two-stage answer, like that of Jesus to the rich young man in the Gospels: 'If thou wilt enter into life, keep the commandments. . . . If thou wilt be perfect, go and sell that thou hast, and give to the poor, and thou shalt have treasure in heaven: and come and follow me' (*Matt.* 19: 16–22). 'Treasure in heaven' is implied by contrast in the *tresor* of 79 and 81.
81. *Treuthe* is to be understood as both objective and subjective: it is at once God's law (and sometimes God himself) and also obedience to God's law.
82. 'I base my case on the text *God is love* [1 *John* 4: 8], to judge truly.' The equation, now to be developed, is: Truth = God = Love.
84–7. The texts referred to are: 'He that is faithful in that which is least is faithful also in much' (*Luke* 16: 10, the parable of the steward), and also, 'My mother and my brethren are these which hear the word of God, and do it' (*Luke* 8: 21).
86. 'He partakes of the divine nature, according to the gospel, and shall be granted salvation.'
89. 'Both Christians and non-Christians claim to have it' (viz. the revelation of divine Truth). The reference is to Mohammedans and Jews rather than to 'heathens'.

Ryden and rappe adoun in reaumes aboute
And take *transgressores* and teyen hem faste,
Til Treuthe hadde termyned here trespas to the ende,
And halden with hem and here that han trewe accion
And for no lordene love leve the trewe partie.   95
Treweliche to take and treweliche to fyghte
Is the professioun and puyr ordre that apendeth to knyghtes,
And whoso passeth that poynt is apostata of knyghthed;
For thei sholde nother faste ne forbere the serk
But feithfullich defende and fyghte for treuthe   100
And never leve for love in hope to lacche sylver.
    David in his daies dobbed knyghtes,
Dede hem swere on here swerd to serve treuthe evere;
And god, whan he bigan hevene in that grete blisse,
Made knyghtes in his couert creatures tene,   105
Cherubyn and seraphyn, such seven and another—
Lucifer, lovelokest tho, ac litel while it dured.
He was an archangel of hevene, on of goddes knyghtes;
He and other with hym helden nat with treuthe,
Lepen out in lothly forme for his fals wille   110
That hadde lust to be lyke his lord that was almyghty.

---

100. *from P : X* But fyghte and fende treuthe (*some disorder in the lineation, 97–101.*)

94–5. 'And (knights should) support all those who act honestly, and not abandon the cause of truth for the sake of pleasing their superiors.'

102. After demonstrating the nature of Truth in chivalric terms as obedience to the laws of knighthood, Langland makes a transition here, via Biblical 'knighthood', to the revolt in heaven, the primal un-Truth, as transgression against a heavenly chivalry. The metaphor works both ways.

105–6. The ten orders of angels (of which seraphim and cherubim constituted the two highest) were reduced to the familiar nine by the defection of the company of Lucifer. The orders of the heavenly hierarchy were authoritatively established by a Greek mystical theologian of the late 5th century known as the Pseudo-Dionysius (to distinguish him from Dionysius the Areopagite, *Acts* 17: 34, to whom the *De Coelesti Hierarchia* and other works were long ascribed).

110. 'Were cast out in hideous shape because of his false desire.' *Lepen out* conveys the wilfulness of the action.

Ponam pedem meum in aquilone, et similis ero altissimo.
Lord! why wolde he tho, that wykkede Lucifer,
Luppen alofte in the north syde
Thenne sitten in the sonne syde there the day roweth?
Nere hit for northerne men, anon I wolde yow telle—   115
Ac I wol lacky no lyf', quod that lady sothly.
'Hit is sikerere bi southe ther the sonne regneth
Then in the north by many notes, no man leve other;
For theder as the fende fly his fote for to sette,
Ther he faylede and ful and his felawes alle,   120
And helle is ther he is, and he there ybounde.
Evene the contrarie sitteth Crist, clerkes wyteth the sothe.
Dixit dominus domino meo, sede a dextris meis.
Ac of this matere no more meven I nelle;
Hewes in the haliday after hete wayten,
Ac thei caren nat thogh hit be cold, knaves, when thei worche.   125
Wonderwyse holy wryt telleth how thei fullen,

123. meven *P* : *X* nemnen

111f. 'I will set my foot in the north, and I will be like the most High'
(cf. *Isaiah* 14: 13–14).
112–25. This gloss on the *north* of the Bible (which Langland quotes
inaccurately, as often), with its exploitation of traditional connotations of *north*
and *south*, and playful apology (115), is in C only. The symbolism is associated
with the earlier (1.14n) use of *east* and *west* (also below, 133) and with *right*
and *left* (below, 122). The Biblical association of Lucifer and the North was
strengthened by Germanic mythology, which also placed Hell in the north
(mount Hecla, in Iceland, according to some ecclesiastical historians), as well
as by a more or less natural geographical prejudice, which can be found
expressed in the ME poem, *The Owl and the Nightingale* (ed. E. G. Stanley,
Nelson's Medieval and Renaissance Library, 1960), 905–22, 995–1030. See
Chaucer's *Friar's Tale*, *CT* III. 1413, and Robinson's note.
116–18. 'But without intending to slander anyone . . . (I would say) that it is
obviously far safer in the south where the sun is powerful than in the north—
let no man believe otherwise.'
122f. 'The Lord said unto my Lord, Sit thou at my right hand' (*Psalm* 110: 1).
Psalm 110 is 109 in the Vulgate; the variation stems from Psalms 9 and 10 in
the English Bible, which are taken as one psalm in the Vulgate.
124–5. 'Labourers look for holy days to be sunny, but don't care if it is
cold on work-days.' The association of God and the sun receives a homely twist.

Summe in erthe, summe in ayr, summe in helle depe,
Ac Lucifer lowest lith of hem alle;
For pruyde ther hym pokede his payne hath non ende.
And alle that worchen that wikked is, wenden thei sholle   130
After here deth-day and dwelle ther Wrong is,
And alle that han wel ywrouhte, wende they sholle
Estward til hevene, evere to abyde
There Treuthe is, the tour that trinite ynne sitteth.
Lere hit thus lewed men, for lettred hit knoweth,   135
That treuthe and trewe love, is no tresor bettre.'

  'I have no kynde knowyng', quod I, 'yut mot ye kenne me
    bettre,
By what wey it wexeth and wheder out of my menynges.'
  'Thow dotede daffe', quod she, 'dulle aren thy wittes;
To lyte lernedest thow, I leve, Latyn in thy yowthe: 140
Heu michi, quod sterilem duxi vitam juvenilem!
Hit is a kynde knowynge that kenneth in thyn herte
For to lovye thy lord levest of alle,
Dey rather then do eny dedly synne:
    Melius est mori quam male vivere.
And this I trowe be treuth; whoso kan teche the bettre,   145
Lok thow soffre hym to seye and so thow myht lerne.
  For Treuthe telleth that love ys triacle to abate synne
And most soverayne salve for soule and for body.
Love is plonte of pees, most precious of vertues,

140. thow *U* : *X* omits

---

  127. Not all the fallen angels fell into Hell. Others inhabited the elements, as (more or less) evil spirits. The traditional lore is fully represented in Shakespeare: see W. C. Curry, *Shakespeare's Philosophical Patterns* (Baton Rouge, La., 1937).

  130–4. These are the terms of the 'pardon' offered to the people in Passus X.

  137–8. 'I have no natural way of knowing—you will still have to teach me better—of how it (i.e. Truth) grows, and whether out of my own efforts or not.' The dreamer cannot understand the equation of line 82n.

  141. 'Ah me, what a useless life I led as a youth!' The line is late Latin, a Leonine hexameter, but its source is not known.

  144f. 'It is better to die than to live in sin' (cf. *Tobit* 3 : 6).

For hevene holde hit ne myghte, so hevy hit first semede,   150
Til hit hadde of erthe ygoten hitsilve.
Was never lef uppon lynde lyhtere ther-after,
As when hit hadde of the folde flesch and blode taken.
Tho was hit portatif and persaunt as is the poynt of a nelde;
May non armure hit lette ne none heye walles.   155
    Forthi is love ledare of oure lordes folke of hevene,
And a mene, as the mayre is bitwene the kyng and the comune;
Ryht so is love a ledare and the lawe shapeth,
Up man for his mysdedes the mercement he taxeth.
    And for to knowe hit kyndly, hit comeseth by myhte,   160
And in the herte—ther is the hed and the heye welle;
For of kynde knowynge of herte ther comseth a myhte
And that falleth to the fader that formede us alle,
Lokede on us with love, let his sone deye
Mekeliche for oure mysdedes, to amende us alle,   165
And yut wolde hem no wo that wrouthe hym al that tene
Bote mekeliche with mouth mercy he bysoughte,
To have pite on that peple that payned hym to dethe.
    Here myhtow se ensaumples in hymself one
That he was myhtfull and meke, and mercy gan graunte   170
To hem that hengen hym hye and his herte thorlede.
Forthy I rede yow riche, haveth reuthe uppon the pore;
Thogh ye be myhty to mote, beth meke in youre werkes,
For the same mesure that ye meteth, amis other elles,
Ye shal be weye ther-with whenne ye wende hennes.   175

    159. he U : X and he

149–55. The richness of metaphor here answers to a concept of love in which overwhelming abundance and delicate fineness, power and humility are combined, in preparation for the paradox of the Incarnation (153).
    151. 'Till it had begotten itself upon an earthly body.'
    157. Christ, as the incarnation of God's love, is here compared, as intercessor and intermediary, to a mayor, and this in turn reintroduces the theme of law.
    159. 'He imposes the fine upon man for his misdeeds.'
    160–3. 'Love can be recognised instinctively, for it begins as a powerful impulse, and the heart is its source and centre. Out of the heart's natural understanding there grows this impulse, one which the Creator is himself subject to.' God's sending his Son into the world is then used as the supreme example of this impulse of love. The example is applied in line 172.

Eadem mensura qua mensi fueritis, remecietur vobis.
For thogh ye ben trewe of youre tonges and trewliche
    wynne
And ben as chast as a child that chyt nother ne fyhteth,
But yf ye lovye leeliche and lene the pore
Of such good as god yow sent goodliche parte,
Ye na haveth na more meryte in masse ne in houres   180
Then Malkyn of here maydenheed when no man here covayteth.
    For James the gentele jugeth in his bokes
That fayth withouten the feet is feblere then naught
And as ded as dore-nayl, but yf the dedes folowe:
    Fides sine operibus mortua est.
Chastite withouten charite worth cheyned in helle;   185
Hit is as lewed thyng as a laumpe that no liht is ynne.
Mony chapeleynes aren chaste, ac charite hem fayleth;
Aren none hardere ne hungriere then men of holy chirch,
Averous and evel-willed when thei ben avaunsed,
Unkynde to here kyn and to alle cristene.   190
Thei chewen here charite and chiden after more,
And ben acombred with coveytise—thei can nought crepe out,
So harde hath avaryce yhasped hem togederes.
And that is no treuthe of the trinite, but triccherye, synne,
And luther ensaumple, leef me, as for the lewed peple.   195
    For this aren wordes ywryten in the evangelie:
Date et dabitur vobis—for I dele yow alle.

177. chyt: *X* chyht   **191.** Thei *omitted in XU*   **197.** dele *S* : *X* telle

---

175f. 'With the same measure that ye mete withal, it shall be measured to you again' (*Luke* 6: 38; cf. *Matt.* 7: 2).

178–81. 'Unless you love truly, and give to the poor a good part of the wealth God has given you, you get no more spiritual benefit from all your devotions than old Maud gets from her maidenhead, when no-one wants it.' The syntax echoes *1 Cor.* 13: 1.

184f. 'Faith without works is dead' (*James* 2: 26).

186. 'It is as useless as an unlit lamp' (with reference to the parable of the wise and foolish virgins, *Matt.* 25: 8).

191–3. 'Their charity is swallowed up in greed and they are always shouting for more; they are burdened with avarice, so firmly shackled by it that they cannot make a movement towards love.'

197. 'Give, and it shall be given unto you' (*Luke* 6: 38, cf. 175, above).

And that is the lok of love and unloseth grace,
That conforteth alle careful, acombred with synne.
  So love is leche of lyf and lysse of alle payne   200
And the graffe of grace and grathest way to hevene.
Forthi I may seye, as I saide eer, by sight of this textes,
Whenne alle tresores ben tried, treuthe is the beste;
Love hit,' quod that lady, 'lette may I no lengere
To lere the what love is'—and leve at me she lauhte.   205

Holy Church stays long enough, however, to point out to the dreamer the
force which perverts men from the way of Truth, personified as Lady Meed,
the desire for gain, the acquisitive instinct, or, in theological terms, *cupiditas*,
the indulgence in worldly goods as an end in themselves. She is about to
marry Falsehood and the nuptial preparations afford Langland the opportunity to portray in allegorical terms the corruption at the heart of English
society. The king summons her to his court to answer the charges against
her, but there she gets to work on court officials and lawyers in her usual
way, and, before the king, tries to blur the distinction between proper
reward ('mesurable hyre') and gain. Conscience speaks out against her, and
his attack merges into a glowing vision of a world ruled by love, humility
and truth and not by Meed. The king rejects Meed, takes Conscience and
Reason as his advisers, and the world's golden age is, it seems, about to begin.

  But the sins of the people must first be purged and, in a significant and
famous addition to the C-text, Langland, drawing near the end of his life,
makes his own 'confession', which, characteristically, blends contrition with
pugnacious self-justification.

3. The Author's Apology for his Life (VI. 1–104)

Thus I wakede, wot god, whan I wonede in Cornehull,

  200–1. 'So love is the healer of life, the relief of all pain, the stem from
which grace grows and the most direct way to heaven.'
  1. Cornhill, in the City, something of a resort, in Langland's day, of
layabouts and failed ecclesiastics. Though 'autobiographical' reminiscence is
mostly literary convention in medieval writings, there is no need to doubt the
accuracy of the details Langland gives (for a full analysis, see Donaldson,
pp. 199–226). What is noteworthy is how small a part actual 'real-life' detail
plays in the passage in proportion to moral evaluation.

Kytte and I in a cote, yclothed as a lollare,
And lytel ylet by, leveth me for sothe,
Amonges lollares of Londone and lewede men, ermytes,
For I made of tho men as resoun me taughte.   5
For as I cam by Consience with Resoun I mette
In an hot hervest whenne I hadde myn hele
And lymes to labory with and lovede wel fare
And no dede to do but to drynke and to slepe.
In hele and in inwitt one me apposede;   10
Romynge in remembraunce, thus Resoun me aratede.
    'Can thow serven,' he sayde, 'or syngen in a churche,
Or koke for my cokeres or to the cart piche,
Mowen or mywen or make bond to sheves,
Repe or been a rypereve and aryse erly,   15
Or have an horn and be hayward and lygge ther-oute nyhtes
And kepe my corn in my croft fro pykares and theves?
Or shape shon or cloth, or shep and kyne kepe,
Heggen or harwen, or swyne or gees dryve,
Or eny other kynes craft that to the comune nedeth,   20
That thou betere ther-by that byleve the fynden?'
    'Certes,' I sayde, 'and so me god helpe,
I am to wayke to worche with sykel or with sythe

21. ther : *X* the

---

2. Langland, like many clerics in minor orders (see Donaldson, pp. 206–8), violated strict canon law by having a wife; this alone would have hindered his advancement in the Church. *Lollare* means more or less what it says, 'idler, vagabond', and is not here connected with 'Lollard', the name given to the followers of John Wycliff. Langland shares many of Wycliff's views on the state of the Church, and approaches him sometimes in anti-clerical invective, but lacks Wycliff's genuine reforming instinct, his intellectual destructiveness, and his venom.

3. 'And not in high favour, believe me truly, among . . .'

5. 'For I judged those men as reason instructed me.'

10–11. '(While I was) in this state of health and good understanding, someone questioned me; as I mused on the past, Reason rebuked me.' *Reason* is the allegorical personified projection of the dreamer's own rational self-analysis.

21. 'By which you may improve the lot of those that provide you with food?'

And to long, lef me, lowe to stoupe,
To wurche as a werkeman eny while to duyren.'   25
  'Thenne hastow londes to lyve by,' quod Resoun, 'or
    lynage ryche
That fynde the thy fode? For an ydel man thow semest,
A spendour that spene mot or a spille-tyme,
Or beggest thy bylyve aboute at men hacches
Or faytest uppon frydayes or feste-day in churches,   30
The whiche is lollarne lyf, that lytel is preysed
Ther ryhtfulnesse rewardeth ryht as men deserveth.
    Reddit unicuique juxta opera sua.
Or thow art broke, so may be, in body or in membre
Or ymaymed thorw som myshap, whereby thow myhte be
    excused?'
  'When I yong was, many yer hennes,   35
My fader and my frendes fonde me to scole,
Tyl I wyste witterly what holy writ menede
And what is best for the body, as the bok telleth,
And sykerest for the soule, by so I wole contenue.
And fond I nere, in fayth, seth my frendes deyede,   40
Lyf that me lykede but in this longe clothes.
And yf I be labour sholde lyven and lyflode deserven,
That laboure that I lerned beste, ther-with lyven I sholde.
    In eadem vocatione in qua vocati estis, manete.
And so I leve yn London and uppe lond bothe;
  44. uppe *U* : *X* ope

---

24. *to long:* 'too tall', cf. 12, 3n.
31-2. 'Which is an idler's life, which will gain little praise when Righteousness comes to reward men exactly as they deserve.'
32f. 'Thou renderest to every man according to his work' (*Psalm* 62: 12).
36. Langland's father (Stacy de Rokayle, a country gentleman of Shipton-under-Wychwood, in Oxfordshire, according to MS. notes) paid for his (illegitimate) son's education (presumably at Malvern priory) until he died, when Langland left the priory, half-trained for a clerical vocation, and sought a living on the ecclesiastical fringes of London society.
39. '. . . provided that I will continue (in well-doing).'
43f. 'let every man abide in the same calling wherein he was called' (I *Cor.* 7: 20).
44. *uppe lond* ('in the country') tells us something important about Langland's life which the familiar misreading of Skeat's text (*on Londone*) obscures.

The lomes that I labore with and lyflode deserve   45
Ys *pater-noster* and my prymer, *placebo* and *dirige*,
And my sauter som tyme and my sevene psalmes.
This I segge for here soules of suche as me helpeth,
And tho that fynden me my fode vouchen-saf, I trowe,
To be welcome when I come, other-while in a monthe,   50
Now with hym, now with here; on this wise I begge
Withoute bagge or botel but my wombe one.
    And also moreover me thynketh, syre Resoun,
Men sholde constrayne no clerc to no knaves werkes,
For by the lawe of *Levyticy* that oure lord ordeynede,   55
Clerkes ycrouned, of kynde understondynge,
Sholde nother swynke ne swete ne sweren at enquestes
Ne fyhte in no vanne-warde ne his foe greve.
    Non reddas malum pro malo.
For hit ben heyres of hevene, alle that ben ycrouned,
And in quor and in kyrkes Cristes mynistres.   60

46–7. The *prymer* is the basic private prayer-book; *placebo* and *dirige* are names given to particular offices of the Dead (derived from initial words of verses from psalms sung in these offices, viz. 116: 9, 5: 8); the *sevene psalmes* are the Seven Penitential Psalms (viz. 6, 32, 38, 51, 102, 130, 143). These are the 'tools' of Langland's trade, which is that of intercession by prayer, particularly intercession for the souls of the dead (to accelerate their progress through Purgatory). Superficially, it looks the kind of parasitic existence scorned by Chaucer's Poor Parson and by Langland himself (1, 83n). The difference is that Langland has no choice, being unbeneficed, and leaves no sheep 'encombred in the myre', and that he sings for food and not for silver.

48–52. These lines show that Langland prayed for the living as well as the dead, 'a sort of itinerant handy man, like a modern neighbourhood gardener who performs odd jobs for a whole suburban block—except, of course, that Langland's odd jobs were prayers' (Donaldson, pp. 218–19).

52. 'With no bag or bottle, but only my stomach.' This is the crucial distinction in Langland's ethics of begging.

55. The reference is very general, to *Levit.* 21.

56–7. 'It is naturally understood that tonsured clerics should neither labour nor sweat, nor have to give evidence on oath in courts of law.' Clerics still had their own ecclesiastical courts and were exempt from the normal processes of law (this custom, much abused, was known as 'benefit of clergy').

58f. 'Render not evil for evil' (1 *Thess.* 5: 15).

59. 'For they are heirs of heaven, all that bear the tonsure.'

Dominus pars hereditatis mee. Et alibi: Clementia non
    constringit.

Hit bycometh for clerkes Crist for to serve
And knaves uncrounede to carte and to worche.
For sholde no clerke be crouned but yf he come were
Of frankeleynes and fre men and of folke ywedded.
Bondemen and bastardus and beggares children,   65
Thyse bylongeth to labory and lordes kyn to serve,
God and good men, as here degre asketh;
Somme to synge masses or sitten and wryten,
Reden and resceyven that resoun ouhte to spene.
Ac sythe bondemen barnes han be made bisshopes   70
And barnes bastardus han be erchedekenes
And soutares and here sones for sulver han be knyhtes
And lordes sones here laboreres and leyde here rentes to wedde—
For the ryhte of this reume ryden ageyn oure enemyes
In confort of the comune and the kynges worschipe—   75
And monkes and monyales, that mendenants sholde fynde,
Ymade here kyn knyhtes and knyhtes-fees ypurchased,
Popes and patrones pore gentel blood refused

---

62. knaves *U* : *X* knave   **76.** mendenants *U* : *X* mendenant

---

60f. 'The Lord is the portion of mine inheritance' (*Psalm* 16: 5, cf. 37: 11, 18). And elsewhere: 'The life of meekness does not constrain a man.' The source of this latter quotation is not known.

63–4. Langland is here extending the argument beyond the personal, unless we assume that the tradition of his own illegitimacy is false.

68–9. Book-keeping and accountancy seem proper enough vocations for the sons of the lower classes, but 'Somme to synge masses' is puzzling. Only priests in full holy orders could conduct Mass. It may refer, however, to serving or assisting (see line 12) in the service, as an acolyte.

70–9. This sentence is dependent on 'Ac sythe' to line 77. Its proliferation of subordinate clauses is a mark of Langland's indignation at the disturbance to traditional social hierarchy caused by money. Social mobility is social sin, in these terms.

78–9. '(Ever since all these things have been happening) ecclesiastical patrons have refused livings to the sons of the impoverished nobility, and have appointed the sons of Simon to look after the church.' *Simony* is called after Simon Magus, who tried to purchase with money the apostles' gift of laying on hands (*Acts* 8: 18). His 'sons' are those who buy office in the church.

And taken Symondes sones seyntwarie to kepe.
Lyf-holynesse and love hath be longe hennes,   80
And wol, til hit be wered out, or otherwyse ychaunged.
    Forthy rebuke me ryhte nauhte, Resoun, I yow praye,
For in my consience I knowe what Crist wolde I wrouhte.
Preyeres of a parfit man and penaunce desirede
Is the levest labour that oure lord pleseth.   85
Non de solo,' I sayde, 'for sothe *vivit homo,*
Nec in pane et in pabulo, the *pater-noster* wittenesseth;
Fiat voluntas dei—that fynt us alle thynges.'
    Quod Conscience, 'By Crist, I can nat se this lyeth;
Ac it semeth no sad parfitnesse in citees to begge,   90
But he be obediencer to prior or to mynistre.'
    'That is soth,' I saide, 'and so I beknowe,
That I have ytynt tyme and tyme myspened;
Ac yut, I hope, as he that ofte hath ychaffared
And ay loste and loste, and at the laste hym happed   95
He bouhte suche a bargayn he was the bet evere,
And sette al his los at a leef at the laste ende,
Suche a wynnyng hym warth thorw wordes of grace.
        Simile est regnum celorum thesauro abscondito in agro, etc.
        Mulier que invenit dragmam, etc.

81. or *omitted in* X
90. begge P : X bygge   **96.** bouhte P : X boute

86–8. 'I said, Indeed, "man shall not live by bread alone" [*Matt.* 4: 6], as the Paternoster shows; "God's will be done" [*Matt.* 6: 10] provides us with all things.' Doing God's will (in this case, living by prayer and penance) is the only thought one needs to take. The text is again (cf. 2.82) used as a grammatical unit, as if in itself it were substantive.

89. Langland's defence satisfies Reason—his life is rationally justifiable—but Conscience, who is concerned with *doing* the right things, not thinking them, catches up his *parfit* (84), and Langland has to confess that he has not truly lived the life he has been defending so forcefully.

98. 'Such a prize he won through the grace destined to him' (*wordes* from *wyrd,* 'fate').

98f. 'The kingdom of heaven is like unto a treasure hid in a field, etc.' (*Matt.* 13: 44). 'The woman that found a piece of silver, etc.' (cf. *Luke* 15: 9). The gospel images, as usual, are Langland's starting-off point in this moving paragraph.

So hope I to have of hym that is almyghty
A gobet of his grace, and bigynne a tyme   100
That alle tymes of my tyme to profit shal turne.'
    'I rede the,' quod Resoun tho, 'rape the to bigynne
The lyf that is louable and leele to thy soule'—
    'Ye, and contynue,' quod Consience; and to the kyrke I wente.

Reason now calls on the folk to repent. This they do, in a symbolic parade
of the seven deadly sins, who each confess and promise amendment, Pride
and Envy first, then Anger.

4. *The Confession of the Folk* (VII. 103–238, 350–441)

Thenne awakede Wrathe, with two whyte eyes
And with a nivilynge nose, nippynge his lippes.
    'I am Wroth,' quod that weye, 'wol gladliche smyte
Bothe with stoon and with staf, and stele uppon myn enemye;
To sle hym sleyliche sleythes ich bythenke.   5
Thogh I sitte this sevene yer I sholde nat wel telle
The harm that I have do with hand and with tonge;
Inpacient in alle penaunces, and pleyned, as hit were,
On god, when me greved auht, and groched of his sonde,
As som tyme in somer and also in hervest,   10
But I hadde weder at my wille, I witte god the cause

2. nivilynge *P* : *X* nivilynges

1–2. The rolling eyeballs, showing only the white, the running nose (he is
too obsessed to wipe it), and the gnawing of lips, are physical symptoms of
Anger. Langland uses both pictorial iconography and dramatic personification
to build up his image of each sin. His technique might be compared with
Spenser's Pageant of the Sins, *Faerie Queene* I. iv. 18–35. The tradition of the
Seven Deadly Sins goes back to pagan descriptions of other-world journeys,
in which the soul has to pass seven perilous spheres, each identified with a
particular temptation or vice, before reaching heaven. Out of such descriptions
grew the Christian codification of sins, for which Evagrius of Pontus, one of
the Desert Fathers of the late 4th century, is chiefly responsible. See M. W.
Bloomfield, *The Seven Deadly Sins* (Michigan, 1952).
    8–9. '(I was) impatient of all suffering, and complained against God whenever
anything upset me, and grumbled about what he sent me.'

In alle manere angres that I hadde or felede.

Amonges alle manere men my dwellyng is som tyme,
With lewed and lered that leef ben to here
Harm of eny man, byhynde or bifore. 15
Freres folewen my lore fele tyme and ofte
And proven unparfit prelates of holy churche;
And prelates pleyneth on hem for they here parschiens shryven
Withoute licence and leve, and herby lyveth wrathe.
Thus thei speke and dispute that uchon dispiseth other. 20
Thus beggares and barones at debat aren ofte
Til I, Wrathe, wexe an hey and walke with hem bothe.
Other til they bothe be beggares and by spiritualte libbe
Or alle riche and ryde, reste shal I nat, Wrathe,
That I ne mot folowe this folk—my fortune is non other. 25

I have an aunte to nonne and to an abbesse;
Here were lever swowe or swelte then soffre eny payne.
I have be cok in here kychene and the covent served,
Mony monthes with hem and with monkes bothe.
I was the prioresse potager and other pore ladies, 30

23. spiritualte *P* : *X* spirituale

14–15. 'With whatever people, educated or ignorant, are glad to hear ill of anyone, behind his back or in his presence.' It is the occasion of Wrath, the source of dispute, that is being specified.

16–20. The traditional enmity of mendicants (friars) and 'possessioners' (holders of ecclesiastical livings, and monks) is here made a source-type of hatred and anger. Friars, with their vows of apostolic poverty, attacked the wealth and luxury of orthodox ecclesiastics, and claimed for themselves a special Papal prerogative as the evangelical spearhead of the Church (the claim was wearing thin in the 14th century). Possessioners responded with a mixture of guilty shame, outrage at what was often blatant hypocrisy, and a very practical dislike of the way the hard-selling professionals creamed off their audiences and their offertories. See 1.56–65.

21. The enmity of mendicants and possessioners is associated with economic inequality, which is bound to produce class-hatred, says Wrath (not Langland).

23–5. 'I shan't rest, I shall go on pursuing these people—it is my fate to do so—either until both (parties to the dispute) are beggars and live by the spirit (i.e. on nothing), or until all grow equally rich and ride on horseback.'

30–1. 'I was cook to the prioress and to other ladies of the convent, and made their stew out of squabblings' (provided them with food for argument). Langland is fond of this kind of food-imagery, cf. 11.43–61.

And made hem joutes of jangelynge: "Dame Jone was a
    bastard,
And dame Clarice a knyhtes douhter, a cokewolde was here
    syre,
And dame Purnele a prestis fyle—prioresse worth she nevere;
For she hadde a childe in the chapun-cote she worth chalenged
    at the eleccion."
Thus sytte they, sustres, sum tyme, and disputen   35
Til "thow lixt" and "thow lixt" be lady over hem alle;
And thenne awake I, Wrathe, and wolde be avenged.
And thenne I crye and crache with my kene nayles,
Byte and bete and brynge forth suche thewes
That alle ladyes me lotheth that lovyeth eny worschipe.   40
    Amonges wyves and wydewes than woned I to sitte
Yparroked in pues; the persone hit knoweth
How lytel I lovye Letyse at the style—
For she had haly-bred ar I, my herte gan change.
Aftur mete aftirward she and she chydde   45
And I, Wrath, was war, and wrathe on hem bothe,
Tyl ayther clepede other "hore" and of with the clothes
Til bothe here hedes were bar and blody here chekes.
    Amonges monkes I myhte be, ac mony tyme I spare,

34. *X* chapun-coke   **40.** lotheth *P* : *X* loteth
47. of *P* : *X* on

33–4. 'Sister Purnel is a priest's concubine—*she* will never be prioress; she gave birth to a child in the hen-house [B, in cherry-time], and she's bound to be accused at the election.' The change from B is maliciously apt, eliminating the air of romance and substituting ludicrous squalor. *Purnel*, a name commonly associated with vulgar overdressed women, is about as appropriate to a nun as Chaucer's Eglantine.

41–4. 'Then again I have been wont to sit amongst wives and widows shut up in their pews; the parson knows how little love there is lost between me and Lettice Stiles; my heart is embittered because she received the holy-bread before me.' Wrath's role shifts later (46) from the representative to the abstract agent of sinfulness.

45. *she and she:* 'she and another woman'.

49–55. The rigorous discipline of monasteries is in striking contrast to the scandal-mongering and squabbling in the convents. Perhaps it is just that anger is one sin to which men are less prone.

For there aren many felle frekes myne aferes to aspye,   50
That ys, priour and suppriour and oure *pater abbas*.
And yf I telle eny tales they taken hem togyderes
And don me faste Fridayes to bred and to water.
Yut am I chalenged in oure chapitre-hous as I a childe were
And balayshed on the bare ers and no brech bytwene.   55
I have no luste, lef me, to longe amonges monkes,
For I ete more fysch then flesshe there, and feble ale drynke.
Ac other-while when wyn cometh and when I drynke late at even
I have a flux of a foul mouth wel fyve daies after,
And al that I wiste wykked by eny of oure covent   60
I coughte hit up in oure cloystre, that al the covent wot hit.'
    'Now repente,' quod Repentaunce, 'and reherce nevere
Consayl that thow knowest, by continaunce ne by speche.
And drynke nat over-delycatly no to depe neyther,
That thy wil ne thy wit to wrethe myhte turne.   65
Esto sobrius,' he saide, and assoiled hym aftur,
And bad hym bid to god, be his help to amende.

    Thenne seyde Lecherye 'Alas!' and to oure lady cryede,
'Lady, to thy leve sone loute for me nouthe,
That he have pite on me, putour, of his puyr mercy,   70
With that I shal,' quod that shrewe, 'Saterdayes, for thy moder
        love,
Drynke but with the doke and dyne but ones.
    I, gulty in gost, to god I me shryve
As in likynge of lecherye my lycames gultes,
In word and in wedes, in waytynge of eyes.   75

70. putour *U* : *X* pitour

---

52. '. . . they take counsel together (about my punishment).'
60–1. 'Everything that I knew to the discredit of any fellow-monk I would
cough up in the cloister, so that it got round the whole monastery.'
66–7. 'Be sober [1 *Peter* 4: 7, 5: 8], he said, and then absolved him, and told
him to pray to God to be his help in amendment.' Each confession ends with
a similar call to repentance, and absolution.
68. The confession of Lechery is shifted and much expanded from B.
71–2. 'And if he does, I promise to drink only water and dine only once on
Saturdays, for thy mother's love' (i.e. he proclaims an extra fast-day).

For eche mayde that I mette I made here a signe
Semyng to synne-ward, and summe I gan taste
Aboute the mouthe, and bynethe bygan I to grope,
Til bothe oure wil was on and to the werk we yeden,
As wel fastyng-dayes and Frydaies and heye-festes evenes,   80
As leef in lente as out of lente, alle tymes ylyche—
Such werkes with us were nevere out of sesoun—
Til we myhte no more; thenne hadde we mery tales
Of putrie and of paramours, and proveden thorw speche
And handlyng and halsyng and also thorw kyssyng,   85
Exited either other til oure olde synne;
Sotiled songes and sende out olde baudes
To wynne to my wille wymmen with gyle,
By sorserie sum tyme and sum tyme by maistrie.
I lay by the lovelokest and lovede here nevere aftur.   90
When I was olde and hoor and hadde ylore that kynde,
I had likyng to lythe of lecherye tales.
Now lord, for thy lewete, on lechours have mercy!'

Thenne cam Covetyse—I can hym nat descreve,
So hungrily and holow, sire Hervy hym lokede.   95
He was bitelbrowed and baburlippid, with two blered eyes,
And as a letherne pors lollede his chekes
Wel syddere then his chyn, ycheveled for elde;
And as a bondemannes bacon his berd was yshave,
With his hood on his heved and his hat bothe,   100
In a tore tabard of twelve wynter age—

84. putrie *U* : *X* putour

---

80. 'Both on special fast-days and eves of high festivals as well as on Fridays.'
Sexual abstinence was recommended on such days as well as fasting in the usual
sense. See *The Book of Vices and Virtues* (a popular handbook of religious
instruction), ed. W. N. Francis (E.E.T.S. 217, 1942), pp. 248–9.

95. *Hervy* ('Harvey'), a traditional name for a covetous rogue, perhaps by
alliterative association with *haft*, 'cheat, graft' (cf. 1.45n), as in Skelton, *Bowge
of Courte* 138: 'Harvy Hafter, that well coude picke a male.'

97–9. 'His cheeks, trembling with age, drooped even lower than his chin,
like old leather bags; his beard was cut like peasants' bacon' (i.e. roughly hacked).

But yf a lous couthe lepe, I leve and I trowe,
He ne sholde wandre uppon that walch, so was hit thredbare.
'I have be covetous,' quod this kaytif, 'I biknowe hit here,
For som tyme I served Symme at the style   105
And was his prentis yplyht, his profit to wayte.
Furste I lerned to lye a lesyng other tweye;
Wykkedliche to waye was my furste lessoun.
To Wy and to Wynchestre I wente to the fayre
With many manere marchandise, as my maister hyhte;   110
Ne hadde the grace of gyle go among my ware,
Hit hadde be unsold this sevene yer, so me god helpe!
    Thenne drow I me amonge drapers, my donet to lere,
To drawe the lyst along, the lenger hit semede.
Amonges the ryche rayes I rendrede a lessoun,   115
To brochen hem with a bat-nelde and bande hem togyderes,
Putte hem in pressoures and pynne hem ther-ynne,
Til ten yerde other twelve tolde out threttene.
    My wyf was a webbe and wollene cloth made;
She spak to the spynnesteres to spynnen oute.   120
The pound that she payede hem by peysed a quarter
More then myn auncel, when I wayed treuthe.
    I bouhte here barly and brew hit to sulle;
Peny-ale and poddyng-ale she poured togederes

---

107. lesyng U : X leef   121. that U : X tho

102-3. 'The cloth was so thread-bare that a louse would have to be pretty good at jumping, I declare, to get about on it.'
109. *Wy*: Weyhill, near Andover in Hampshire, site of a famous fair.
113-14. 'I spent some time amongst drapers, learning the elements of my craft, such as stretching the edge of the cloth so that it would measure longer.' *Donet* is the elementary Latin grammar of Donatus (4th cent.), universal in medieval schools, and widely applied in this kind of synecdoche.
115-18. 'I could teach them something about handling fine striped cloths: I would stitch the pieces loosely together, using a large needle, then pin them out in the presses till ten or twelve yards stretched out to thirteen.' Langland's knowledge of technical detail is an element in the *density* of his writing, and also in its compelling moral power: there is no escaping this eye.
121-2. 'The pound that she paid them by weighed a quarter more than a pound correctly weighed on my own scales.'
124. *Peny-ale*, thin ale (a penny a gallon); *poddyng-ale*, thick, or strong ale.

For laboreres and for louh folke that lay by hemsulve.   125
Ac the beste ale lay in my bour and in my bed-chaumbre
And who-so bommede ther-of he bouhte hit ther-after
A galon for a grote—and yut no grayth mesure
Whanne it cam in coppe-mele; this crafte my wyf usede.
Rose the regrater was here ryhte name;   130
She hadde holde hokkerye this elevene wynter.'
   'Repentedest nevere?' quod Repentaunce, 'ne restitucioun
      madest?'
   'Yus, ones I was herberwed,' quod he, 'with an heep of
      chapmen;
I ros and ryflede here males when they a reste were.'
   'That was a ruful restitucioun,' quod Repentaunce, 'for sothe;   135
Thow wolt be hanged heye ther-fore, here other in helle!'

   The confession of Avarice continues at length, amplified in C by the incor-
   poration of passages from the confession of Haukyn (B. XIII) and from
   elsewhere in B. Gluttony follows.

Now bygynneth Glotoun for to go to shryfte
And kayres hym to-kyrke-ward, his coupe to shewe.
Fastyng on a Friday forth gan he wende
By Betene hous the brewestere, that bad hym good morwen,   140
And whedeward he wolde the breuh-wyf hym askede.
   'To holy churche,' quod he, 'for to here masse,
And sennes sitte and be shryve and synege no more.'
   'I have good ale, gossip Glotoun, woltow assaye?'
   'Hastow,' quod he, 'eny hote spyces?'   145
   'I have peper and pyonie and a pound of garlek,

138. coupe U : X conpte

126-9. 'I kept the best ale in my own quarters, and anyone who tasted it
would buy it at a groat (4d.) a gallon, and even then get no true measure when
it came by the cupful—this was one of my wife's tricks.'

132. Restitution (of ill-gotten gains) is the practical demonstration of sin-
cerity of repentance in confessions of avarice (it is used of other sins too, but
not in the same physical sense). The sinner thinks it is a French word for
'robbing', as the B-text explains (or perhaps for robbing people when they are
at *rest*).

140. 'Past the house of Betty the ale-wife, who bade him good morrow.'

A ferthyng-worth of fenkelsedes, for fastyng-dayes I bouhte hit.'
 Thenne goth Glotoun in and grete othes aftur.
Sesse the souhteres sat on the benche,
Watte the wernare and his wyf dronke,   150
Tymme the tynekare and tweyne of his knaves,
Hicke the hackenayman and Hewe the nedlare,
Claryce of Cockes-lane, the clerc of the churche,
Syre Peres of Prydie and Purnele of Flaundres,
An hayward, an heremyte, the hangeman of Tyborne,   155
Dawe the dikere, with a doseyne harlotes
Of portours and of pikeporses and pilede toth-draweres,
A rybibour and a ratoner, a rakere and his knave,
A ropere and a redyngkynge and Rose the disshere,
Godefray the garlek-monger and Gryffyth the Walshe,   160
And of uphalderes an heep, erly by the morwe
Geven Glotoun with glad chere good ale to hansull.
 Clement the coblere cast of his cloke
And to the newe fayre nempnede forth to sull.

---

147. of omitted in X

---

147. Fennel-seed was taken to get rid of wind—Glutton's only penance on fast-days.

148. *grete othes.* Swearing is one of the 'sins of the tavern' traditionally associated with gluttony, along with drunkenness and gambling (see 163–80), in homiletic literature, as in the sermon of Chaucer's Pardoner (*CT* VI. 463–660).

152–4. 'Hick the horse-dealer and Hugh the needle-seller, Clarice of Cock's Lane [a street of brothels], the parish clerk, Father Peter of Prie-Dieu [an imaginary abbey, named after kneeling-desk] and Purnel of Flanders.' Incongruity of collocation, collision of detail, is the satiric technique here, as in Pope's description of Belinda's toiletries: 'Puffs, powders, patches, Bibles, billet-doux' (*Rape of the Lock* i. 138). Note the repetition of the women's names from the episode of the nuns (32–3, above). Flemish women were notorious as prostitutes.

156–60. 'Davy the ditcher, with a dozen villainous porters and pickpockets and bald-headed tooth-drawers, a fiddler and a ratcatcher, a scavenger (street-sweeper) and his boy, a rope-maker and a horse-soldier and Rose the dish-seller, Godfrey the garlic-dealer and Griffith the Welshman.'

164. *newe fayre.* The game of 'New Market' seems to have been a cross between a blind auction and a guess-the-weight competition. The two articles, in this case a cloak and a hood, are put 'to market' for exchange, their value is assessed by (supposedly impartial) arbitrators, and the winner makes up the

D

Hicke the hackenayman hit his hod aftur   165
And bade Bitte the bochere ben on his syde.
There were chapmen ychose this chaffare to preyse,
That who-so hadde the hood sholde nat have the cloke,
And that the bettre thyng, be arbitreres, bote sholde the worse.
Tho rysen up rape and rounned togyderes   170
And preisede this peniworths apart by hemsulve,
And there were othes an heep, for on sholde have the worse.
Thei couthe nat be here consience accorde for treuthe
Tyl Robyn the ropere aryse they bisouhte
And nempned hym for a noumper, that no debat were.   175
   Hicke the hostiler hadde the cloke,
In covenaunt that Clement sholde the coppe fulle,
And have Hickes hood the hostiler and holde hym yserved;
And who-so repentede hym rathest shold aryse after
And grete syre Glotoun with a galon of ale.   180
   There was leyhing and louryng and 'lat go the coppe!'
Bargaynes and bevereges bygan tho to awake,
And seten so til evensong, and songen umbywhile,
Til Glotoun hade yglobbed a galoun and a gylle.
His guttes gan to gothly as two grydy sowes;   185
He pissede a potel in a *pater-noster*-whyle,
He blew his rownd ruet at his rygebones ende,
That alle that herde the horne helde here nose after
And wesched hit hadde be wasche with a weps of breres.

---

189. be *omitted in* X

---

difference with drinks all round (probably the main point of the game for the
spectators).
   169. 'The (winner of the) article judged more valuable by the arbitrators
should make up the difference in value' (with a round of drinks).
   172. 'There were oaths in plenty, in case one or the other got the worse of
the bargain.'
   175. 'And nominated him as umpire, so that there should be no more
argument.'
   179. 'And the first to complain . . .'
   182. 'There was always some new bargaining and drinking starting up.'
   183. Again the ironic collision of detail (cf. 186).
   187. 'And blew off the round horn at the backbone's end.'
   189. 'And wished it had been scoured with a bunch of briar-twigs.'

He myhte nother steppe ne stande til he a staf hadde,   190
And thenne gan he go lyke a glemans byche,
Sum tyme asyde and sum tyme a-rere,
As who-so layth lynes for to lacche foules.
    And when he drow to the dore, thenne dymmede his yes,
And thromblede at the thresfold and threw to the erthe,   195
And Clement the coblere cauhte hym by the myddel
And for to lyfte hym aloft leyde hym on his knees;
Ac Gloton was a greet cherl and greved in the liftynge
And cowed up a caudel in Clementis lappe;
Ys none so hungry hound in Hertfordshyre   200
Durste lape of that levynge, so unlovely hit smauhte.
    With alle the wo of this worlde his wyf and his wenche
Beren hym to his bed and brouhten hym ther-ynne;
And aftur al this exces he hadde an accidie after,
He sleep Saturday and Sonenday til the sonne yede to reste.   205
Then gan he wake wel wanne and wolde have ydronke;
The furste word that he spak was 'Who halt the bolle?'
His wif and his inwit edwitede hym of his synne;
Ywax ashamed that shrewe, and shrofe hym as swythe
To Repentaunce ryht thus: 'Have reuthe on me,' he saide,   210
Thow lord that aloft art and alle lyves shope!
    To the, god, I, Glotoun, gulty I me yelde
Of that I have trespased with tonge, I can nat telle how ofte,
Sworn "Godes soule and his sides!" and "So helpe me, god
    almyhty!"
There no nede ne was, many sythe falsly;   215
And over-sopped at my soper and som tyme at nones
More then my kynde myhte deffye,

---

207. word *omitted in* XU; Who U : X to

191-3. '. . . like a blind minstrel's bitch . . . or like someone laying lines to
catch birds.'
    207. 'Who's got the bowl?'
    211. 'Thou, Lord, that art on high and created all living creatures.'
    215. Idle, false, and violent swearing were condemned, but not swearing
itself. For the orthodox view, and the Biblical texts, see Chaucer's *Parson's
Tale*, *CT* X. 587.

And as an hound that eet gras, so gan I to brake,
And spilde that I aspele myhte—I kan nat speke for shame
The vilony of my foule mouthe and of my foule mawe—   220
And fastyng-dayes bifore none fedde me with ale
Out of resoun, among rybaudes, here rybaudrye to here.
　　Her-of, gode god, graunte me foryevenesse
Of all my luyther lyf in al my lyf-tyme.
For I vowe to verray god, for eny hunger or thurste,   225
Shal nevere fysch in the Fryday defyen in my wombe
Til Abstinence myn aunte have yeve me leve—
And yut have I hated here al my lyf-tyme.'

> Sloth, appropriately, brings up the rear of the procession. Repentance now
> leads the people in a prayer of Penitence.

5. The Prayer of Repentance and the Guide to Truth (VIII. 120–291)

　　Tho was Repentaunce aredy and redde hem alle to knele:
'I shal byseke for alle synneful oure saviour of grace,
To amende us of oure mysdedes, do mercy to us alle.
　　God, that of thi goodnesse gonne the world make
And madest of nauhte auhte and man liche thysulve,   5

---

228. hated U : chasted

218–19. 'And like a dog that eats grass I would throw up, and waste what
might have been saved.'

222. '(Drank) to unreasonable excess, surrounded by profligates, eager to
hear more of their filthy stories.'

227. *Abstinence myn aunte.* Exigencies of alliteration often create weird and
arbitrary collocations of this kind.

228. Gluttony's last words are a backward look at the old life. His penitence
is of the morning-after kind, and seems peremptory and mechanical, like that
of all the Sins, besides the enormous relish and vigour of his sinfulness. The
allegorical suggestion is that this kind of penitence is too easy; we are prepared
for backsliding, and for subsequent penetration to deeper levels of awareness.

2–3. Repentance announces the prayer, which then follows (4–32), in the
form of an invocation to God to have mercy on the penitent sinners, for
Jesus' sake. The structure of the prayer, the syntax, and the language are all
deeply liturgical, rich in quotation and echo from the Scriptures.

And sethe soffredeste hym to synege, a sykenesse to us alle,
And for oure beste, as I beleve, what-so the book telle.
    O felix culpa, O necessarium peccatum Ade!
For thorw that synne thy sone ysent was til erthe
And bicam man of a mayde, mankynde to amende,
And madest thysulve, with thy sone, oure soule and oure body
    ilych.   10
    Ego in patre, et pater in me est; et qui videt me, patrem
      meum videt.
And sethe in oure secte, as hit semed, deydest,
On a Friday, in forme of man, feledest oure sorwe.
    Captivam duxit captivitatem.
The sonne for sorwe ther-of lees liht for a tyme
Aboute mydday, when most liht is, and mel-tyme of sayntes;
Feddest tho with thy flesch and blood oure forfadres in helle.   15
    Populus qui ambulabat in tenebris, lucem magnam vidit.
The lihte that lup oute of the, Lucifer hit blente
And brouhte thyne yblessed fro thennes into the blisse of hevene.

---

6. Certain patterns in the structure of Langland's alliterative line, certain syntactical moulds, soon impose themselves on the ear. This one is significantly echoed in B. XVI. 163: 'Justed in Jerusalem, a joye to us alle'.

7. *for oure beste.* The blessed paradox of the *felix culpa,* happily embroidered in one of the most famous of Middle English lyrics, *Adam lay ibounden,* and more soberly by Milton in *Paradise Lost* XII. 469–78.

7f. 'O happy fault, O necessary sin of Adam!' (necessary, for without it Christ would not have been necessary). Not from the Bible, but from the Missal, or mass-book—the Canticle for Easter Eve.

10f. 'I am in the Father, and the Father in me; he that hath seen me hath seen my Father' (cf. *John* 14: 9–10).

12f. 'He led captivity captive' (*Ephes.* 4: 8), i.e. he put an end to the thraldom of the flesh to sin.

14-15. 'About midday, when the sun's light is strongest, a time of spiritual refreshment for holy men, (for this was the time when) you fed with your flesh and blood our forefathers in hell.'

15f. 'The people that walked in darkness have seen a great light' (*Isaiah* 9: 2). This passage was the source in prophecy of the apocryphal gospel narrative of the Harrowing of Hell, the descent of Christ into Hell to release the souls of the patriarchs. See 15.272n.

17. *brouhte* replaces *blewe* in B. Langland's characteristic energy, like Shakespeare's (see Donald Davie, *Articulate Energy,* London, 1955), is a freedom and

The thridde day ther-aftur thow yedest into oure sekte;
A synful Marie the saw ar seynte Marye thy dame,
And al to solace synful thow soffredest hit so were.   20
    Non veni vocare justos, sed peccatores ad penitenciam.
And al that Mark hath ymade, Matheu, Johan and Lucas,
Of thy douhtiest dedes, was don in oure sekte.
    Verbum caro factum est.
And by so muche hit semeth the sykerloker we mowe
Bidde and biseche the, yf hit be thy wille,
That art furste oure fadur and of flesch oure brother,   25
And sethen oure savyour, and seydest hit with thy tonge
That what tyme we synneful men wolden be sory
For dedes that we han don ylle, dampned sholde we ben nevere,
Yf we knowlechede and cryde Crist ther-fore mercy.
    Quandocumque ingemuerit peccator, omnes iniquitates eius non
      recordabor amplius.
And for thi muchel mercy and Marie love thi moder,   30
Have reuthe of alle these rybaudes that repenten hem sore
That evere thei gulte ageyn the, god, in gost or in dede.'
    Thenne hente Hope an horn of *Deus, tu conversus vivificabis nos,*

20. al *P* : *X* also	**22.** *X* douhtiokest
30. *first* thi *omitted in* *X*	**33.** Hope *U* : *X* I

---

vigour in the use of verbs. The change in C is a neat demonstration of its occasional tendency to rationalize the poetry out of existence.

19. Referring to the meeting with Mary Magdalene in the garden.

20f. 'I am not come to call the righteous, but sinners to repentance' (*Matt.* 9: 13).

22. *in oure sekte.* The threefold repetition of this phrase (B uses three different words, *secte*, *sute* and *armes*) is designed to focus the prayer on the central mystery and the central hope of the Incarnation, at once to acknowledge God's love in becoming incarnate, and to make a claim upon it.

22f. 'The Word was made flesh' (*John* 1:14).

23-4. 'And with this in mind we may all the more confidently pray to thee and beseech thee . . .'

29f. 'And when the sinner shall repent, I will remember his sins no more' (cf. *Jeremiah* 31:34).

30. 'And because of thy great mercy, and for the love of Mary thy mother.'

33. 'Lord, thou shalt quicken us again' (*Psalm* 71:20).

And blewe hit with *Beati quorum remisse sunt iniquitates et quorum*
    tecta sunt peccata,
That alle seyntes for synful songen with David: 35
    Homines et jumenta salvabis, domine, quemadmodum multiplicasti
      misericordiam tuam, deus!
A thousend of men tho throngen togyderes,
Criede upward to Crist and to his clene moder
To have grace to go to Treuthe—god leve that they mote!
Ac ther ne was wye non so wys that the way thider couthe,
But blostrede forth as bestes over baches and hulles,   40
Til late was and longe that thei a lede mette,
Aparayled as a paynyem in pilgrimes wyse.
  He bar a bordon ybounde with a brood liste,
In a wethewynde wyse ywrithe al aboute;
A bolle and a bagge he bar by his syde;   45
An hundret of ampolles on his hat sette,
Signes of Syse and shelles of Galys,

---

34. 'Blessed are they whose transgressions are forgiven, and whose sins are covered' (*Psalm* 32:1).

35f. 'O Lord, thou preservest man and beast. How excellent is thy loving-kindness, O God!' (*Psalm* 36: 6–7).

38. The prayer of penitence and the hope of salvation prompt the pilgrimage to Truth, the search for the good Christian life, which in one form or another occupies the rest of the poem.

42. *as a paynyem:* 'like a Saracen'. Pilgrims to the holy land would dress, for comfort, like the local inhabitants. Jerusalem had been in the hands of the Saracens since 1187, but Christian pilgrims had free access by Frederick II's treaty of 1229.

43–4. 'He carried a pilgrim's staff bound with a broad strip of cloth, twisted all round like convolvulus.' This is probably a relic of the custom of carrying a slender rod bound to the pilgrims' staff, perhaps a penitentiary's rod in token of the indulgence gained at a particular shrine, or perhaps a formalized palm-branch, in general token of pilgrimage. There seems to be an original association with St. James of Compostella, but its significance is elusive. See G. McN. Rushforth, *Medieval Christian Imagery* (Oxford, 1936), pp. 93–6. (I am indebted for help with this note to Dr. Peter Newton.)

45. *ampolles:* small phials containing holy water or oil from shrines he had visited.

47. *Signes of Syse:* 'souvenirs from Assisi'. Each place of pilgrimage had its special 'sign' or souvenir, such as the scallop-shells of St. James of Compostella in Galicia (St. James the Greater, brother of John the Evangelist, who according

And many a crouch on his cloke, kayes of Rome,
And the vernicle bifore, for men sholde yknowe
And se by his signes wham he sought hadde.   50
    This folke frayned hym furste fro whennes he come?
'Fro Sinaye,' he sayde, 'and fro the sepulcre of oure lord.
In Bedlem and in Babiloyne I have be in bothe,
In Armonye, in Alisaundre, and in Damascle.
Ye may se be the signes that sitten on my cappe,   55
I have souht gode seyntes for my soule helthe
And ywalked ful wide in wete and in drye.'
    'Knowest thow auht a cor-seint,' quod they, 'that men calleth
        Treuthe?
Kouthest wissen us the way whoder out Treuthe woneth?'
    'Nay, so me god helpe,' sayde the gome thenne,   60
'I saw nevere palmere with pyk ne with scrippe
Axen aftur hym, but now in this place.'

    'Peter!' quod a ploghman, and putte forth his heved,
'I knowe hym as kyndely as clerk doth his bokes.

54. and in Damascle *P* : *X* I have be in bothe
59. the way *P* : *X* today

---

to a late tradition preached the gospel in Spain; Compostella is near the N.W.
coast, which probably accounts for the tradition of the shells), the *crouch* or
cross, sewn on the cloak as a sign of a visit to the holy land, and the keys of
St. Peter (guardian of heaven's gate) of Rome.
    49. *vernicle:* a copy of the handkerchief of St. Veronica (whence the name,
from Latin *veronicula*), which, according to legend, was miraculously impressed
with a likeness of Christ when she wiped his face with it as he was led to
crucifixion. The original was preserved in St. Peter's.
    52–4. The palmer had visited the convent of St. Katherine in the desert of
Sinai (not far from the place where, according to tradition, Moses received the
Ten Commandments), the Holy Sepulchre in Jerusalem, Bethlehem, Babylon
the Less (i.e. Cairo, with its shrine of St. Barbara, and church of Our Lady,
who dwelt there after the flight into Egypt), Armenia (where he would have
seen the Ark), Alexandria, home of the martyred St. Katherine, and Damascus,
where God created Adam before planting him 'eastward in Eden'.
    60–2. The ignorance of Truth displayed by the palmer is not intended as
an indictment of professional pilgrims, but rather to emphasise the interior
nature of the pilgrimage. Dramatically, as a direction of attention from outer
to inner, it is akin to the Pardon episode (Passus X).

Consience and Kyndewyt kenned me to his place   65
And maden me sykeren sethen to serven hym for evere,
Bothe to sowe and to sette the while I swynke myhte,
And to sowen his seed, suewen his bestes,
Withynne and withouten to wayten his profyt.
I have ybe his foloware al this fourty wynter   70
And yserved Treuthe sothly, somdel to paye.
In alle kyne craftes that he couthe devise
Profitable as for the plouh, he putte me to lerne,
And, thogh I sey hit mysulf, I serve hym to paye.
I have myn huyre of hym wel and other whiles more;   75
He is the presteste payere that eny pore man knoweth;
He with-halt non hewe his huyre over even.
He is as louh as a lombe and leel of his tonge,
And who-so wilneth to wyte where that Treuthe woneth,
I wol wissen yow wel, ryht to his place.'   80
    'Ye, leve Peres,' quod thise pilgrimes, and profrede Peres mede.
    'Nay, bi the perel of my soule!' Peres gan to swerie,
'I ne wol fonge a ferthynge, for seynt Thomas shryne!
Were it itolde Treuthe that I toke mede
He wolde love me the lasse a long tyme after.   85
    Ac who-so wol wende ther Treuthe is, this is the way theder.

66. sykeren *U* : *X* sykerenesse

---

69. 'To look after his interests both indoors and out.' There is no need to allegorize this as 'in both spiritual and material matters', since the whole passage describing the honest ploughman labouring in his vocation is at once real *and* also allegorical of the spiritual life in the most obvious way. It is a true *figure* (see Introd.). The Christian significance of the ploughman-archetype needs no explanation, which is why Langland chose it. Cf. Chaucer's Plowman, *CT* I. 529–41.

77. 'He never fails to pay the labourer his wage when evening comes.' The reference is to the parable of the Vineyard (*Matt.* 20: 1–16), though the reward spoken of here is spiritual grace and fulfilment on earth (as well as, *literaliter*, a living) and not salvation.

83. '... not for all the riches on St. Thomas a Becket's shrine' (in Canterbury).

84. *mede.* After three whole Passus (III–V) devoted to the exposure of *Mede* (desire for gain, the 'profit-motive') as the source of social corruption, the word for Piers is like a goad.

D*

Ye mote go thorw Mekenesse, alle men and wommen,
Til ye come into Consience, yknowe of god sulve,
That ye lovye hym as lord leely above alle;
That is to sey sothly, ye sholde rather deye   90
Thenne eny dedly synne do, for drede or for preyere.
And thenne youre neghebores next in none wyse apayre
Otherwyse then ye wolden they wrouhte yow alle tymes.

And so goth forth by the brok, a brugge as it were,
For to ye fynde a ford, Youre-fader-honoureth;   95
Wadeth in at that water and wascheth yow wel there
And ye shal lepe the lihtloker al youre lyf-tyme.

   Honora patrem et matrem.

And thenne shalt thow se Swere-nat-but-if-it-be-for-nede-
And-nameliche-an-ydel-the-name-of-god-almyhty.

   Thenne shalt thow come by a croft, ac com thow nat ther-
      ynne;   100
The croft hatte Coveyte-nat-menne-catel-ne-here-wyves-
Ne-none-of-here-servauntes-that-nuye-hem-myhte;
Loke thou bere nat there aweye, but yf hit be thyn owene.

   Two stockes ther stondeth, ac stynte thow nat there;
Thei hatte Stel-nat and Sle-nat—stryk forth by bothe   105
And leveth hem on the lift hand and loke nat therafter,
And hold wel the haliday heye til even.

---

100. nat *omitted in XU*   **104.** Two *U* : *X* Tho
106. nat *omitted in XU*

---

91. '. . . even though fear or the beseeching of others press you to it.'

94. The first part of the journey to Truth takes the pilgrim through a countryside dotted with allegorical reminders of the Ten Commandments (*Ex.* 20) and the Gospel glosses on them (e.g. *Matt.* 19: 17–19; *Luke* 10: 27); the fifth, third, tenth, eighth, sixth, fourth and ninth are referred to specifically, in that order. The allegory is stiff and mechanical: there is no inherent symbolic aptness in the representation of the fifth commandment, for instance, as a ford over a river. The countryside is stark, dry and colourless. But this itself is apt, for Piers does not wish to disguise from the pilgrims the fact that the basis of Christian truth is a hard-won rectitude of life, and that the rich rewards of Christian grace, love and mercy have to be deserved. The journey is through the Old Testament to Christ.

97f. 'Honour thy father and thy mother (that thy days may be long upon the land)' (*Ex.* 20: 12).

Thenne shaltow blenche at a berw, Ber-no-fals-witnesse,
Ys frithed in with floreynes and othere fees monye;
Loke thow plokke no plaunte there, for perel of thy soule.   110
    Thenne shaltow se Say-sothe-so-hit-be-to-done-
In-none-manere-elles-nat-for-no-mannes-preyere,
And so shaltow come to a court as cleer as the sonne;
The mote is of Mercy, the manere in the myddes,
And al the wallyng is of Wyt, for Wil ne sholde hit wynne.   115
The carneles ben of Cristendom, that kynde to save,
Ybotresed with Bileve-so-or-thow-best-not-ysaved;
And alle the hous been yheled, halles and chaumbres,
With no leed but with Love, and with Lele-speche.
The barres aren of Buxumnesse, as brethrene of o wombe.   120
The brygge hatte Byde-wel-the-bet-may-thow-spede;
Eche a piler is of Penaunces and preyeres to seyntes;
The hokes aren Almes-dedes that the gates hange on.
    Grace hatte the gate-ward, a gode man for sothe;
His man hatte Amende-yow, many man hym knoweth.   125
Tel hym this ilke tokene: "Treuthe wot the sothe,
I am sory of my synnes and so I shal evere,
And performed the penaunce that the prest me hihte."
Biddeth Amende-yow to meke yow to his maister Grace,
To opene and undo the hye gate of hevene   130

---

117. thow *U* : *X* two   121. thow *U* : *X* they

---

109. 'It is wooded around with florins and many other bribes.'

111–12. 'Then you shall see Tell-the-truth-as-you-ought-to-and-nothing-but-the-truth-whatever-anyone-says.'

113. The 'court' is the castle of Truth, of man dwelling in God, built of and inhabited by the Christian virtues of the soul redeemed by Christ. The allegory here is different in style, rich, intricate and meaningful in a manner made possible by the long allegorical tradition of the 'castle of the soul'. See *Sawles Warde* (ed. R. M. Wilson, Leeds, 1938), a free early 13th c. translation from the *De Anima* of Hugh of St. Victor (d. 1146;) and the *Castle of Love* (ed. C. Horstmann, in EETS, OS 98, 1892), translated from a French poem attributed to Robert Grosseteste, bishop of Lincoln.

115. 'Wit' and 'Will' are traditionally paired as moral contraries, representing the divine gift of reason and free ordering control pitted against the instinctual drives of fallen nature—what Milton calls 'Reason' and 'Passion'. See 2.5n.

That Adam and Eve agenes us alle shette.

> Per Evam janua celi cunctis clausa est, et per Mariam
> virginem iterum patefacta est.

A ful leel lady unlek hit of grace,
And she hath the keye and a clycat, thogh the kynge slepe,
And may lede in that she loveth as here lef lyketh.

And yf Grace graunte the to go in in this wyse,   135
Thow shalt se Treuthe sitte in thy sulve herte,
And solace thy soule and save the fram payne,
And charge Charite a churche to make
In thyne hole herte, to herborwe alle trewe
And fynde alle manere folke fode to here soules,   140
Yef love and leute and owre lawe be trewe:

> Quodcumque petieritis in nomine meo, dabitur enim vobis.

Be war thenne of Wrath, that wikkede shrewe,
For he hath envye to hym that in thyn herte setteth
And poketh forth pruyde to preyse thysulven.
The boldenesse of thy been-fetes maketh the blynd thenne,   145

---

135. *second* in *omitted in XU*
141. be *omitted in XU*   **142.** that *P* : *X* nat that

---

131. B has the more familiar 'Tho Adam and Even eten apples unrosted'.
The change is a good example of C's tendency to excise 'poetic' irrelevances,
however charming.

131f. 'Through Eve the door of heaven was closed to all men, and through
the Virgin Mary it was opened again.' The idea is familiar, but the source of
the quotation is not identified.

132-3. 'A true woman [the Virgin] graciously unlocked the gate, and she
has the latch-key, though the king himself [God] may be asleep.'

136. The journey to Truth ends in self-discovery, in the recognition of the
divine within, the soul's part in God. Langland here touches on a theme frequent
in mystical writing. See Elizabeth Zeeman, 'Piers Plowman and the Pilgrimage
to Truth', *Essays and Studies* XI (1958), 1–16.

138-41. 'And let Love make your heart a sanctuary of Truth, and a source
of spiritual nourishment, in accordance with what we believe true of Love,
Faith and the Law'.

141f. 'Whatsoever ye shall ask in my name, it shall be given unto you'
(cf. *John* 16: 23).

145-6. 'Rash confidence in your good deeds produces a kind of spiritual
blindness, and you will be cast out as swiftly as the dew fades' (a Biblical image:
see *Hosea* 13: 3).

So worth thow dryven out as deux, and the dore yclosed,
Ykeyed and yclyketed to close the withouten,
Hapliche an hundred wynter ar thow eft entre.
Thus myhte thow lesen his love, to lete wel by thysulven,
And geten hit agayne thorw grace, ac thorw no gifte elles.   150
    Ac ther ben sevene susteres that serven Treuthe evere
And aren porters over the posternes that to that place bilongen.
That on hatte Abstinence and Umbletee annother,
Charite and Chastite ben his chief maydenes,
Pacience and Pees muche peple thei helpe,   155
Largenesse that lady lat in ful monye—
None of hem alle helpe may in betere,
For she payeth for prisones in places and in peynes.
And who is sib to this sevene, so me god helpe,
Is wonderliche welcome and fayre underfonge.   160
Who is nat syb to this sevene, sothly to telle,
Hit is ful hard, be myn heved, eny of yow alle
To geten ingang at eny gate, bote grace be the more.'
    'By Crist,' quod a cutte-pors, 'I have no kyn there.'

---

153. *X* Astinence

149. 'Thus you might lose his love by thinking a lot of yourself.'
150. Despite the Langlandian emphasis on good works, on the practice of
virtue, Grace is shown, in accordance with orthodox doctrine, to transcend,
even to ignore (see 163) human desert. The doctrine of Grace, evolved by
St. Augustine (d. 430) in his treatises against Pelagius, was designed to arrogate
to God an absolute and arbitrary free-will in judgment. Grace cannot be won
nor deserved, but only given. To Langland's charitable eye, this makes it an
instrument of potential universal salvation; in a narrower context, it produced
the Calvinist doctrine of Election.
151. These are the seven Christian virtues, first formulated in penitential
literature as *remedia* for the seven deadly sins. They are to be distinguished
from the three spiritual virtues, Faith, Hope and Charity, and the four cardinal
(Aristotelian) virtues, Prudence, Temperance, Justice and Fortitude, which have
independent origin, and constitute another 'seven', though the categories
sometimes cross. All testify to the medieval passion for a schematization of
moral activity, a kind of grid-reference for experience, which in turn is
prompted by a belief in the absolute coherence of the revealed system. Cf.
J. Huizinga, *The Waning of the Middle Ages*, chap. xv.
157. 'None of them all can better help people to get in, for she ransoms
prisoners from places of suffering.'

'Ne I,' quod an apeward, 'by auht that I know!'   165
'Wyte god,' quod a wafrestere, 'wiste I this for sothe,
Wolde I nevere forthere no fot for no frere prechynge!'
  'Yus,' quod Peres the ploghman, and pokede hem alle to gode,
'Mercy is a mayden there hath myhte over hem alle,
And she is sib to alle synful, and here sone bothe.   170
And thorw the helpes of hem two, hope thow non other,
Thow myhte gete grace there, so thow go by-tymes.'

Piers Plowman offers to act as their guide on the way to Truth, but first
they must help him plough his half-acre, an allegorical way of indicating
the need to face social and economic realities. To all ranks of society he allots
the task appropriate for their station, and all work well for a while, but
soon malcontents and idlers begin to disrupt the ordered pattern of society.
Piers calls in Hunger to coerce them into submission, but when the threat
of famine recedes, they return to their old selfish ways. At this point, in an
atmosphere dark with ominous prophecy, Piers receives a Pardon from
Truth, to be awarded to all those who help Piers in his work, whatever their
estate. Its terms are specified, as gradually Langland works his way down
to the dregs and outcasts of society, amongst whom his sympathy so naturally moves.

6. *The Pardon sent from Truth* (X. 61–186)

Beggares and biddares beth nat in that bulle

166–7. 'God defend (us),' said a woman cake-seller, 'if I were sure this was
all true, I wouldn't stir a foot further, not for any friar's preaching' (with
reference to the traditional skill of friars in persuasive preaching).

168. *Peres* and *ploghman* are erased in *X*, and so throughout the MS, though
not consistently. This may be the work of a 15th c. anti-Lollard fanatic, since
the name of Piers the Ploughman had become, however mistakenly, something
of a revolutionary rallying-call in the late 14th century, judging by John Ball's
letter to the men of Essex, and political and religious heresy were not much
distinguished.

169–70. The encompassing quality of God's mercy is our final image of the
castle of Truth, as well as the first (114). It is here indentified with the Virgin
Mary as intercessor.

1. Having dealt with the estates within society—knights, bishops, merchants,
lawyers, labourers—Langland turns now to beggars, distinguishing the professional from the truly needy with a scrupulous compassion.

Bote the sugestion be soth that shapeth hym to begge.
For he that beggeth or biddeth, but yf he have nede,
He is fals and faytour and defraudeth the nedy
And also gileth hym that gyveth and taketh ageynes his wille.   5
For he that gyveth for goddes love wolde nat gyve, his thankes,
Bote ther he wiste were wel grete nede
And most meritorie to men that he yeveth fore.
Catoun accordeth ther-with: *Cui des videto*.
  Wot no man, as I wene, who is worthy to have;   10
Ac that most neden aren oure neyhebores, and we nyme
      gode hede,
As prisones in puttes and pore folke in cotes,
Charged with childrene and chief lordes rente;
That they with spynnyng may spare, spenen hit on hous-huyre,
Bothe in mylke and in mele, to make with papelotes   15
To aglotye with here gurles that greden after fode.
And hemsulve also soffre muche hunger,
And wo in wynter-tymes, with wakynge on nyhtes
To rise to the reule to rokke the cradel,
Bothe to carde and to kembe, to cloute and to wasche,   20
And to rybbe and to relye, rusches to pylie,

---

3. *second* he P : X they   8. to U : X and to

---

6. '. . . would not give, of his choice.'

9. 'Take care whom you give alms to.' The Roman sage Cato was the reputed author of a series of Distichs or moral sayings, of wide circulation in the Middle Ages, to which are prefixed a number of pithy apophthegms. This is one of them.

10. From here to line 101 is new in C, a long meditation upon the plight of the poor, the oppressed and the outcast, an attempt to answer the unanswerable question of this line. Serious, unsentimental, unwavering in its honesty, it is something new, indeed unique, in literature, not only as an expression of 'social conscience', but for a quality of heroism, even gaiety, which Langland's optimism produces out of sub-human suffering.

11. 'If we look hard, we can find need enough among our neighbours.'

14-16. 'The money that they can put aside from their spinning they spend on rent, on milk and meal to make porridge with, to feed their children, who cry out for food.'

21. 'To scrape flax (with a flat iron tool, to remove particles of core) and to wind yarn on to the reel, and to peel rushes' (to make rushlights from the pith).

That reuthe is to rede or in ryme shewe
The wo of this wommen that wonyeth in cotes;
And of monye other men that moche wo soffren,
Bothe a-fyngred and a-furste, to turne the fayre outward,   25
And ben abasched for to begge and wollen nat be aknowe
What hem nedede at here neyhebores at noon and at eve.
   This I wot witterly, as the world techeth,
What other byhoveth that hath many childrene
And hath no catel but his craft to clothe hem and to fede,   30
And fele to fonge ther-to, and fewe panes taketh.
There is payne and peny-ale as for a pytaunce ytake,
And colde flesche and fische as venisoun were bake;
Fridays and fastyng-days a ferthing-worth of moskeles
Were a feste for suche folke, or so fele cockes.   35
These are almesse, to helpe that han suche charges
And to comforte such coterelles and crokede men and blynde.
   Ac beggares with bagges, the whiche brewhous ben here
      churches,
But they be blynde or to-broke or elles be syke,
Thouh he falle for defaute that fayteth for his lyf-lode,   40
Reche ye nevere, ye riche, thouh suche lollares sterven.
For alle that han here hele and here ye-syhte
And lymes to labory with, and lollares lyf usen,
Lyven agen goddes lawe and the lore of holi churche.
   And yut ar ther other beggares, in hele, as hit semeth,   45
Ac hem wanteth wyt, men and women bothe,
The whiche aren lunatyk lollares and lepares aboute,
And madden as the mone sit, more other lasse.

28. I *U* : *X* he

25-7. 'Though racked by hunger and thirst, they keep up a respectable appearance, being ashamed to beg, and refuse to admit to their neighbours what they go short of at every meal.'
28-9. 'I know for certain, from my experience of the world, what falls to the lot of other men . . .'
32-3. 'Bread and penny-ale are a special treat for them, cold meat and fish regarded like roast venison.'
36. 'It would indeed be an act of charity to help folk so oppressed.'
48. 'And grow more or less mad, according to the moon's phase '

Careth they for no colde ne counteth of non hete,
And aren mevynge after the mone; moneyeles they walke,   50
With a good will, witteles, mony wyde contreyes,
Riht as Peter dede and Poul, save that they preche nat
Ne none muracles maken—ac many tymes hem happeth
To prophecye of the peple, pleyinge, as hit were,
And to oure syhte, as hit semeth, seth god hath the myhte   55
To yeve uch a wyht wyt, welth, and his hele,
And suffreth suche go so, it semeth, to myn inwyt,
Hit aren as his postles, suche peple, or as his prive disciples.
For he sent hem forth selverles in a somer garnement
Withoute bagge and bred, as the book telleth: 60

　　Quando misi vos sine pane et pera.

Barfoot and bredles, beggeth they of no man.
And thauh he mete with the mayre ameddes the strete,
He reverenceth hym ryht nauht, no rather then another.

　　Neminem salutaveritis per viam.

Suche manere of men, Matheu us techeth,
We sholde have hem to house and helpe hem when they come.   65

　　Et egenos vagos induc in domum tuam.

For hit aren merye-mouthed men, munstrals of hevene,
And godes boys, bordyors, as the book telleth.

　　Si quis videtur sapiens, fiet stultus ut sit sapiens.

　And alle manere munstrals, men wot wel the sothe,
To underfongen hem fayre byfalleth for the ryche,

53–67. The inspired wisdom of fools is traditional, and had Biblical warrant, but this whole passage is striking for the divine sanction Langland extends to lunatics, allowing their irrationality to work its leaven on society, and not insulating society from the uncomfortable truth of their existence and their vision. Like much else in Langland, it reminds one of Blake, and expresses a half-mystical apprehension of a divine 'carelessness'. There are elements of self-portrayal (62–3 is vividly personal, cf. B. XV. 5).

60f. 'I have sent you forth without bread or scrip' (cf. *Luke* 10: 3–4, Christ's admonition to the disciples).

63f. 'Salute no man by the way' (*Luke* 10: 4).

65f. 'And bring the poor that are cast out to thy house' (*Isaiah* 58: 7). The general reference is to *Matt.* 25: 31–46.

67f. 'If any man among you seemeth to be wise in this world, let him become a fool, that he may be wise' (1 *Cor.* 3: 18).

For the lordes love or the ladyes that they with longen.   70
Men suffreth al that suche sayen and in solace taketh,
And yut more to such men men doth ar they passe;
Men gyveth hem giftes and gold for grete lordes sake.
   Ryht so, ye ryche, yut rather ye sholde
Welcomen and worschipen and with youre good helpen   75
Godes munstrals and his mesagers and his mery bordiours,
The whiche arn lunatyk loreles and lepares aboute,
For under godes secret seal here synnes ben kevered.
   For they bereth none bagges ne boteles under clokes,
The whiche is lollarne lyf and lewede ermytes,   80
That loken louhliche to lache men almesse,
In hope to sitte at even by the hote coles,
Unlouke his legges abrood or ligge at his ese,
Reste hym and roste and his rug turne,
Drynke druie and depe and drawe hym thenne to bedde;   85
And whenne hym lyketh and luste, his leve is to ryse,
And when he is rysen, rometh out and right wel aspyeth
Where he may rathest have a repast or a ronde of bacoun,
Sulver or sode mete and sum tyme bothe,
Loof or half-loof other a lompe of chese;   90
And caryeth hit hom to his cote and cast hym to lyvene
In idelnesse and in ese and by otheres travayle.
   And what freke on this folde fisceth aboute
With a bagge at his bak a begyneld wyse,
And can eny craft in cas he wolde hit use,   95

---

77. arn *omitted in* X   81. That *omitted in* X

69–70. 'It is the responsibility of the rich to welcome them gladly, for the sake of the lords and the ladies with whom they dwell.' The mention of 'minstrels of heaven' prompts a digression on a favourite subject. See 1.37n.

71. 'Men tolerate all that such minstrels say, and take it in good part.'

76. *Godes munstrals*, cf. *joculatores Domini*, the name applied to the early followers of St. Francis, who also exhibited this 'carelessness' of the world.

79. Langland returns to the theme of the professional idler.

81. 'Who put on a very abject expression, to obtain men's alms.'

93–8. 'And whoever wanders about like this, with a bag on his shoulder in the fashion of a beggar—knowing some trade which he could use if he wanted to earn bread and ale and, what's more, a suit of clothes to cover his bones with—whoever yet lives like an idler is condemned by God's law.'

Thorw which craft he couthe come to bred and to ale
And over-more to an hater to hele with his bonis,
And lyveth lyke a lollare, goddes lawe hym dampneth.

'Forthy lollares that lyven in sleuthe and over-land strikares
Beth nat in this bulle,' quod Peres, 'til they ben amended,   100
Ne no beggare that beggeth, but yf they have nede.'
The bok banneth beggarie and blameth hit in this manere:

> *Junior fui, etenim senui. Et alibi: Infirmata est virtus mea in*
>   *paupertate.*

Hit nedeth nat nouthe anoon for to preche
And lere this lewede men what this Latyn meneth,
For hit blameth all beggarie, be ye ful certayn.   105
For they lyve in no love, ne no lawe holden;
They weddeth none wymmen that they with deleth,
Bringeth forth bastardus, beggares of kynde,
Or the bak or som bon they breke of here children
And gon and fayten with here fauntes for everemore after.   110
Ther aren mo mysshape amonges suche beggares
Then of many other men that on this molde walken;
And tho that lyveth thus here lyf, leve ye non other,
Thai have no part of pardoun, ne of preyeres ne of penaunces.

Ac olde and hore, that helples ben and nedy,   115
And wymmen with childe that worche ne mowe,
Blynde and bedredne and broken in here membres,
And alle pore pacient, apayed of goddes sonde,
As mesels and mendenantes, men yfalle in meschief,
As prisones and pilgrimes and paraunter men yrobbed   120
Or by-lowe thorw luther men and lost here catel after,

---

97. an hater *U* : *X* han astor   **107.** They *U* : *X* he

---

99. '. . . and those who wander around the country' (tramps).

102f. 'I have been young, and now am old (yet have I not seen the righteous forsaken, nor his seed begging bread)' (*Psalm* 37: 25). And elsewhere: 'My strength faileth because of my poverty' (cf. *Psalm* 31: 10).

108. '. . . beggars by nature, from birth.'

115. The recurrent movement of this whole passage is of strict moral judgment constantly wrought upon and qualified by compassion.

118. 'And all poor patient sufferers who are content with what God has sent them.'

Or thorw fuyr other thorw flood yfalle into poverte,
That taketh thise meschiefes mekeliche and myldeliche at herte,
For love of here lowe hertes oure lord hath hem ygraunted
Here penaunce and here purgatorie uppon this puyre erthe,   125
And pardon with the Plouhman *a pena et a culpa.*

The terms of the Pardon are further specified in relation to hermits true
and false. A priest now asks to see the pardon, and points out that it is no
more than the familiar verses from the Athanasian creed—*Et qui bona
egerunt, ibunt in vitam eternam; qui vero mala, in ignem eternam.* (The C-text
here suppresses a dramatic episode in B, where Piers tears the pardon in a
rage, and determines to devote himself to a life of prayer and penance and
to leave his plough. The significance of this paradoxical act seems twofold:
impatience with the dry eschatology of the Church; and a disillusioned
recognition of the failure of the attempt to reform society.) The dreamer
wakes with the noise of Piers and the priest arguing and contemplates his
dream, concluding that pardons and indulgences, triennials and pilgrimages,
are nothing beside *Dowel*, the good Christian life honestly led (the term is
first used to translate 'qui bona egerunt' and soon generates *Dobet* and
Dobest as well). This realization prompts a new vision, virtually a new
poem, the *Visio de Dowel*, in which the problems of community recede and
the theme of search is more deeply interiorized.

7. *The Quest for Dowel* (XI. 1–126)

Thus yrobed in russet I romede aboute
Alle a somer seson for to seke Dowel,

---

125. This view of poverty and suffering, patiently borne, as purgatorial,
effectively stifled any political response to it as a social evil, and made it a
martyrdom to be embraced, like chronic illness. Langland, for all his compassion, never suggests doing anything about it—in fact, at one point he sternly
reproves labourers for demanding higher wages (C. IX. 336). It is strange that
the name of Piers Plowman was used as a rallying-cry by leaders of the Peasants'
Revolt in 1381. See 5.168n.

126. '. . . both from punishment and from guilt', i.e. a plenary remission of
sins. Properly, only the sacrament of penance offered total absolution, while
pardons and indulgences remitted merely the temporal punishment. But the
distinction was not much observed in the 14th century (least of all by
pardoners).

1. Quite deliberately, here and in the dream-prologue (61–7, below),

And fraynede ful ofte of folke that I mette
Yf eny wiht wiste where Dowel was at ynne,
And what man he myhte be of mony men I askede.   5
  Was nevere wihte in this worlde that me wisse couthe
Where that he longed, lasse ne more,
Til hit biful in Fryday two freres I mette,
Maystres of the menores, men of gret witte.
I haylsede hem hendly, as I hadde ylered,   10
And preyde hem pur charite ar they passede forthere
Yf they knewe eny contre other costes aboute
Wher that Dowel dwelleth, 'Dere frendes, telleth me,
For ye ar men of this molde that moste wyde walken
And knowen contrees and courtes and many kynne plases,   15
Bothe princes paleis and pore menne cotes,
And Dowel and Do-evele, where thei dwellen both.'
  'Sothly,' saide the frere, 'he sojourneth with us freres
And evere hath, as I hope, and evere wol here-aftur.'
  'Contra,' quod I as a clerke, and comsed to despute,   20
And saide sothly, 'Septies in die cadit justus,
Fallyng fro joye, Jesu wot the sothe!
"Sevene sithe," sayth the bok, "synegeth day by day
The rihtfulleste reng that regneth in erthe."

7. that he P : X this   9. X menore

Langland echoes the opening of the poem. It is a fresh start, to the same search,
on a different level. *Russet* is a coarse woollen cloth, reddish-brown in colour,
a traditional garb of shepherds.
  9. 'Masters of divinity in the order of the Friars Minors', i.e. the Franciscans,
from Latin *fratres minores*, 'lesser brothers', a name taken by early followers
of St. Francis as a mark of humility. Franciscans were the great scholars and
theologians of the 13th and 14th centuries, especially in England (there was a
famous Franciscan school at Oxford), and Roger Bacon, John Duns Scotus and
William of Ockham were all members of the order.
  20. *Contra:* 'I dispute that', a term used in scholastic debate. Immediately,
the poet takes up an aggressive tone, symptomatic of the kind of intellectual
obstinacy and self-sufficiency which obstructs spiritual illumination in these
middle passus of the poem.
  21. 'The just man falls seven times a day' (cf. *Proverbs* 24: 16).
  22. This line, added in C, is a parenthetic exclamation playing on the double
meaning of *cadit*, 'falls' and 'sins'.
  24. 'The most righteous man of all that live upon earth.'

And who-so synegeth,' I saide, 'certes, he doth nat wel;   25
For who-so synegeth, sikerly doth evele,
And Dowel and Do-evele may nat dwelle togyderes.
Ergo, he is nat alwey at hom amonges yow freres;
He is other-while elleswher to wisse the peple.'
    'I shal sey the, my sone,' sayde the frere thenne,   30
How sevene sithes the sad man synegeth on the day.
By a forbisene,' quod the frere, 'I shal the fayre shewe.
    Lat bryng a man in a bot amydde a brood water;
The wynde and the water and wagyng of the bote
Maketh the man many tyme to stomble, yf he stande;   35
For stonde he nevere so stifliche, thorw steryng of the bote
He bendeth and boweth, the body is unstable,
And yut is he saf and sound; and so hit fareth by the rihtful.
Thogh he falle, he falleth nat but as who-so ful in a bot
That ay is saf and sound, that sitte withynne the borde.   40
So hit fareth,' quod the frere, 'by the ryhtful mannes fallynge;
Thogh he thorw fondynges falle, he falleth nat out of charite,
So dedly synne doth he nat, for Dowel hym helpeth.
The water is likned to the world, that wanyeth and waxeth;
The godes of this grounde ar like the grete wawes,   45
That as wyndes and wederes waleweth aboute;
The bot is liknet to oure body, that bretil is of kynde,
That thorw the fend and oure flesch and this freel worlde
Synegeth sevene sithes the saddest man on erthe,
And lyf-holiest of lyf that lyveth under sonne.   50

37. He *U* : *X* Ai   39. as *omitted in XU*
50. lyf-holiest *U* : *X* lyfliost

---

28. *Ergo*: the argument has all the trappings of scholarly disputation, but it
is of course specious and hair-splitting.
    33. The allegorical illustration that follows is an example of the clarity and
economy of Langland's technique of homiletic exposition. The ultimate source
of the parable is a passage in a sermon of St. Augustine, in which the allegory
of the Ship of the Church is evolved from the story of Jesus stilling the storm
on the sea of Galilee (*Luke* 8: 22–5).
    43. 'Provided he commits no mortal sin, for Dowel (i.e. the New Law, of
redemption) is on his side.'
    45-6. 'The powerful forces and influences of this world are compared to
great waves, tossing about turbulently like winds and storms.'

Ac fre wil and fre wit foleweth man evere
To repenten and to arise and rowe out of synne
To contricion, to confessioun, til he come til his ende.
For rather have we no reste til we restitue
Oure lyf to oure lord god for oure lycames gultes.'   55
    'I have no kynde knowlechyng to conseyve al this speche,
Ac yf I may lyve and loke I shal go lerne bettere.'
    'I bykenne the Crist,' quod he, 'that on the cross deyede;'
And I sayde, 'The same save yow fro meschaunce,
And gyve me grace on this grounde with good ende to deye.'   60
    I wente forth wyde-whare, walkynge myn one,
By a wilde wildernesse and by a wode-syde.
Blisse of the briddes abyde me made,
And under lynde upon a launde lened I a stounde
To lythen here layes and here lovely notes.   65
Murthe of here mouthes made me ther to slepe,
And merveilousliche me mette amyddes al that blisse.
    A muche man, as me thoghte ylike to mysulve,
Cam and calde me be my kynde name
'What art thow?' quod I, 'that thow my name knowest?'   70
'That wost thou, Wille,' quod he, 'and no wyht bettere.'
'Wot I,' quod I, 'who art thow?' 'Thouhte,' sayde he thenne;
'I have sued the this seven yer, saw thow me no rather?'
    'Art thow Thouhte?' quod I tho, 'thow couthest me wisse

71. That wost thou P : X What thou

54-5. 'We have no rest until (lit. sooner than) we yield up our lives to God for our body's sins' (i.e. die).

56. 'I have no natural understanding to enable me to grasp what you say.' Ignorance, suspicion, intellectual resistance, the desire for easy answers, all hamper the dreamer in his search. The position expounded by the Friar is 'true'—nothing can happen to cancel its truth, for the movement of the poem is ruminant and cumulative, not dialectic—but its truth has the unlived quality of objective statement, and no pressure of imaginative experience. Note that the meeting with the Friar is a waking episode.

61. 'I went forth, wandering by myself, far and wide.'

68. Each allegorical character he meets is an aspect, a focusing, of his own mind and experience, formally isolated to give the kind of linear analysis of total psychological experience characteristic of allegory.

73. 'I have been with you for a long time; haven't you noticed me before?'

Where that Dowel dwelleth, and do me to knowe?'   75
   'Dowel and Dobet,' quod he, 'and Dobest the thridde
Aren thre fayre vertues and ben nat fer to fynde.
Who is trewe of his tonge and of his two handes
And thorw lele labour lyveth and loveth his emcristene
And therto trewe of his tayl and halt wel his handes   80
And is nat dronklewe ne dedeynous, Dowel hym foleweth.
   Dobet doth al this, ac yut he doth more;
He is logh as a lomb and loveliche of speche,
And helpeth alle men of that he may spare.
The bagges and the bigerdeles he hath to-broken hem alle,   85
That the erl Averous held, and his ayres,
And of Mammonas money maked hym many frendes,
And is ronne into religioun and hath rendred the bible
And precheth to the peple seynt Paules wordes:

80. halt wel his *P* : *X* of his two

---

76. Here, for the first time, the perspective of the poem is extended through the degrees of Dowel, in a grammatical amplification of the good life. Thought's analysis of the three lives is the first of many such definitions, through which full understanding is gradually evolved by a process of accretion.

78–98. Dowel is the life of obedience to the Law and labour in one's vocation (the original 'Piers Plowman' concept); Dobet adds to this a greater degree of humility and charity; while Dobest puts all these qualities to the active service of the organized Church. There is reference here to the traditional division of the Active, Contemplative and 'Mixed' lives (see Introduction, p. 30), though Langland, as usual, expands the sense of the middle term.

80. 'And (who) is also honest in his reckoning, and keeps his hands to himself.'

84. '. . . with what he can afford.'

85–6. This vivid image, casually thrown off, is an example of the instinctively allegorical nature of Langland's mode of thought.

87. Cf. 'Make to yourselves friends of the mammon of unrighteousness' (*Luke* 16: 9, *of* = 'by means of '). The personification of Mammon (Lat. 'riches'), and the glossing of the text so that it refers to charitable giving rather than profitable stewardship, are usual.

88. 'And has entered a religious order, and explains (*or* translates) the Scriptures.'

89f. 'For ye suffer fools gladly, seeing ye yourselves are wise' (2 *Cor.* 11: 19). Paul intended this as an ironical rebuke, but Thought translates it as an exhortation. It is probable that Langland is following a (still) current and charitable misinterpretation, rather than that he is deliberately mistranslating 'in character' in order to undermine Thought's reliability.

Libenter suffertis insipientes, cum sitis ipsi sapientes.
"Ye worldliche wyse, unwyse that ye soffre, 90
Lene hem and love hem," this Latyn is to mene.
  Dobest bere sholde the bisshopes crose
And halie with the hoked ende ille men to gode,
And with the pyk pulte adoun *prevaricatores legis.*
Lordes that lyven as hem lust and no lawe acounten, 95
For here mok and here mebles suche men thenketh
Sholde no bisshop be, here biddynges to with-sitte.
Ac Dobest sholde drede hem nat, but do as god hihte.
  Nolite timere eos qui possunt occidere corpus.
  Thus Dowel and Dobet demede as Dobest
And crounede one to be kyng, to kull withoute synne 100
That wolde nat do as Dobest devinede and tauhte.
Thus Dowel and Dobet and Dobest the thridde
Crounede one to be a kyng and kepen us alle,
And to reule alle reumes by here thre wittes,
But othere wise ne elles nat, but as they thre assentede.' 105
  I thonkede Thoght tho, that he me so tauhte:
'Ac yut savereth nat me thy sawes, so me Crist spede;
A more kyndere knowynge coveyte I to here
Of Dowel and Dobet and who doth best of alle.'
  'Bote yf Wit wol the wisse,' quod Thouhte, 'where tho thre
    dwelleth, 110
Elles knowe I non that can, in none kyneryche.'

92. *X* corose   **93.** ille *U* : *X* alle   **99.** as *U* : *X* a

---

94. 'And with the sharp end strike down wilful evaders of the law.'

96–7. 'Because they've got money (*lit.* muck) and property, these men think that bishops should never oppose their wishes.'

98f. 'Fear not them which kill the body (but are not able to kill the soul)' (*Matt.* 10: 28).

100–1. 'And crowned a man as king, so that he can make lawful execution of those who disobey the decrees and teaching of Dobest.' The inseparability of Church and State is orthodox political doctrine in the Middle Ages (it is basic, for instance, to Dante's imperial theme). It has no connection with the subsequently developed personal myth of 'divine right'.

107–8. 'Yet what you say does me no good, Christ help me; I long for a real, basic understanding ...'

Thouht and I thus thre dayes we yeden,
Disputyng uppon Dowel day after other,
And ar we ywar were, with Wit gan we mete.
He was long and lene, ylyk to noon other,   115
Was no pruyde on his parail, no poverte noythere;
Sad of his semblant, with a softe speche.
I durste meve no matere to maken hym to jangle,
Bote as I bad Thouht tho to be mene betwene
And putte forth som purpos to proven his wittes,   120
What was Dowel fro Dobet and Dobest fro hem bothe.
    Thenne Thouht in that tyme sayde this wordes:
'Whare Dowel and Dobet and Dobest ben in londe,
Here is one wolde ywyte, yf Wit couthe teche,
And what lyves they lyve and what lawe thei usen,   125
And what they drede and doute, dere sire, telleth.'

Wit explains Dowel, or the good life, in the familiar terms of the allegorical
castle. For him it consists in rational obedience to rational law (this is illustrated in a long passage on the institution of marriage), whilst Dobet is love
and Dobest is active love. Wit's wife, Dame Study, scolds him for feeding
intellectual pride by answering the speculative questioner in such terms, and
attacks the barren disputations of theology.

8. The Speech of Dame Study (XII. 1–92)

Thenne hadde Wit a wyf, was hote dame Studie,
That ful lene lokede and lyf-holy semede;
She was wonderly wroth that Wit me so tauhte.
Al staryng dame Studie sterneliche sayde:
'Wel artow wyse,' quod she to Wyt, 'suche wysedomes to shewe   5
To eny fol or to flaterere or to frentike peple;'
And sayde, '*Nolite mittere*, ye men, margerie-perles

---

114. 'Thought' (intellectual activity) leads imperceptibly to 'Wit' (rational
understanding).

118–20. 'I didn't dare to broach any subject, to provoke him to argument,
except to ask Thought to act as mediator, to put forward some case so as to
test his wisdom.'

7. 'Do not cast (pearls before swine)' (*Matt.* 7: 6).

Among hogges that han hawes at wille;
They do bote drevele theron—draf were hem levere
Then al the preciouse perye that eny prince weldeth.   10
I syg hit by suche,' quod Studie, 'that sheweth by here werkes
That they lovyen lond and lordshipe and lykynge of body
More then holynesse or hendenesse or al that seyntes techeth.
  Wysdom and wit now is nat worth a carse
Bote hit be cardet with coveytise, as clotheres kemben here wolle.   15
Who can contreve and caste to disseyve the rightful
And lette with a love-day treuthe, and bigile,
That coveite can and caste thus ar cleped into the consayle.
Qui sapiunt nugas et crimina lege vocantur,
Qui recte sapiunt, lex jubet ire foras.   20
He is reverensed and yrobed that can robbe the peple
Thorw fallas and fals questes and thorw fikel speche.
  Job the gentele in his gistes witnesseth
What shal worthen of suche when thei lyf leten:
    Ducunt in bonis dies suos, et in fine descendunt ad infernum.
The sauter saith the same of alle suche ryche: 25
    Ibunt in progenies patrum suorum, et usque in eternum non
        videbunt lumen.
    Et alibi: Ecce ipsi peccatores, &c.

  11. Studie *P* : *X* Wit   **12.** they *omitted in XU*

---

  8. 'Haws' are later (83) explained as symbolic of the pleasures of the world.
  11. 'I am referring to those . . .'
  14–15. 'Wisdom is not now regarded unless its teachings can be tailored to
the profit-motive, as wool is combed and dressed to make it look attractive.'
This was an accusation frequently levelled against friars, particularly (see 1.58n).
  17. 'And hinder and deceive truth by holding love-days.' A 'love-day' was
a day set aside for the peaceful arbitration of disputes and feuds. The clergy
were very active in organising them (e.g. Chaucer's Friar, *CT* I. 258), and it is
clear that it was often money that did the talking.
  19–20. 'Those who know about trifles and slanders are called in by the law,
but the law turns away those who are truly wise.' The source of this quotation
is not known.
  24f. 'They spend their days in wealth, and in a moment go down to the
grave' (*Job* 21: 13).
  25f. 'He shall go to the generation of his fathers; they shall never see light'
(*Psalm* 49: 19). And elsewhere: 'Behold, these are the ungodly (who prosper
in the world)' (*Psalm* 73: 12).

"Lo!" saith holy letrure, "whiche lordes beth this schrewes!
Tho that god most good yeveth, greveth most riht and treuthe."
        Que perfecisti, destruxerunt.
Harlotes for here harlotrye aren holpe ar nedy pore;
And that is no riht ne resoun, for rather men sholde
Help hem that hath nauhte then tho that han no nede.   30
    Ac he that hath holy writ ay in his mouth
And can telle of Treuthe and of the twelve aposteles
Or of the passioun of Crist or of purgatorie the peynes,
Litel is he loved or leet her-fore among lordes at festes.
    Nowe is the manere at the mete, when munstrals ben stille,   35
The lewed agen the lered the holy lore to dispute,
And tellen of the trinite how two slowe the thridde
And brynge forth ballede resones, taken Bernard to witnesse,
And putten forth presompciouns to preve the sothe.
Thus they drevele at the deyes, the deite to knowe,   40
And gnawen god with gorge when here guttes fullen.
    Ac the carful may crye and quake at the gate,
Bothe a-fyngred and a-furst, and for defaute spille;

---

36. *XU* dispite	**37.** two *U* : *X* tho
40. at *U* : *X* as	**41.** fullen *U* : *X* fallen

27f. 'What thou hast perfected, they have destroyed; (and what hath the righteous done?)' (*Psalm* 11: 3, Vulgate only).

37. An example of idle, dangerous, hair-splitting speculation, concerning here the doctrine of the unity of the Trinity. Dame Study is using the idea of high-table chat as a contemptuous allegory of secular intrusion into the traditional domains of theology. The 14th century was an age of vigorous growth away from the Thomist synthesis, free, ingenious, often destructive. Langland approved none of it. Scribes of the B-text were so shocked by the violence and daring of this line that they substituted, for the second half, the innocuous 'a tale other tweyne'.

38. 'And trot out their threadbare arguments, misusing the writings of St. Bernard in their support'. St. Bernard of Clairvaux (d. 1153) was the effective founder of the Cistercian order of monks, and the greatest single spiritual influence on the Middle Ages.

40-1. 'With this sort of high-table drivel they seek to understand the Deity, and try their teeth on God when their bellies are full.'

42. In this stark image, Langland focuses the contrast between well-fed intellectual speculation and the need for active well-doing and charity.

Ys non so hende to have hym yn, but hote hym go ther god is!
Thenne semeth hit to my siht, to suche that so biddeth,   45
God is nat in that hom, ne his helpe nother.
Lytel loveth he that lord that lente hym al that blisse
That so parteth with the pore a parsel, when hym nedeth.
Ne were mercy in mene men more then in riht riche,
Mony tymes mendenauntes myhte gon a-fyngred;   50
And so saith the sauter, I saw hit in *Memento:*
    Ecce audivimus eam (i.e. caritatem) in Effrata; invenimus eam
      in campus silve.
  Clerkes and knyhtes carpen of god ofte
And han muche in here mouth, ac mene in herte.
Freres and faytours han founde up suche questions
To plese with proude men sennes this pestelences,   55
And prechyng at seynt Poules in puyr envye of clerkes,
That folk is nat ferme in the faith ne fre of here godes,
Ne sory for here synnes; so is pruyde enhanced
In religion and in al the reume among riche and pore,
That preyeres han no power this pestilences to lette.   60

---

44. yn *omitted in XU*   **56.** in S: X and   **58.** is *omitted in XU*

---

44. 'No one is kind enough to have him in; instead they tell him to seek comfort in heaven.'

47–8. 'The man who shares his goods in this way with the poor, when they are in need, shows little return of love to the Lord who gave him all that happiness.'

51. *Memento*, 'remember', is the first word of the psalm referred to; psalms and texts were often briefly identified in this way. 'Lo, we heard of it (i.e. charity) at Ephratah: we found it in the fields of the wood' (*Psalm* 132: 6). The literal reference is to the Ark of the Covenant, symbol of God's truth revealed to Israel. Langland's gloss carries the suggestion that charity is found amongst the poor and lowly.

56. St. Paul's cross in London was a famous open-air preaching place. Friars were skilful preachers, and the suggestion is that they used sermons not only to lull their audiences into a false complacency about sin and retribution, but also to attack their traditional enemies, the 'clerkes' or possessioners (see 1.62n, 4.16n).

60. The successive waves of plague (see 1.82n) were seen as God's punishment on the sinful commonalty. They contribute to, are perhaps the original inspiration of, the monitory quality of Langland's vision.

For god is deef nowadayes and deyneth us nat to here
And gode men for oure gultes he al to-grynt to deth;
And yut this wreches of this world is none ywar by other,
Ne for drede of eny deth withdraweth hem fro pruyde
Ne parteth with the pore, as puyr charite wolde,   65
Bote in gaynesse and in glotonye for-glotten here godes
And breketh nat here bred to the pore, as the bok hoteth:
    Frange esurienti panem tuum.
Ac the more he wynneth and hath the world at his wille
And lordeth in ledes, the lasse gode he deleth.

    Tobie techeth nat so, taketh hede, ye ryche,   70
How he tolde in a tyme and tauhte his sone dele:
    Si tibi sit copia, abundanter tribue; si autem exiguum, illud
        impertiri libenter stude.
And is to mene no more bote "Who muche gode weldeth,
Be large ther-of whil hit lasteth to ledes that ben nedy;
And yf thow have litel, leve sone, loke by thy lyve
Get the love ther-with, thogh thow worse fare."   75
Ac lust no lord now ne lettred man of suche lore to here,
Bote lythen how they myhte lerne leest god spene.
And that loveth lordes now and leten hit a Dowel,
For is no wit worth now but if hit of wynnynge soune.
Forthy, Wit,' quod she, 'be war holy writ to shewe   80
Amonges hem that han hawes atten wille,

67f. 'Deal thy bread to the hungry (and bring the poor that are cast out to thy house)' (*Isaiah* 58: 7).

71f. 'If thou hast abundance, give alms accordingly; if thou have but a little, be not afraid to give according to that little' (*Tobit* 4: 8).

78-9. 'And this is what lords enjoy now, and this is what they consider "doing-well"; for no wisdom is regarded now, unless it has to do with profit.'

80-2. Dame Study recapitulates her argument, that a little learning is a dangerous thing, that the Christian truths and mysteries are only profaned and abused if they are disseminated among the laity. For them, simple faith, charity, penitence (57-8), are enough. True learning can only be sought within the strict clerical regime of the universities (this is the difference between *Wit* and *Study*), and with particular reference to Theology (*Clergy*) and Biblical studies (*Scripture*). These are not necessarily Langland's views: on one level, what he is doing here is to canvas the value of a university education, which is something of a preoccupation for a man who hasn't had one.

The which is a lykyng and a luste and love of the world.'
    And when Wit was ywar what Studie menede,
I myhte gete no grayn of Wittes grete wittes,
But al lauhynge he louted and loked uppon Studie,   85
Semyng that I sholde bysechen here of grace.
    And when I was war of his wille, to that womman gan I
        louten,
And saide, 'Mercy, ma dame youre man shal I worthen
As longe as I lyve, bothe late and rathe,
And for to worche youre wille the while my lyf duyreth,   90
With that ye kenne me kyndeliche to knowe what is Dowel.'

The dreamer, as a reward for his meek acceptance of her rebuke, is directed
to her cousin, Clergy, and his wife, Scripture, for further enlightenment.
Clergy offers a brief analysis of the three lives (of Dowel, Dobet and
Dobest), but Scripture seems to mock the dreamer's ignorance, and in his
anger and hurt intellectual pride he turns from her, and from the search,
and falls into an inner dream of a Land of Longing where he is led by
Fortune (allegorically, the dreamer's real life). The spokesman for this
superficial, worldly, complacent self is Recklessness, who rehearses familiar
arguments about the salvation of the righteous heathen in order to refute
non-pragmatic theology. (It is at this point, 'in wandering mazes lost', that
the A-text gives up, and falls back on the idea of the simple honest ploughman as the exemplar of Dowel. The wide variations between B and C also
help to indicate the complexity and fluidity of the poem's development in
this crucial section.) The dreamer is brought back to his senses by approach-
ing Age and by Scripture's sermon on the uncomfortable theme, 'Many are
called', but the intellectual fabric of the quest (all the abstractions so far have
been intellectual) is abruptly shattered by the intervention of Trajan (' "Ye,
baw for bookes!" quath on, was broken out of helle'), the great example
of the redeemed heathen, saved by love and not by law. From the discourse
that follows, with its eulogy of poverty, emerge the distinctive lineaments
of Dowel, the life of humility, patient poverty and love. The following
passage is in C only.

82. *second* and *P* : *X* the

9. *The Praise of Patient Poverty* (XIII. 140–248, XIV. 1–25)

'And alle the wyse that evere were, by auhte I can aspye,
Preisede proverte for beste, if pacience hit folowe,
And bothe bettere and blessedere by manyfold then richesse.
Althouh he be sour to soffre, ther cometh a swete after.
As on a walnote withoute is a bittere barke   5
And after that bittere barke, be the scale aweye,
Is a cornel of confort, kynde to restore;
So aftur penaunce and poverte, pacientliche ytake,
Maketh man to have mynde in god and his mercy to crave,
The which is the cornel of confort for alle cristene soules.   10
And wel sikerere he slepeth, the segg that is pore,
And lasse drat by day or in derke to ben yrobbed,
Then he that is rihte ryche, reson bereth witnesse:
Pauper ego ludo, dum tu dives meditaris.
    Holy churche witnesseth, "Who-so forsaketh   15
His fader or his frendes, fremde other sybbe,
Or eny welthe in this world, his wyf or his childrene,
For the love of our lord loweth hym to be pore,
He shal have an hundred fold of hevene-ryche blisse
And lyf lastyng for evere, byfore oure lord in hevene."   20
    Quicunque reliquerit patrem et matrem, &c.
Crist acordeth efte her-with, clerkes wyteth the sothe,
What god saide hymsulve to a segg that he lovede:
"Yf thow likest to lyve," quod god, "the lyf that is parfit,

18. loweth *P*, loueth *U* : *X* lotheth

---

1. The whole of this extract is spoken by the 'I' of the poem, further identified in C as 'Rechelessnesse'. The purpose of C here is to isolate the dreamer's discourse as a phase in growing understanding, so as not to give it authorial warrant. Recklessness has good qualities, particularly his freedom from worldly pressures, which enables him to see certain things very clearly, but he lacks comprehensive insight and is prone to get carried away (see the beginning of the next extract, and Donaldson, pp. 170–5).

14. 'I am poor and free from care, while you are rich and full of anxiety.' The quotation is unidentified.

15. From here to the end of the extract is new in C.

20f. 'Everyone that hath forsaken father and mother, etc.' (*Matt.* 19: 29).

XIII

Al that thow haste here, hastly go and sulle hit;
Yef pore peple the panes, therof pors thou none,   25
Ac yef hem forth to pore folk that for my love hit aske;
For-sak al and sue me and so is thi beste."
　　Si vis perfectus esse, vade et vende omnia que habes.
Yut conseileth Crist in commen us all:
"Who-so coveiteth to come to my kyneriche
He mot forsaken hymsulve his suster and his brother   30
And al that the world wolde, and my will folowe."
　　Nisi renunciaveritis omnibus que possidetis, &c.
Mo proverbes I myhte have of mony holy seyntes
To testifie for treuthe the tale that I shewe,
And poetes to preven hit, Porfirie and Plato,
Aristotel, Ennedy, enlevene hundred,   35
Tulius, Tolomeus, I can nat tell here names,
Preveth pacient poverte prince of alle vertues.
And by the grayn that groweth god us all techeth
Mischiefes on molde mekeliche to soffren:
　　Nisi granum frumenti cadens in terra mortuum fuerit, ipsum,
　　solum manet.

27f. 'If thou wilt be perfect, go and sell that thou hast' (*Matt.* 19: 21). This whole passage in Matthew, Christ's words to the young man and to the disciples, is crucial to an understanding of the shift in the poem from the good life to the perfect life (see 2.80n), from 'mesurable' use of worldly goods to renunciation. The movement of the second part of the poem often parallels that of the first, but on a deeper spiritual level; the treatment of povery here corresponds to the Lady Meed episodes earlier.

31f. 'Whosoever forsaketh not all that he hath, (he cannot be my disciple)' (*Luke* 14: 33).

34-6. Rhetorical amplification by random citation of learned 'authorities'. Porphyry (a Greek philosopher, d. 306), Plato, Aristotle, Ennodius (a Christian-Latin poet of the 5th century; other texts have *Ovidius*, which looks like a simple scribal substitution), Tullius (Cicero) and Ptolemy the astronomer (*c.* A.D. 150) were probably little more than names to Langland, but he may be remembering scraps from some of them culled from *florilegia* or collections of *sententiae* or apophthegms, which were the source of much medieval knowledge of classical writers. One such saying, relevant here, is quoted by Chaucer, from a collection attributed to Ptolemy, in *CT* III. 324.

39f. 'Except a corn of wheat fall into the ground and die, it abideth alone: (but if it die, it bringeth forth much fruit)' (*John* 12: 24).

E

Bote if the seed that sowen is in the sloo sterve,   40
Shal nevere spir sprynge up, ne spike on straw kerne;
Sholde nevere whete wexe but whete furste deyede.
And other sedes also in the same wyse,
That ben layd in louhe erthe, ylore as hit were,
And thorw the grace of god and grayn dede on erthe   45
At the laste launceth up, where-by we lyven all.

   Ac sedes that ben sowen and mowen soffre wyntres
Aren tidiere and towere to mennes byhofte
Then sedes that sowe ben and mowen nat with forstes,
Ne wynde ne wederes, as in wynter tymes;   50
As lyn-sed, lek-sed, and lente-sedes all
Aren not so worthy as whete, ne so wel mowe
In the feld with the forst, and hit frese longe,
Riht so, sothly, that soffry may penaunces
Worth allowed of oure lord at here laste ende   55
And for here pacience ben ypreised as for puyr martir,
Or for a confessor ykud, that counteth nat a rusche
Fere ne famyne ne fals mennes tonges.
But as an hosebonde hopeth after an hard wynter,
Yf god gyveth hym the lyf, to have a gode hervest,   60
So preveth this profetes that pacientliche soffren.
Mescheves and myshappes and many tribulaciouns

---

43. And *U* : *X* On   **47** Ac *P* : *X* As
48. towere *P* : *X* tououre   **62.** *X* tribulacoes

40–1. 'Unless the seed that is sown die in the earth, no blade shall ever grow
nor ear ripen to grain on the straw'. The image of 'death' is from the analogy
of burial underground, and has archetypal resonance. The Gospel text suggests
a spiritual 'dying into life' (and St. Paul uses the same text of the resurrection
of the body, 1 *Cor.* 15: 35–44), but Langland's application is more practical.

48–9. 'Are tougher and more suitable to man's needs than seeds that are
sown and may not (endure) against frosts . . .'

54. *that:* 'those that'.

57. 'Or acknowledged as (equal in holiness to) a confessor . . .'

59–60. Cf. *James* 5: 7, 'Behold the husbandman waiteth for the precious
fruit of the earth, and hath long patience for it, until he receive the early and
latter rain.' The whole passage in *James* (5: 1–11) is a fundamental source for
this discussion of riches and patient poverty.

Bitokeneth treuly in tyme comyng after
Murthe for his mornyng and that muche plentee.
For Crist saide so to seyntes that for his sake tholeden   65
Poverte and penaunce and persecucion of body;
Then angelis in here anger on this wyse hem grette:
    Tristitia vestra vertetur in gaudium.
"Youre sorwe into solace shal turne at the laste
And out of wo into wele youre wirdes shal chaunge."

  Ac who-so rat of the ryche, the revers may fynde,   70
How god, as the gospelle telleth, gyveth fole to name,
And that his gost shal go and gode bileve,
And asketh after, "Who shal hit have,
The catel that he kepeth so in coffres and in bernis,
And art so loth to leve that lete shal thow nedes?   75
    O stulte, ista nocte anima tua egredietur; que congregasti,
      cuius erunt? Thesaurizat, et ignorat cui, &c.
An unredy reve thy residue shal spene,
That many mothe was maister ynne, in a mynte whyle;
Upholderes on the hulle shal have hit to sulle."

  Lo, lordes, lo! and ladyes, taketh hede,
Hit lasteth nat longe that is lycour swete,   80
As pesecoddes, pere-jonettes, plomes and cheries.
That lihtlich launceth up litel while dureth,
And that rathest rypeth rotieth most sonnest.

---

65. so *omitted in* X   **73.** after *omitted in* X

---

67. 'Then, in their moment of agony, angels greeted them thus.' The line demonstrates Langland's habit of elaborating a Biblical text in pageant-form, suggesting a scene with angels bearing scrolls to welcome the martyr at the moment of death.

67f. 'Your sorrow shall be turned into joy' (*John* 16: 20).

71–2. '. . . gives him the name of fool, and (continues by saying that) his spirit shall pass away and his goods be left behind.'

75f. 'Thou fool, this night thy soul shall be required of thee: then whose shall those things be which thou has provided?' (*Luke* 12: 20). 'He heapeth up riches, and knoweth not who (shall gather them)' (*Psalm* 39: 6).

76–7. 'An improvident steward shall spend all that is left—what moths alone had charge of before—in a moment.'

83. Proverbial: 'Soon ripe, soon rotten'.

On fat lond ful of donge foulest wedes groweth;
Riht so, sothly, suche that ben bischopes,   85
Erles and erchedekenes and othere riche clerkes,
That chafferen as chapmen and chide bote they wynne,
And han the world at her wille, otherwyse to levene.
Riht as wedes waxeth in wose and in donge,
So of rychesse uppe rychesse ariste alle vices.   90
Lo, lond overleyd with marl and with donge,
Whete that theron wexeth worth lygge ar hit rype;
Riht so, sothly, for to segge treuthe,
Over-plente pruyde norischeth, ther poverte hit distrueth.
    For how hit evere be ywonne, but hit wel despeneth,   95
Worldly wele ys wykked thyng to hem that hit kepeth.
For if he be fer ther-fro, ful ofte hath he drede
That fals folke fecche awaye felonliche his godes;
And yut more hit maketh man mony tymes and ofte
To synege, and to souche sotiltees of gyle,   100
For coveytyse of that catel to culle hym that hit kepeth.
And so is many man ymorthred for his moneye and his godes
And tho that dede the dede ydampned ther-fore after,
And he for his hard holdyng in helle, paraunter.
So coveytise of catel was combraunce to hem alle.   105
Lo, how pans purchaseth fayre places and grete,
That rote is of robbares the rychesses withynne.

    Ac wel worth Poverte! for he may walke unrobbed
Among pilours in pees, yf pacience hym folwe.
Oure prince Jesu poverte chees, and his apostles alle,   110
And ay the lengere they lyvede the lasse gode they hadde.
    Tanquam nihil habentes, et omnia possidentes.

    90. uppe: *X* ope   **106.** grete *U* : *X* deede

----

    84. Cf. 2 *Henry IV* IV. iv. 54.
    88. 'And have it in their power to live otherwise if they wanted to.'
    92. 'Wheat that grows on it will fall (under its own weight) before it grows
ripe.' The idea is still of poverty as a spiritual toughener, but the image is now
of hard soils rather than hard weather.
    107. 'The riches within which are the source of all covetousness.'
    108. 'But well may it be for Poverty', i.e. Poverty will be better off.
    111f. 'Having nothing, and yet possessing all things' (2 *Cor.* 6: 10).

Yut ret men that Abraham and Job weren wonder ryche,
And out of nombre tho men many mebles hadden.
Abraham for his hadde moche tene,
For in greet poverte he was put; a prince, as hit were, 115
Bynome his hosewyf and heeld her hymself,
And Abraham not hardy ones to letten hym
Ne for brihtnesse of here beaute here spouse to be byknowe.
And for he soffrede and saide nauht, oure lord sente tokene,
That the kynge criede to Abraham mercy 120
And delyverede the weye his wyf, with moche welthe aftur.
  Job the gentele, what joye hadde he on erthe!
And how bittere he hit abouhte, as the book telleth.
And for he song in his sorwe, "*Si bona accepimus a domino,*
Dereworthe and dere god! do we so *mala,*" 125
Alle his sorwe to solace thorw that song turnede,
And Job bykam as a jolyf man, and al his joye newe.
  Lo, how pacience in here poverte thise patriarkes relevede
And broughte hem all above, that in bale rotede.
As grayn that lith in the greut, and thorw grace, at the laste, 130
Spryngeth and spredeth, so spedde the fader Abraham
And the gentel Job; here joye hath non ende.'

Humility, however, is a difficult lesson to learn, and the berating of the clergy that follows the discourse on poverty betrays the old aggressive and rebellious self. Another vision follows.

10. *The Vision of Middle-Earth* (XIV. 129–249)

Thus Rechelessnesse in a rage aresenede Clergie
And Scripture scornede, that many skilles shewede,
Til that Kynde cam, Clergie to helpe,

116. and heeld her hymself *omitted in XU*
120. to Abraham *P* : *XU* hym   **128.** in here *P* : *XU* and

---

115. The story of Abraham and Abimelech is told in *Genesis* 20.
124–5. 'If we receive good at the hand of God, (let us also receive evil)' (*Job* 2: 10). For the example of Job, cf. *James* 5: 11.
  1. See 9.1n, above.

And in the myrour of Mydel-erthe made hym efte to loke,
To knowe by uch a creature Kynde to lovye.   5
    And I bowed my body, bihelte al aboute,
And saw the sonne and the see and the sond after,
And where that briddes and bestis by here make thei yeden,
Wilde wormes in wodes and wonderful foules
With flekede fetheres and of fele colours.   10
Man and his make I myhte se bothe,
Poverte and plente, bothe pees and werre,
Blisse and bale, bothe I saw at ones,
And how that men mede toke and mercy refusede.
    Resoun I saw sothly sewe alle bestes   15
In etynge and drynkyng, in engendrure of kynde;
Aftur cors of concepcion noon toke kepe of other,
As when thei hadde roteyed anon they reste after.
Males drow hem to males a morwenynge by hemsulve,
And femeles to femeles ferddede and drowe.   20
Ther ne was cow ne cow-kynde that conseyved hadde,
That wolde bere after bole, ne bore aftur sowe.
Ther ne was no kyne kynde that conseyved hadde,
That ne lees the lykynge of lust, of flesch, as hit were,
Save man and his make; and ther-of me wondrede,   25
For out of resoun they ryde and rechelesliche taken on,
As in derne dedes, bothe drynkyng and elles.

---

14. men *omitted in* X   **19.** a *U* : *X* and
21. was *omitted in* X   **26.** taken *P* : *X* token

---

4. *Mydel-erthe*, i.e. between heaven and hell. The world of Nature (*Kynde*), or natural order, is the *myrour* of the order in the mind of the Creator. God can be 'read' in his creation.

23–5. Sexual intercourse during pregnancy was condemned by the Church. See the *Book of Vices and Virtues*, ed. Francis (EETS 217), p. 249. The whole contrast between the 'natural' sexual behaviour of animals and the unnatural lustfulness of man was homiletic commonplace. It is frequently used to provoke sexual disgust, as in the early 13th c. treatise on virginity, *Holy Maidenhood*, ed. Furnivall (EETS, OS 18, 1922), p. 35.

26–7. 'For they have intercourse at unnatural times, and continue in it without restraint, with secret practices stimulated by drink and the like.'

Briddes I beheid in bosches made nestes,
Hadde nevere weye wyt to worche the leste.
I hadde wonder at whan and where the pye   30
Lernede to legge stikkes that ley on here neste;
Ther is no wriht, as I wene, sholde worch here nest to paye.
If eny mason made a molde therto, moche wonder me thynketh.
    And yut I merveylede more, mony of the briddes
Hudden and helede here egges dernely   35
For no foul sholde hit fynde but his fere and hymsulve.
And som treden, I toke kepe, and on trees bredde,
And brouhte forth here briddes al above the grounde.
In mareys and in mores, in myres and in watres,
Dompynges dyvede; 'Dere god,' I sayde,   40
'Where hadde thise wilde suche wit, and at what scole?'
And how the pocok caukede, therof toke I kepe,
How un-corteysliche that cok his kynde forth strenede,
And ferlyede of his fayrenesse and of his foul ledene.
    And sethe I lokede on the see and so forth on sterres; 45
Mony selcouthes I saw, aren nat to segge nouthe,
Ne what on floures on felde, and of here fayre coloures,
And how out of greut and of gras growe so many hewes,
And some soure and some swete, selcouthe me thouhte.
Of here kynde and of here colours to carpe hit were to longe. 50
    Ac that moste mevede me and my mod chaungede
Was that I saw Resoun sewen alle bestes
Save man and mankynde; mony tymes me thoughte

---

31. legge *U* : *X* begge   43. forth *U* : *X* for
44. ledene *U* : *X* lenede   48. greut *U* : *X* greent

---

29. 'No man would have the skill to make even the simplest.'
33. 'It would be a wonderful builder who could make a mould for it.'
The domed nest of the magpie is notably elaborate.
42-4. 'I watched carefully how the peacock mated, how aggressive the bird
was in the act of procreating its kind, and I marvelled at its beauty and its
raucous cry.' The dreamer uses the peacock as an illustration of the rich and
complex variety of animal creation. In a later passage (C. XV. 173), Imaginative
counters such eccentricity by likening the peacock to a rich but useless man.
Animals, in the orthodox view, are not for wondering at, have indeed no
existence but as examples and figures. Medieval bestiaries are not books of
natural history, but homilies spiced with fancy.

Resoun ruled hem nat, nother ryche ne pore.
Thenne I resonede Resoun and ryht til hym I sayde: 55
'I have wonder in my wit, so wys as thow art holden,
Wherefore and why, as wyde as thow regneste,
That thow ne reuledest rather renkes then other bestes?
I se non so ofte sorfeten, sothly, so mankynde;
In mete out of mesure and mony tymes in drynke,   60
In wommen, in wedes, and in wordes bothe,
They overdon hit day and nyhte and so doth nat other bestes;
They reule hem al by resoun, ac renkes ful fewe.
And therfore merveileth me, for man, as in makynge,
Is most yliche the of wit and of werkes,   65
Why he ne loveth thy lore and liveth as thou techest?'
    And Resoun aresounede me and sayde: 'Reche the nevere
Why I soffre or nat soffre—certes,' he sayde,
'Uch a segge for hymsulve, Salamon us techeth:
    De re que te non molestat, noli certare.
Who soffreth more then god?' quod he; 'no gome, as I leve!   70
He myht amende in a mynte-while al that amys standeth,
Ac he soffreth, in ensaumple that we sholde soffren alle.
    Ys no vertue so fair, ne of valewe ne profit,
So is soffrance sovereynliche, so hit be for godes love.
And so witnesseth wyse and wisseth the Frenche: 75

---

54. ruled *U* : *X* relevede   64. as in makynge *omitted in XU*

---

63. *by resoun:* 'by natural instinct'. The equivocation is quite deliberate: the dreamer is meant to seem confused.

69f. 'Strive not in matter that concerneth thee not' (*Ecclesiasticus* 11:9). *Ecclesiasticus* is one of the Apocryphal books of the Bible, being the Wisdom of Jesus, son of Sirach, and is distinct from *Ecclesiastes.* The Apocrypha are those Hebrew books which did not form part of the Hebrew Bible, but which were incorporated in the Greek Bibles of the 4th and 5th centuries. Attitudes to these books varied in the Middle Ages—Jerome, for instance, though he translated them for the Vulgate, regarded them as inferior in authority—but generally they were accepted as canonical. The Protestant church has tended to reject them.

70–85. Reason offers no rational 'arguments' to answer the dreamer—to do so would be to admit the validity of such intellectual questioning—but shifts the ground of the debate.

75. *wyse:* 'wise men', e.g. Solomon, in *Ecclesiastes* 7:8 ('The patient in spirit is better than the proud in spirit').

Bele vertue est suffraunce, mal dire est petit vengeance;
Ben dire e ben suffrer fait lui suffrable a bien venir.
Forthy,' quod Resoun, 'I rede thow reule thy tonge evere,
And ar thow lacke eny lyfe, loke who is to preyse.
For is no creature under Crist that can hymsulve make,   80
And if creatures Cristene couth make hemsulve
Uche a lede wolde be lacles, leef thow non other !
Man was made of such matere he may nat wel asterte
That some tyme hym bitit to folewen his kynde;
Caton acordeth ther-with—*nemo sine crimine vivit.*'   85

Tho cauhte I colour anon and comesede to ben aschamed,
And awaked therwith; wo was me thenne
That I ne hadde met more, so merye as I slepte,
And saide anon to mysulve, 'Slepynge, hadde I grace
To wyte what Dowel is, ac wakynge nevere!'   90

And thenne was ther a wyhte, what he was I ne wiste:
'What is Dowel?' quod that wyhte. 'Ywis, syre,' I saide,
'To se moche and soffre al, certes, is Dowel.'

'Haddestow soffred,' he sayde, 'slepyng tho thow were,
Thow sholdest have yknowe that Clergie can, and more
          conseyved thorw Resoun;   95
For Resoun wolde have rehersed the riht as Clergie seide.
Ac for thyn entermetynge her artow forsake:
          Philosophus esses, si tacuisses. Et alibi: Locutum me
          aliquando penituit, tacuisse nunquam.

91. ne wiste *U* : *X* neste   **95.** thorw *P* : *X* then

76–7. 'Patience is a fair virtue, cursing is a petty vengeance; gentle speech and forbearance bring the patient man to a good end.' A quatrain of unknown origin on a familiar theme (see 11.138n).

79. 'And before you start blaming anyone, see whether you've got anything to be proud of yourself.'

85. 'No man can live without offending.' From Cato's *Distichs*: see 6.9n.

95. 'You would have known what Clergy was getting at, and understood still more from Reason.'

97f. 'You might be a philosopher, if you could hold your tongue' (Boethius, *Consolation of Philosophy*, book II, prose 7; in Chaucer's translation, line 138). And elsewhere: 'I have sometimes regretted having spoken, but never (regretted) having kept silent' (from Cato's *Distichs*, book I).

E*

Adam, the whiles he spak nat, hadde paradys at wille,
Ac when he mamelede aboute mete and musede for to knowe
The wisdom and the wit of god, he was put out of blisse.   100
Rihte so ferde Resoun by the for thy rude speche,
And for thow woldest wyte why of Resones pryvete.
   For pruyde and presompcion of thy parfit lyvynge
Resoun refusede the and wolde nat reste with the,
Ne Clergie of his connynge kepeth the nat shewe.   105
For shal nevere, ar shame come, a shrewe wel be chaste.
For lat a dronkene daffe in a dykke falle,
Lat hym lygge, lok nat on hym, til hym luste to aryse;
For thogh Resoun rebuke hym thenne, recheth he nevere,
Ne of Clergie ne of Kynde wyt counteth he nat a rusche;   110
To blame hym or to bete hym thenne I halde hit but synne.
Ac when Nede nymeth hym up, anon he is aschamed,
And thenne wot he wherfore and why he is to blame.'
   'Ye seggeth soth, by my soule,' quod I, 'I have sey hit ofte:
Ther smyt no thyng so smerte, ne smelleth so foule   115
As Shame; ther he sheweth hym, uch man shoneth his companye.
Why ye worden to me thus was for I aresonede Resoun.'
   'Ye, certes,' quod he, 'that is soth', and shop hym to walke;
And I aros up riht with that and reverensed hym fayre,
And yf his wille were, he wolde his name telle?   120

The newcomer is Imaginative (the accumulated wisdom of experience),
who deals with the questions of the righteous heathen and the order of
creation, and with Langland's anti-clericalism, in terms which are at once
a solution to the dreamer's problems and a salutary rebuke to his intellectual
and anti-intellectual conceit. Imaginative thus brings to an end the period
of intellectual uncertainty and aridity. The dreamer wakes, and ponders on
his dream.

102. of *omitted in XU*; pryvete *U : X* prevede
103. For *omitted in XU*; and *U : X* or   **105.** the *U : X* he
106. be *omitted in X*   **119.** I *omitted in XU*

---

99. *mete:* 'food', i.e. the apple.
103. 'Because of your presumptuous pride in assuming that you knew all
about the "perfect life" . . .'
106. 'A wretch like you can only be brought to his senses by being made to
feel ashamed.'

11. *The Feast of Patience* (XVI. 1–184)

And I awakede therwith, witteles ner-hande,
And as a freke that fay were forth can I walken
In manere of mendenaunt mony yer after.
And many tymes of this meteles moche thouhte I hadde;
Furste how Fortune me faylede at my moste nede   5
And how elde manased me—so myhte happe
That I lyvede longe—leve me byhynde
And vansche alle my vertues and my fayre lokes.
And how that freres folewede folk that was ryche
And peple that was pore at litel pris setten,   10
Ne no cors of pore comune in here kyrke-yerde most lygge
Bote quyke he byquath hem auht or wolde helpe quyte here dettes.
And how this coveytyse overcome al kyne sectes,
As wel lered as lewede, and lorde as the bonde.
And how that lewede men ben lad, but oure lorde hem helpe,   15
Thorw unkunynge curatours to incurable peynes.
And how that Ymaginatyf in dremeles me tolde
Of Kynde and his connynge, and what connynge he yaf bestes,
And how lovyng he is to uch a lyf, a londe and o watere,
For alle he wisseth and yeveth wit that walketh other
    crepeth.   20
And I merveyle in herte how Ymaginatyf saide
That *justus* bifore Jesu *in die judicii*
Non salvabitur bote if *vix* helpe;
And when he hadde ysaide so, how sodeynliche he vanschede.
And so I musede uppon this matere, that me lust to slepe.   25

6. *X* manced

6–8. 'And how Old Age threatened me that, if it might happen that I lived long, he would abandon me, and cause all my powers to waste away, and my fine locks.'

14. 'Both learned and ignorant, the lord like the peasant.'

22–3. Cf. 'The righteous shall scarcely (*vix*) be saved on the day of judgment' (1 *Peter* 4: 18). The play on words depends on the interpretation of *vix* as the Five (*V*) Wounds of Jesus (*I*) Christ (*X*).

And thenne cam Concyence, and Clergie after,
And beden me ryse up and rome, and with Reson sholde I dyne.
And I aroos and romede forth and with Resoun we mette.
We reverensede Resoun and romede forth softly
And metten with a mayster, a man lyk a frere.   30
Concience knewe hym, welcomede hym fayre;
They woschen and wypeden and wenten to the dyner.
    And there cam Pacience as a pore thyng and preyede mete
        par charite,
Ylyk Peres the Ploghman, as he a palmere were,
Cravede and cryede, for Cristes love of hevene,   35
A meles mete for a pore man, or moneye, yf they hadde.
Conscience knewe hem wel and welcomede hem alle;
They woschen and wipeden and wenten to sytten.
    The maister was made sitte furste, as for the moste worthy;
Resoun stod and styhlede, as for styward of halle.   40
Pacience and I was put to be mettes,
And seten by ouresulve at a syde-table.
    Clergie cald after mete and thenne cam Scripture
And served hem thus sone of sondrye metes monye,
Of Austyn, of Ambrose, of alle the foure evangelies,   45
    Edentes et bibentes que apud illos sunt.
Ac of this mete that mayster myhte nat wel chewe;

---

38. They *omitted in XU*   **46.** chewe *U* : *X* shewe

26-7. All these characters have been met before, and have dealt with Will pretty harshly. The invitation to dinner is a probationary reward.

30. *mayster:* a Master (or *doctor*) of Divinity. Friars were the professional intellectuals of the day (see 7.9n).

33. *Patience* is the significant guest—an active virtue, not an abstraction, and the developing theme of these last books. The resemblance to Piers Plowman prepares us for the resurrection and metamorphosis of Piers (last mentioned in C. X. 299) as the embodiment, successively, of the lives of Dowel, Dobet and Dobest.

42. The virtue is to be 'actively' tested.

45. St. Augustine and St. Ambrose, two of the Church Fathers whose work had almost equal authority with the Scriptures.

45f. 'Eating and drinking such things as they have in the house' (cf. *Luke* 10: 7), Christ's advice to the disciples to receive hospitality readily, 'for the labourer is worthy of his hire'.

Forthy eet he mete of more cost, mortrewes and potages.
Of that men mys-wonne they maden hem wel at ese;
Ac here sauce was over-soure and unsaverly ygrounde
In a morter, *post-mortem*, of many bittere peynes,   50
Bote yf they synge for tho soules and wepe salte teres.

> *Vos qui peccata hominum comeditis, nisi pro eis lacrimas*
> *effuderitis, ea que in deliciis comeditis, in tormentis*
> *evometis.*

Thenne Resoun radde, anoon-riht after,
That Consience comaunde sholde to do come Scripture,
And bringe breed for Pacience, bytynge apartye,
And to me that was his mette tho, and other mete bothe.   55
He sette a sour lof, and saide, '*Agite penitentiam,*'
And sethe he drow us drynke, *diu-perseverans:*
'As longe,' quod he, 'as lyfe and lycame may duyre.'
'This is a semely servyce!' saide Pacience.
Thenne cam Contricion, that hadde coked for hem all,   60
And brouhte forth a pytaunce, was *Pro-hac-orabit-omnis-*
      sanctus-in-tempore-oportuno.
Thenne Consience confortede us, bothe Clergie and Scripture,
And saide, '*Cor contritum et humiliatum, deus, non despicies.*'

---

52. *XU* Thenne as Resoun

49–51. The sharp and pungent sauces which the learned divine needs to savour the wholesome diet of Scripture (already made easy in 'potted' versions) are associated by the pun on *morter* with the pangs the unrighteous will feel after death (*post mortem*) unless they repent. The allegory here explodes in a characteristic profusion of detail.

51f. 'You who feast upon the sins of men, unless you pour out tears for them, you shall vomit up amid torments the food you now feast on amid pleasures'. The source of the quotation is not identified.

56. 'Repent ye' (*Matt.* 3: 2).

57. 'Long-enduring' (cf. *Matt.* 10: 22, 'He that endureth to the end shall be saved').

61. 'For this shall every one that is godly pray unto thee in a time when thou mayest be found' (*Psalm* 32: 6).

63. 'A broken and contrite heart, O God, thou wilt not despise' (*Psalm* 51: 17). This text, like the last, is from one of the seven penitential psalms (3.46n), the 'food of repentance' for the dreamer.

Pacience was wel apayed of this propre service,
And made mery with this mete; ac I mournede evere,   65
For a doctour that at the hey deys dranke wyn faste—
  Ve vobis qui potentes estis ad bibendum vinum—
And ete manye sondry metes, mortrewes and poddynges,
Brawen and blod of gees, bacon and colhoppes.
Thenne saide I to mysulve, so Pacience hit herde:
'Hit is nat thre daies don, this doctour that he prechede   70
At Poules byfore the peple what penaunce they soffrede,
Alle that coveyte to come to eny kyne joye;
And how that Poul the apostel, what penaunce he tholede
For oure lordes love, as holy lettre telleth:
  In fame et frigore, &c.
Ac me wondreth in my witt why that they ne preche   75
As Poul the apostle prechede to the peple ofte:
  Periculum in falsis fratribus!
Holy writ byt men be war and wysly hem kepe
That no fals frere thorw flatrynge hem bygyle;
Ac me thynketh loth, thogh I Latyn knowe, to lacken eny secte,
For alle be we brethrene, thogh we be diversely clothed.   80
  Ac I wiste nevere freek that frere is ycald, of the fyve
      mendynants,
That tok this for his teme and tolde hit withoute glose.
They preche that penaunce is profitable to the soule,
And what meschief and mal ese Crist for man tholede;
Ac this doctour and dyvynour,' quod I, 'and decretistre of
      canon   85
(And also a gnedy glotoun with two grete chekes)

66f. 'Woe unto you that are mighty to drink wine' (*Isaiah* 5: 22).
71. *Poules*, see 8.56n.
74f. 'In hunger and cold . . .' (see 2 *Cor.* 11: 24–7).
76f. 'Peril among false brethren' (2 *Cor.* 11: 26), with the pun on *fratres*, 'friars'.
79. The dreamer exhibits Patience, somewhat painfully.
81. *fyve:* usually four orders of friars are referred to (see 1.56n). The fifth is the order of Crutched (*Cruciferi*) Friars, or Friars of the Cross, whose habit bore a cross on the breast.
82. *withoute glose*, see 1.58n.

Hath no pyte on us pore, he performeth evele;
That he precheth he preveth nat,' to Pacience I tolde,
And wischede witterly with will ful egre
That in the mawe of that mayster alle tho metes were,   90
Bothe disches and dobelares, with alle the deyntees after!
     'I schal jangle to this jurdan, with his juyste wombe,
And apose hym what penaunce is and purgatorie on erthe,
And whi he lyveth nat as he lereth!' 'Lat be,' quod Pacience,
And saide, 'Thow shalt se thus sone, when he may no more,   95
He shal have a penaunce in his foule paunche, and puffe at uch
     a worde;
And thenne shal gothelen his guttes, and gynnen to galpe.
Now he hath dronke so depe he wol devyne sone,
And preven hit by here Pocalips and the passioun of seynt Averoy,
That nother bacon ne brawn ne blaun-manger ne mortrewes   100
Ys nother fische ne flesche, but fode for penantes;
And take wittenesse at a trinite, and take his felowe to witnesse,
What he fond in a forel of a freres lyvynge;
And bote the furste leef be lesynges, leve me nevere after!
And thenne is tyme to take to apose this doctour   105
Of Dowel and of Dobet, and yf Dobet do eny penaunce.'
     I sat stille, as Pacience wolde, and thus sone this doctour,   ◆
As rody as a rose, rodded his chekes,
Coughede and carpede, and Consience hym herde

88. *second* he U : X and; to Pacience P : X compacience
90. the U : X that   **102.** to U : X no
105. take U : X take and   **109.** X cowhede

___

99. *here Pocalips:* 'their version of the Apocalypse', the *Apocalipsis Goliae*, a
parody of St. John, satirizing corrupt and gluttonous clergy, and attributed to
Walter Map (*c.* 1180). *Seynt Averoy* is St. Avoya, who was fed in her torment
with fine bread from heaven—a useful twist to the doctor's argument that good
food and suffering go together (though not quite in the way that Patience
suggested, 96). The mistake in the spelling of the saint's name is readily attribut-
able to a scribal misreading of *u* = (*v*) as *u*+*er* contraction, and to the fact that
her cult was not widespread (though there is evidence from N. France from the
early 15th century).
102–3. '. . . and appeal to the evidence of a friend, of what (poor) fare he
found in a friar's box of provisions.'
     105. 'And then is the time to set about questioning this doctor . . .'

And tolde hym of a trinite and toward me he lokede.   110
'What is Dowel, sire doctour?' quod I. 'Is Dobet eny penaunce?'
  'Dowel?' quod this doctour, and he dronke after,
'Do thy neyhebore non harm ne thysulve nother,
And thenne dost thow wel and wysly, I dar hit wel avowe.'
  'Certes, sire,' thenne saide I, 'hit semeth nouht here,   115
In that ye parteth nat with us pore, that ye passeth Dowel,
Ne lovyeth nat as ye lereth, as oure lorde wolde.
      Et visitavit et fecit redemptionem plebis sue.
And ye fare thus with youre syke freres, ferly me thynketh
Bote Dowel wol endite yow *in die judicii.*'
  Thenne Consience ful corteyslyche a continaunce he made   120
And preynte uppon Pacience to preie me be stille,
And saide hymsulve, 'Sire doctour, by so hit be youre wille,
What is Dowel and Dobet? ye devynours knoweth.'
  'I have yseide,' quod that segg, 'I can sey no bettre,
Bote do as doctours techeth for Dowel I hit holde;   125
That travayleth to teche othere I halde hit for a Dobet;
And he that doth as he techeth, I halde hit for the beste.
      Qui facit et docuerit, magnus vocabitur.'
  'Now thou, Clergie,' quod Consience, 'carpe what is Dowel.'
  'Have me excused,' quod Clergie, 'be Crist, but in scole,
Shal no such motyf be meved for me, bote there,   130

---

111. Dobet *P* : *X* Dobest (*cf.* 106)
119. Bote *P* : *X* That   **130.** there *P* : *X* othere

---

113. 'Love thy neighbour as thyself' (*Matt.* 19: 19) is the text, but the doctor's wording gives it a dubious slant.

117f. 'He hath visited and redeemed his people' (*Luke* 1: 68, the words of Zacharias at the naming of his son, John the Baptist).

118–19. 'If this is how you treat your sick brothers, I shall be surprised if Dowel doesn't call you to account on the day of judgment.'

125–7. Plausible, but again dubious in its implication that *not* practising what you preach is Dobet. For an analysis of the Feast of Patience, see Goodridge's translation of *Piers Plowman*, pp. 299–308.

127f. 'Whosoever shall do and teach them, the same shall be called great (in the kingdom of heaven)' (*Matt.* 5: 19).

129–30. 'I would not wish to speak on such a subject, except in the context of a scholarly debate.' Clergy has the academic's reluctance to speak on large questions before a lay audience, as well as humility before the teaching of Piers Plowman (Christ).

For Peres love the palmare, that inpugnede ones
Alle kyne konnynges and alle kyne craftes,
Save love and leute and lowenesse of herte,
And no tixt ne taketh to preve this for trewe
Bote *dilige deum et proximum*, and *domine, quis habitabit in
    tabernaculo;* 135
And preveth by puyre skyle inparfyt alle thynges,
    Nemo bonus,
Bote lele love and treuth, that loth is to be founde.'

Quod Peres the Ploghman: '*Pacientes vincunt*.
Byfore perpetuel pees I shal preve that I saide
And avowe byfore god, and forsaken hit nevere, 140
That *disce, doce, dilige deum*
And thyn enemy helpe emforth thy myhte.
Caste hote coles on his heved of alle kyn speche,
Fond thorw wit and word his love to wynne,
Yef hym eft and eft, evere at his nede, 145
Conforte hym with thy catel and with thy kynde speche,
And ley on hym thus with love til he lauhe on the;

131. *X* palmare gent (*U* yut)

---

135. 'Love God and thy neighbour' (*Matt.* 22: 37, 39) and 'Lord, who shall abide in thy tabernacle?' (*Psalm* 15: 1—it is the answer to the question in the next two verses that is important to the argument here).

136f. 'There is none good (but one, that is, God)' (*Mark* 10: 18).

138. The mysterious and dramatic appearance of Piers Plowman is new in C, a crucial breakthrough. He represents Christ in his life upon earth, and enforces the idea of Dowel (patience, humility, love) as an aspect of the life of Christ, in which all three lives are ultimately to be found united. *Pacientes vincunt*, 'the patient conquer', is proverbial, as much indebted to Cato's *Distichs* as to *Matt.* 10: 22.

139. 'In the presence of the everlasting peace . . .', i.e. *byfore god*.

141. 'Learn; teach; love God.' C here cuts through the riddles of the B-text, and some complex redefinitions of the three Lives, sweeping all aside in a demonstration of the ruthlessness of perfect love: 'Love your enemies' (see *Matt.* 5: 43–8—the whole passage, with its final injunction, 'Be ye therefore perfect', is fundamental to an understanding of the redirection of the poem's movement at this point).

143. See *Romans* 12: 20, *Prov.* 25: 22.

And bote he bowe for this betynge, blynde mote he worthen!'
  And whan he hadde yworded thus, wiste no man after
Where Peres the Ploghman bycam, so priveliche he wente.   150
And Resoun ran after and riht with hym yede;
Save Concience and Clergie I couthe no mo aspye.
  And Pacience properliche spak, tho Peres was thus ypassed:
'That loveth lely,' quod he, 'bote litel thyng coveyteth.
I wolde, and I will hadde, to wynnen all Fraunce   155
Withoute bruttenynge of burne or eny blod-shedynge;
I take wittenesse,' quod he, 'of holy writ a partye:
    Pacientes vincunt.
For, by hym that me made, myhte nevere poverte,
Meseyse ne meschief, ne man with his tonge,   160
Tene the eny tyme and thou take Pacience
And bere hit in thy bosom aboute wher thou wendest
In the corner of a cart-whel, with a crowe croune.
Shal nevere burne be abasched that hath this abouten hym,
Ne nevere hete ne hayl ne helle-pouke hym greve,
Nother fuyr ne flod, ne be aferd of enemye.   165
    Caritas expellit omnem timorem.
Ne ther is wyht in this world that wolde the lette
To have alle londes at thy likyng, and the here lord make
And maister of alle here mebles and of here moneye after,
The kyng and alle the comune and clergie to the loute
As for here lord and here ledare, and live as thow techest.'   170

153. And *P* : *X* Save   **162.** cart *U* : *X* car
170. live *U* : *X* love

147-8. 'Oppress him thus with love till he smiles upon you; and if his resistance can't be beaten down by such love, may he be blinded for ever!'

155-6. 'I could, if I chose, conquer all France without any man being killed or any blood shed' (a literal illustration of *pacientes vincunt*).

162. The line is a puzzle, perhaps a deliberate bit of mystification. Langland seems to be thinking of an emblematic badge of patience, in the shape of a spoked wheel (a symbol of the martyrdom of St. Katherine), with a crow's head (the priest's tonsure?) in one of the sectors. The badge would thus associate the patient man with the martyrs of the Church.

165f. 'Love casteth out all fear' (1 *John* 4: 18). Patience is an aspect of Charity, in which all three Lives are identified.

'This is a *Dido*,' quod this doctour, 'a dysores tale!
Al the wit of this worlde, and wyhte menne strenghe,
Can nat performe a pees of the pope and his enemyes
Profitable for bothe parties'—and putte the bord fro hym,
And tok Clergie and Consience to conseyle, as hit were.   175
   Ac Concience, I tok kepe, conjeyed sone this doctour,
And sethe he saide to Clergie, so that I hit herde,
'By Crist,' quod Consience, 'Clergie, I wol nat lye,
Me were levere, by oure lorde, and I live sholde,
Have pacience parfitlyche then half thy pak of bokes!   180
Lettrure and long studie letteth ful monye,
That they knoweth nat,' quod Concience, 'what is kynde Pacience.
Forthy,' quod Concience, 'Crist I the byteche,
With Pacience wol I passe, parfitnesse to fynde.'

Conscience and Patience meet with *Activa Vita*, a representative of common
humanity, which is thus symbolically gathered up again into the quest.
(The whole section is much shorter in C, as a result of the transfer of
Haukyn's confession to the earlier confession of the Folk. It is also totally
depersonalized.) His presence is made the opportunity for further exposition
of the nature of perfect Patience and the virtues of Poverty: the seven deadly
sins are associated explicitly and in detail with love of worldly riches.
   All this accumulated understanding is now embodied in a new abstraction,
variously called *Liberum-Arbitrium* (Free Will) and *Anima* (the Soul), maybe
what we should call Intuition, the whole intellectual and mental faculty
divinely illumined. The way is prepared for Dobet with a preliminary
outline of the nature of true Charity.

172. the *U* : *X* this

---

171. *Dido:* a tale of Dido, a mere story.
   173. The Doctor is a 'man of the world' and takes the sourly practical view
that abstractions like Patience are irrelevant to the real problems of the world,
like the Papal schism. His impatient dismissal of the whole conversation (174),
and turning to 'business', is a vivid gesture.
   180. Conscience speaks on the limitations of learning with an authority
denied to the dreamer, even to Dame Study, in the poem's hierarchy of witness.
See also later, C. XVII. 206–33.
   184. 'Be ye therefore perfect, even as your Father which is in heaven is
perfect' (*Matt.* 5: 48).

12. *The Definition of Charity* (XVII. 284–372)

'Charite,' quod I tho, 'That is a thyng forsothe
That maistres comenden moche; where may hit be yfounde?
I have ylyved in Londone monye longe yeres
And fonde I nevere, in faith, as freres hit precheth,
Charite, that chargeth naught, ne chyt, thogh men greve hym,   5
As Poul in his pistul of hym bereth wittenesse:
    Non inflatur, non est ambiciosa, non querit que sua sunt.
I knewe nevere, by Crist, clerk nother lewed
That he ne askede aftur his and othere-whiles coveytede
Thyng that nedede hym nauhte, and nyme hit, yf he myhte!
For thogh men souhte alle the sektes of sustrene and of
    bretherne,   10
And fynde hym, but figuratyfly, a ferly me thynketh;
    Hic in enigmate, tunc facie ad faciem.
And so I trowe treuly, by that men telleth of Charite.'
  'Charite is a childische thyng, as holychurche witnesseth,
    Nisi efficiamini sicut parvuli, non intrabitis in regnum
    celorum,
As proud of a peny as of a pounde of golde,
And as glad of a goune of a gray russet   15
As of a cote of camaca or of clene scarlet.
He is glad with alle glad, as gurles that lawhen alle,
And sory when he seth men sory—as thow seest childerne
Lawhe ther men lawheth and loure ther othere louren.

---

3. The B-text has 'I have lyved in londe, quod I, my name is Longe Wille', usually taken to be Langland's 'signature'.

6f. '(Charity) vaunteth not itself, is not puffed up, seeketh not her own' (1 *Cor.* 13: 4–5).

11f. 'For now we see through a glass, darkly; but then, face to face' (1 *Cor.* 13: 12). The dreamer uses Paul's text to suggest that only 'figures', mirror-images, of Charity are to be found here below, but the poem is now opening to a higher vision, of Charity crowned and made manifest in the life of Christ.

12. 'And so truly I believe, judging by what people say of Charity.'

13. The speaker is *Liberum-Arbitrium.*

13f. 'Except ye become as little children, ye shall not enter into the kingdom of heaven' (*Matt.* 18: 3).

And when a man swereth for soth, for sooth he hit troweth; 20
Weneth he that no wyhte wolde lye and swere,
Ne that eny gome wolde gyle othere, ne greve,
For drede of god that so gode is, and thus-gates us techeth:
Quodcunque vultis ut faciant vobis homines, facite eis.
Hath he no lykynge to lawhe, ne to likene men to scorne.
Alle seknesses and sorwes for solaces he hit taketh, 25
And alle manere meschiefs as munstracie of hevene.
Of deth ne of derthe drad he nevere,
Ne mysliked thogh he lore, or lened that ilke
That nevere payed peny ageyn in places there he borwede.'
    'Who fynt hym his fode?' quod I, or what frendes hath he, 30
Rentes other richesse to releve him at his nede?'
    'Of rentes ne of othere rychesse ne reccheth he nevere.
A frende he hath that fynd him, that faylede hym nevere:
One *Aperis-tu-manum* alle thynges hym fyndeth;
Fiat-voluntas-tua festeth hym uch a daye. 35
And also he can clergie, *credo-in-deum-patrem*,
And portraye wel the *pater-noster* and peynten hit with *avees*.
And other-while his wone is to wende in pilgrimages
There pore men and prisones ben, and paye for here fode,
Clotheth hem and conforteth hem and of Crist precheth hem, 40
What sorwe he soffrede in ensaumple of us alle
That poverte and penaunce, pacientlyche ytake,

---

30. Who *U* : *X* He   **31.** *line supplied from U* (releve *P* : *U* rule)
38. wende *U* : *X* wynde

23f. 'Whatsoever ye would that men should do to you, do ye even so to them' (*Matt.* 7: 12).
24-6. 'He takes no pleasure in laughing at men, nor in mocking them scornfully. He takes all sickness and sorrows as favours, and accepts all kinds of misfortune as grace-notes to the divine harmony.' The last phrase has an untranslatable felicity.
34-7. 'One called Thou-openest-thine-hand [a daily grace] provides him with everything; Thy-will-be-done is a daily feast for him. He is not without learning—of the kind I-believe-in-God-the-Father—and can do a good illumination of the Paternoster, painting it about with Aves' (i.e. knows his Rosary well).
38. *pilgrimages:* errands of mercy, not 'pilgrimages', which Langland had little time for.

Worth moche meryte to that man that hit may soffre.
And when he hath visited thus fetered folke and other folke
    pore,
Thenne yerneth he into youthe and yeepliche he secheth   45
Pruyde, with alle portinaunces, and pakketh hem togyderes
And laveth hem in the lavendrie, *laboravi-in-gemitu-meo*,
Bouketh hem at his breste and beteth hit ofte,
And with warm water of his yes woketh hit til hit white.
    Lavabis me, et super nivem dealbabor.
And thenne syngeth he when he doth so, and som tyme
    wepynge: 50
    Cor contritum et humiliatum, deus, non despicies.'
  'Were I with hym, by Crist,' quod I, 'I wolde nevere fro hym,
Thogh I my bylive sholde begge aboute at menne hacches.
Where clerkes knowe hym nat,' quod I, 'that kepen holy-churche?'
  'Peres the Plouhman,' quod he, 'moste parfitlyche hym
    knoweth.
    Et vidit deus cogitationes eorum.
By clothyng ne by carpynge knowe shaltow hym nevere,   55
Ac thorw werkes thow myhte wyte wher-forth he walketh.
    Operibus credite.
He is the murieste of mouthe at mete ther he sitteth,
And compenable in companye, as Crist hymsulve techeth:
    Nolite tristes fieri, sicut ypocrite.

---

49. *second* hit *U* : *X* he   **50.** wepynge *U* : *X* wypynge

---

45–9. The passage describes, with characteristically uninhibited concretion, the cleansing of Pride and other sinfulness from the soul through penitential groans ('I am weary with my groaning', *Psalm* 6: 6) and tears.
    49f. 'Wash me, and I shall be whiter than snow' (*Psalm* 51: 7).
    50f. See 11.62n.
    53. 'Do the clergy not know him . . . ?'
    54f. 'And God saw their thoughts' (cf. *Matt.* 9: 4). Piers Plowman's knowledge of Charity is associated with Christ's knowledge of men's hearts, thus helping to build up a creative identification (which in B is baldly stated, 'Petrus, id est Christus', XV. 206; see 1 *Cor.* 10: 4).
    56f. 'Believe the works' (*John* 10: 38)—and so recognize God in man, i.e. in Christ and in Piers.
    58f. 'Be not, as the hypocrites, of a sad countenance' (*Matt.* 6: 16).

I have ysey hym mysulve somtyme in russet,
Bothe in gray and in grys and in gult harneys,   60
And also gladliche he hit gaf to gomes that hit nedede.
Edmond and Edward, ayther were seyntes,
And cheef charite with hem, and chaste all here lyves.
I have yseye Charite also syngen and rede,
Ryden, and rennen in raggede clothes;   65
Ac biddyng als a beggare byhelde I hym nevere.
Ac in riche robes rathest he walketh,
Ycalled and ycrimyled and his croune yshave.
And in a frere frocke he was founde ones,
Ac hit is fer and fele yer, in Franceys tyme;   70
In that sekte sethe, to selde hath he be founde.
Riche men he recomendeth, and of here robes taketh,
Of tho that lelelyche lyven, and loven, and byleyven.
       Beatus est dives sine macula.
In kynges court he cometh, yf his consaile be trewe;
Ac yf covetyse be of his consaile he wol nat come therynne.   75
Amonges the comune in court he cometh bote selde,
For braulyng and bac-bitynge and berynge of fals witnesse.
In constorie bifore comissarie he cometh nat ful ofte,
For over-long is here lawe but yf thay lacche sulver.
With bisshopes he wolde be, for beggares sake,   80
Ac avarise other-whiles halt hym withoute the gate.

69. frocke *U* : *X* flocke   **71.** that *omitted in X*
72. here *omitted in X*

59–60. '. . . in coarse russet, in grey cloth and rich fur, and in gilded armour',
i.e. among all classes.

62. St. Edmund, king of East Anglia (d. 870) and St. Edward the Confessor
(d. 1066)—examples to show that Charity can rule kings too.

64. *syngen and rede*, i.e. act as a priest.

68. 'With skull-cap and anointed hair and with tonsured crown', i.e. as a
monk or other member of the regular clergy.

70. '. . . in the time of St. Francis of Assisi.'

72. '. . . and receives gifts of clothes from them.'

73f. 'Blessed is the rich man that is found without blemish' (*Ecclesiasticus*
31: 8).

79. 'For their law-suits go on for ever unless they get money (bribes).'
Money rules the law-courts, not Charity.

Kynges and cardynals knewen hym sum tyme,
Ac thorw coveytyse and his consaile ycongeyed is he ofte.
   And who-so coveyteth to knowe hym, such a kynde hym
      foleweth
As I tolde the with tonge, a litel tyme ypassed;   85
For nother he ne beggeth ne biddeth, ne borweth to yelde.
He halt hit for a vyce and a foul shame
To begge or to borwe, but of god one.
   Panem nostrum cotidianum da nobis hodie.'

   Free Will continues with a long account of where Charity is and is not to
   be found, gathering up previous speculation about Saracens and Jews and
   others outside the Law into a charitable doctrine of potential universal
   salvation, and redefining traditional anti-clericalism in terms of a distinction
   between the Church and its officers. The donation of Constantine (the
   original secular 'establishment' of the Church) is seen as the source of abuses
   within the Church, and here occurs the famous warning of expropriation
   (XVIII. 227) which made Langland popular at the time of the Reformation.
   The dreamer returns to his question.

13. *The Tree of Charity* (XIX. 1–137)

'Leve *Liberum Arbitrium*,' quod I, 'I leve, as I hope,
Thow couthest telle and teche me to Charite, as I leve?'
   Thenne louh *Liberum Arbitrium* and ladde me forth with tales
Til we cam into a contre, *Cor-hominis* hit heihte,
Erber of alle pryvatees and of holynesse.   5
Evene in the myddes an ympe, as hit were,
That hihte *Ymago-dei*, graciousliche hit growede.

   84. *first* hym *omitted in* X

---

   84. 'And whoever is eager to know him (may recognize him by) a certain
nature that he has . . .'
   88f. 'Give us this day our daily bread' (*Matt.* 6: 11).
   7. The tree that grows in the heart of man (*Cor-hominis*) is the image of
God (*Ymago-dei*), a graft (*ympe*) from God's love, set and supported by the
Trinity against the winds of the World, the Flesh and the Devil, and bearing
the fruit of charitable deeds and charitable souls. The tree is thus the divine
potential implanted in man, and also the expression of that potential in history

Thenne gan I aske what hit hihte, and he me sone tolde:
'The tree hatte Trewe-love,' quod he, 'the trinite hit sette;
Thorw lovely lokynges hit lyveth and launseth up blosmes,　　　　10
The whiche blosmes burnes Benigne-speche hit calleth.
And ther-of cometh a gode fruyt, the whiche men calleth Werkes-
Of-holynesse, of hendenesse, of helpe-hym-that-nedeth,
The whiche is *Caritas* ykald, Cristes oune fode,
And solaceth alle soules sorwful in purgatory.'　　　　15
　'Now, certes,' I sayde, and sighte for joye,
'I thonke yow a thousend sethe that ye me hider kende,
And sethen that ye vouchen-saf to sey me as hit hoteth.'
And he thonkede me tho. Bote thenne toke I hede,
Hit hadde schoriares to shuyven hit up, thre shides of o lenghe　　20
And of o kyne colour and kynde, as me thoghte,
Alle thre yliche long and yliche large.
Moche merveyled me on what more thei growede,
And askede eft of hym of what wode they were?
　'Thise thre shorriares,' quod he, 'that bereth up this plonte,　　25
Bytokeneth trewly the Trinite of hevene,
Thre persones indepartable, perpetuel were evere,
Of o will, of o wit; and here-with I kepe

24. eft *U* : *X* ofte

(i.e. the Church). The style of the allegory here is formal, pictorial, numero-
logical, a method of explaining and informing, not of persuading. Debate,
speculation, uncertainty, are over; the poem is now on a plateau, preparing
its assault on the just-visible peak of Christ's sacrifice by mapping and displaying
the terrain. A similar moment in Dante, at the end of the *Purgatorio* (xxix. 43),
just before the ascent through the spheres, produces the same kind of 'old-
fashioned' allegorical pageantry. The tree itself is a favourite medieval pictorial
device for presenting relationship (e.g. trees of vices and virtues) or causal
sequence (e.g. the tree of Jesse, *Is.* 11 : 1) in spatial terms. There are also symbolic
connections with the tree of Knowledge (and *its* apples), the tree of Life, and
the tree of Christ's cross, with its three stems, of cedar, cypress and pine,
symbolic of the Trinity. See *Legends of the Holy Rood*, ed. R. Morris (*EETS, OS*
46, 1871), esp. pp. 70, 77.
　10. 'It lives on looks of love . . .'
　20. 'It had props to support it, three beams of the same length.'
　28. *I kepe. Liberum-arbitrium* tends the tree of Charity (in B, as a tenant-farmer
of Piers Plowman), since Free-will is 'that part of man which bears the impress
of the image of God to which man was created' (Donaldson, p. 189).

The fruyt of this faire tre fro thre wikkede wyndes,
And fro falling the stok, hit faile not of his myght.　30
The World is a wikkede wynd to hem that wolde treuthe;
Covetyse cometh of that wynde, and *Caritas* hit abiteth
And for-fret that fruyt thorw many fayre sihtes;
And with the furste planke I palle hym down, *Potencia-dei-patris*.
Thenne is the Flesch a fel wynde, and in flouryng-tyme;　35
Thorw lecherie and lustes so loude he gynneth blowe
That hit norischeth nice sihtes and som tyme wordes
And many wikkede werkes, wormes of synne,
And al for-bit *Caritas* rihte to the bare stalke;
Thenne sette I the seconde planke, *Sapiencia-dei-patris*,　40
The which is the passioun and the penaunce and the parfitnesse
　　of Jesus,
And ther-with I warde hit other-while til hit waxe rype.
And thenne fondeth the Fende my fruyte to destruye,
And leyth a laddere ther-to, of lesynges ben the ronges,
And with alle the wyles that he can, waggeth the rote　45
Thorw bak-bitares and brauleres and thorw bolde chidares,
And shaketh hit; ne were hit under-shored, hit sholde nat stande.
So this lordeynes lithereth ther-to, that alle the leves falleth,
And feccheth away the fruyt som tyme byfore bothe myn yes.
And thenne palle I adoune the pouke with the thridde shoriere,　50
The whiche is *Spiritus-sanctus* and soth-faste bileve,
And that is grace of the Holy Gost; and thus gete I the maystrye.'
　I toted upon that tree tho, and thenne toke I hede
Where the fruyt were fayre or foul for to loke on.
And the fruyt was fayre, non fayrere be myhte;　55
Ac in thre degrees hit grewe, grete ferly me thouhte,

---

30. *line omitted in X*　　　　**46.** *XU* braules

---

30. 'And (keep) the stem from falling, so that it does not fail in strength.'

33. The greed aroused by the fine appearances of things eats away at Charity.

34. 'With the first stave, the power of God the Father, I beat him down.' Langland's 'active' imagination immediately transforms props into weapons. See 5.17n.

40. Sapience, or Wisdom, is traditionally identified with the second person of the Trinity.

45. '. . . shakes the base of the tree.'

And askede efte tho, where hit were all o kynde?
  'Ye, certes,' he sayde, 'and sothliche leve hit.
Hit is al of o kynde, and that shal I preven,
Ac somme ar swettere then somme and sonnere wollen rotye.   60
Men may se on an appul-tre, mony tyme and ofte,
Of o kynde apples aren nat iliche grete,
Ne suynge smale, ne of o swettenesse swete.
Tho that sitten in the sonne-syde sonnere aren rype,
Swettere and saveriere and also more grettere   65
Then tho that selde han the sonne and sitten in the north halfe;
And so hit fareth sothly, sone, by oure kynde.
Adam was as tre, and we aren as his apples,
Somme of us soothfaste and some variable,
Summe litel, some large, ylike apples of kynde.   70
As weddede men and wedewes and riht worthy maydenes,
The whiche the Seynt Spirit seweth, the sonne of al hevene,
And conforteth hem in here continence that lyven in
    contemplacion,
As monkes and monyals, men of holy-churche;
These han the hete of the Holi Gost as hath the crop of tre
    sonne.   75
Wedewes and wedewares, that here ownere wil forsaken

63. o *omitted in XUP*   75. hete *P : X* gyfte

---

63. 'Nor smaller in regular gradation, nor sweet with the same sweetness.'
72. 'With whom dwells the holy spirit.'
75. 'These receive "warmth" of the Holy Ghost as the top of the tree receives
the sun' (see 64).
76–80. Chaste widowhood was placed above marriage and below virginity
in the hierarchy of heavenly reward; see, for example, *Holy Maidenhood*
(EETS, OS 18), p. 32; also M. W. Bloomfield, '*Piers Plowman* and the Three
Grades of Chastity', *Anglia* 76 (1958), 227–53. Widowhood is here associated
with the Contemplative life of the recluse or monk as against the Active life
of the Christian in the world. The association is new in C (like the whole
passage, 58–103) and slightly puzzling, for there *is* a third quality of life beyond
the Active and the Contemplative, namely the Mixed or Apostolic life, which
brings the fruits of contemplation to the life of action. The dreamer's apparent
ignorance of this third and highest quality of life is perhaps a dramatic device,
to draw our attention, by implicit association with another 'best' life, Virginity,
to the existence of a perfection of life in which active and contemplative are

And chaste leden here lyf, is lyf of contemplacioun,
And more lykynde to oure lorde then lyve as kynde asketh
And folewe that the flesche wole and fruyt forth brynge,
That *Activa* lyf lettred men in here langage hit calleth.'   80
  'Ye, sire,' I sayde, 'and sethen ther aren but tweyne lyves
That oure lorde alloweth, as lered men us techeth,
Activa Vita and *Contemplativa Vita*,
Why growth this fruyt in thre degres?' 'A gode skil,' he saide;
'Here beneth I may nyme, yf I nede hadde,   85
Matrimonye, a moist fruyt, that multiplieth the peple.
And thenne above is bettere fruyt (ac bothe two ben gode),
Wydewhode, more worthiere then wedlok, as in hevene.
Thenne is Virginite, more vertuous, and fayrest, as in hevene,
For that is evene with the angelis, and angeles pere.   90
Hit was the furste fruyte that the fader of hevene blessed,
And bad hit be, of a bat of erthe, a man and a maide,
In menynge that the fayrest thyng the furste thyng shold honour,
And the clennest creature furste creatour knowe.
In kynges court and in knyhtes, the clenneste men and fayreste   95
Shollen serve for the lord sulve, and so fareth god almyhty.
Maydenes and martres ministrede hym here on erthe
And in hey hevene is priveeste and next hym by resoun,
And for the fayrest fruyte byfore hym, as of erthe,
And swete withoute swellynge, sour worth hit nevere.'   100
  'This is a propre plonte,' quod I, 'and priveliche hit bloweth,
And bryngeth forth fruyt, folke of alle nacion,
Bothe parfit and inparfit; puyr fayn I wolde
Assay what savour hit hadde,' and saide that tyme,

---

94. creatour *U* : *X* creature   **97.** hym *omitted in X*

---

united, that is, in the life of Christ. (The three Lives have often been used as
a basis for interpreting Dowel, Dobet and Dobest, for instance by Wells and
Coghill; see Bibl., and Introd., p. 30; also 7.78n.)

86. *a moist fruyt*: and therefore more productive, but also liable to rot sooner.

92-4. 'And created from a lump of earth a man and a maid, in token that
the First Cause should honour the loveliest thing [Virginity], and that the
purest creature should be first to acknowledge the Creator.'

97. *hym*: Christ.

99-100. 'As being the fairest fruit, in his sight, that earth had produced,
sweet without over-ripeness, never to grow sour.'

'Leve *Liberum Arbitrium*, lat some lyf hit shake.'   105
   And anoon he hihte Elde an hy for to clymbe,
And shaken hit sharpeliche, the rype sholden falle.
And Elde clemb to the crop-ward, thenne comsed hit to crye:
He waggede Wedewhed, and hit wepte after;
He meved Matrimonye, hit made a foule noyse;   110
For evere as Elde hadde eny down, the devel was redy,
And gadered hem alle togyderes, bothe grete and smale,
Adam and Abraham and Ysaye the prophete,
Sampson and Samuel and seynt John the Baptiste,
And bar hem forth baldly, nobody hym lette,   115
And made of holy men his hord in *limbo inferni*,
There is derkenesse and drede, and the devel maister.
   Thenne moved hym mod *in majestate dei*,
That *Libera-Voluntas-Dei* lauhte the myddel shoriar
And hit aftur the fende, happe how hit myhte.   120
Filius, by the fadres wille, fley with *Spiritus Sanctus*
To go ransake that ragman and reve hym of his apples,
That thorw fals biheste and fruyt furste man disseyved.
   And thenne spak *Spiritus Sanctus* in Gabrieles mouthe
To a mayde that hihte Marie, a meke thyng with-alle,   125
That one Jesus, a Justices sone, moste jouken in here chaumbre,

---

106. The allegory here takes on its other dimension, of time—time in relation to man's life and in relation to history.

116. *limbo inferni*: the borderlands of hell, where the souls of the patriarchs and prophets dwelt until released by Christ.

118-20. 'Then God in his majesty was moved to anger, and of his own Divine Free-will seized the middle prop [the Son] and struck out at the Devil in all directions.' Man's Free-will, his divine potential, is suddenly made absolute in God's Free-will, and realised in the Incarnation.

122. 'To rob that cowardly villain (the Devil) . . .'

124. The Annunciation is the moment of the intersection of the timeless with time, of God's entry into human time. It is the most stupendous moment in Christian history, and Langland, by his sudden and brilliant shift from allegorical abstraction to historical reality, makes it seem so.

126-30. '(And said) that one Jesus, son of a Judge, must dwell in her womb till the fulness of time [*Gal.* 4: 4] was come, when Age should have caused the fruit to fall or it should have happened to grow ripe, and that then Jesus would joust for it, to decide by force of arms who should have this fruit, the Devil or Jesus himself.'

Til *plenitudo temporis*, tyme ycome were,
That Elde felde efte the fruyt, or full to be rype,
That Jesus sholde jouste ther-fore, and by jugement of armes,
Who sholde fecche this fruyt, the fende or Jesus sulven.   130
The mayde myldeliche the messager she grauntede
And saide hendely to hym, 'Lo, me, his hondmayden,
For to worchen his wille withouten eny synne.
     Ecce ancilla domini, fiat mihi secundum verbum tuum.'
And in the wombe of that wenche was he fourty wokes,
And bycam man of that maide, mankynde to save,   135
Byg and abydyng, and bold in his barn-hod
To have yfouhte with the fende ar ful tyme come.

A brief life of Christ hints at the nature of Dobet, that is, perfect Charity, but first the dreamer meets with Abraham, the type of Faith, who explains to him, though not very clearly, the doctrine of the Trinity, and then with Moses, the type of Hope. These two represent the old Law, about to be crowned in the New, and also, in Pauline terms, the two spiritual virtues which are nothing without Charity, as the following episode shows.

14. *The Good Samaritan* (XX. 46–110)

And as we wenten in the way, thus wordyng of this matere,
Thenne saw we a Samaritan, cam sittynge on a muyle,

133f. 'Behold the handmaid of the Lord; be it unto me according to thy word' (*Luke* 1: 38).

136–7. 'Strong and enduring and brave enough even in his youth to have fought with the Devil, even before his time was fully come.'

1. The rehandling of the parable of the good Samaritan (*Luke* 10: 25–37) is one of Langland's most brilliant inspirations, and one of the few instances where his allegorical technique can profitably be investigated in terms of the traditional four levels of Scriptural exegesis (see Coghill, Roberston and Huppé, in Bibl., and Introd., pp. 5–7), from which, indeed, it derives. Literally, it is meaningful in terms of the historical situation of Samaritans in Judaea; allegorically, it demonstrates the precept, 'Love thy neighbour'; tropologically (in terms of abstract morality), it shows the meaninglessness of Faith and Hope without Charity; and anagogically, or spiritually, it tells with great moving power of Christ's redeeming love for mankind, sick of sin (8). Langland is aware of all four levels, and uses, them, in their context, to penetrate to the vision of Christ's humanity as the perfect exemplar of Charity.

Rydynge ful raply the right way we yeden,
Comynge fram a contreye that men callide Jerico,
To joust in Jerusalem he jaced awey ful faste.   5
Bothe Abraham and *Spes* and he mette at ones
In a wilde wildernesse where theves hadde ybounde
A man, as me tho thouhte, to moche care they brouhte;
For he ne myhte stepe ne stande, ne stere fot ne handes,
Ne helpe hymsulve sothly, for *semyvyf* he semede,   10
And as naked as a nedle, and non helpe abouten.

    Fayth hadde furst of hym siht, ac he fleyh asyde,
And wolde nat neyhele hym by nyne londes lenghe.

    Hope cam huppynge aftur, that hadde so ybosted
How he with Moyses maundement hadde mony men yholpe;   15
Ac when he hadde sihte of this syke, asyde he gan hym drawe,
And dredfully withdrow hym tho and durste go no nerre hym.

    Ac so sone so the Samaritan hadde sihte of this careful,
Alihte anon of lyard and ladde hym in his handes
And to this wey he wente, his woundes to byholde.   20
He perseyvede by his pous he was in perel to deye,
And bote if he hadde recover the rather that ryse sholde he
    nevere,
And unbokelede his boteles and bothe he atamede;
With wyn and with oyle his woundes he can lithe,
Enbaumed hym and bond his heved and on bayard hym sette   25
And ladde hym forth to *lavacrum-lex-dei*, a grange,
Is syxe myle or sevene bisyde the newe market,
And lefte hym there a-lechyng, to lyve yf he myhte;
And tok two pans the hostiler to take kepe to hym,
'And that more goth for his medicyne I make the good
    ageynward,   30

12. hadde *omitted in XU*   **24.** lithe *U* : *X* lihte   **27.** *X* marcat

---

    13. 'And would not come within nine furrows' width of him' (*lond* is here the ridge of land between furrows in a ploughed field).
    22. 'And unless he made a recovery quickly, he would never rise again.'
    26–8. 'And took him to *Lavacrum-lex-dei* [a baptismal font, symbolic of entry into the Law or Church of Christ], a lone farm-house, six or seven miles from the local market-town, and left him there to convalesce, if he might live.'
    30. 'And whatever more his medicine costs, I will repay.'

For I may nat lette,' quod that lede, and lyard he bystrideth,
And rapede hym to ryde the rihte way to Jerusalem.
Bothe Fayth and his felawe *Spes* folewede faste aftur,
Ac I sewede the Samaritan and saide how they bothe
Were afered, and flowe fram the man ywounded.   35
   'Have hem excused,' quod he, the Samaritan, 'here helpe may
     nat availe,
Ne no medicyne under molde the man to hele brynge,
Nother Faith ne fyn Hope, so festred aren his woundes.
Withoute the blod of a barn he beth nat ysaved,
The whiche barn mote nedes be born of a mayde,   40
And with the blod of that barn enbaumed and ybaptised.
And thouh he stande and steppe, right stronge worth he nevere
Til he have eten al that barn and his blod dronken,
And yut be plastered with pacience when fondynges hym priketh,
(For wente nevere man this way that he ne was here yryfled,   45
Save mysulve sothly, and suche as I lovede),
And yut bote they leve lelly upon that litel baby,
That his lycame shal lechen at the laste us alle.'
   'Ah, sire,' I saide, 'shal nat we bileve,
As Faith and his felawe *Spes* enformede me bothe,   50
In thre persones, a parceles departable fram other,
And alle thre bote a god? Thus Abraham me tauhte.
And Hope afturward of o god more me tolde,
And lered me for his love to lovye al mankynde
And hym above alle and hem as mysulve;   55
Nother lacke ne alose, ne leve that ther were
Eny wikkedere in the worlde then I were mysulve,
And most imparfit of alle persones, and pacientliche soffre
Alle manere men, and thogh I myhte venge,
I sholde tholye and thonken hem that me evel wolden.'   60
   'He saide soth,' quod the Samaritan, 'and so I rede the also.
And as Abraham the olde of o god the taughte,
Loke thow lovye and bileve al thy lyf-tyme.
   44. be *U* : *X* he

---

43. A reference to the sacrament of the Eucharist.
   44. 'And, what is more, be prepared to accept a poultice of patience, when temptations assail him' (referring to the sacrament of Penance).

And yf Kynde Wit carpe here-agen, or eny kyne thouhtes,
Other eretikes with argumentis—thin hond that thow hem
    shewe!'   65

> This last startling injunction introduces the image of the Trinity as a hand
> (fist, palm, and fingers), which is followed by the image of the Trinity as
> a taper (wax, wick and flame). The Samaritan concludes his discourse with
> the affirmation of God's mercy to all except those guilty of 'unkyndenesse'
> or lack of Charity. The dreamer wakes.

15. *The Crucifixion and the Harrowing of Hell* (Passus XXI)

Wolleward and watschod wente I forth aftur
As a recheles renke that recheth nat of sorwe,
And yede forth ylike a lorel al my lyf-tyme,
Til I waxe wery of the world and wilnede efte to slepe
And lened me to lenten and long tyme I slepte.   5
  Of gurles and of *gloria laus* greetliche me dremede
And how *osanna* by orgene olde folke songe.
One semblable to the Samaritan, and somdeel to Peres the
    Plouhman,
Barfot on an asse bake botles cam prikynge
Withouten spores other spere—sprakeliche he lokede,   10
As is the kynde of a knyhte that cometh to be dobbet,
To geten here gult spores and galoches ycouped.
And thenne was Faith in a fenestre and criede '*A, filii David!*'

64-5. 'And if common sense, or any other kind of thoughts, argue against
this, or heretics with their arguments, show them your hand.'

6-7. 'I dreamt much of children singing "Glory, praise (and honour to
thee)" [a procession hymn sung on Palm Sunday] and of older people singing
"Hosanna" to the sound of the organ.' This part of the poem is less like a
sermon (2.25n) than a dramatization of the liturgy for Holy Week.

10-12. '. . . and lusty and eager he looked, as is the nature of a knight who
comes to be dubbed, to receive his gilt spurs and his cut-away shoes.' The
imagery of knighting ceremonies relates to the idea of Jesus' fight with the
devil as a 'joust'.

13, 15f. 'Hosanna to the son of David'; 'Blessed is he that cometh in the
name of the Lord' (*Matt.* 21: 9, but suggested here by the antiphons to the
procession hymn for Palm Sunday).

F

As doth an heraud of armes when auntres cometh to joustes.
Olde Jewes of Jerusalem for joye they songen, 15
    Benedictus qui venit in nomine domini.
Thenne I afraynede at Fayth what al that fare bymente,
And who sholde jouste in Jerusalem? 'Jesus', he saide,
And feche that the fende claymeth, Pers fruyt the Plouhman'.
    'Is Peres in this place?' quod I, and he prente on me:
'*Liberum-dei-arbitrium* for love hath undertake 20
That this Jesus of his gentrice shal jouste in Pers armes,
In his helm and in his haberjon, *humana natura*,
That Crist be nat yknowe for *consummatus deus*;
In Peres plates the Plouhman this prikiare shal ryde,
For no dynt shal hym dere as *in deitate patris.*' 25
    'Who shal jouste with Jesus', quod I, 'Jewes, or scribes?'
    'Nay', quod Faith, 'bote the fende, and Fals-dom-to-deye.
Deth saith he wol for-do and adown brynge
Alle that lyveth or loketh, a londe or a watere.
Lyf saith that he lyeth and hath leide his lyf to wedde, 30
That for al that Deth can do, withynne thre dayes to walke
And feche fro the fende Peres fruyt the Plouhman,
And legge hit ther hym liketh and Lucifer bynde

25. dynt *U* : *X* dount

---

18. 'And bring back what the devil claims as his, the fruit of Piers the Plowman', i.e. the souls of the righteous, the apples on the tree of Charity, which have fallen and been seized by the Devil (see 13.112). Free-Will looked after the tree in the C-text, but in B it was Piers Plowman, whence this reference.

20-25. 'God, in his Free Will, and out of love, has undertaken that this Jesus, in accord with his noble nature, shall joust in Piers' coat-armour [i.e. the flesh], in the helmet and coat-of-mail of Human Nature, in order that Christ shall not be recognized as God Almighty; he will ride as a knight in the armour of Piers Plowman, for no blow shall injure him in his divine nature as the Father.' To say that Christ *is* Piers Plowman would do scant justice to this subtle and creative handling of the mystery of the Incarnation.

27. '. . . and the false judgment of death upon mankind.'

28. The idea of the Crucifixion as a combat between Death and Life is best known in the sequence *Victimae paschali laudes*, for Easter Sunday ('Death with life contended: combat strangely ended. Life's own champion slain, yet lives to reign'). It is the theme of a fine 15th c. alliterative poem, *Death and Life* (ed. Gollancz, *Select Early English Poems*, 1930).

And forbete and bringe adown bale and deth for evere.
   O mors, ero mors tua!'
 Thenne cam Pilatus with moche peple, *sedens pro tribunali*,   35
To se how douhtyliche Deth sholde do, and demen ther beyre
   rihte.
The Jewes and the justices ageyns Jesus they were,
And alle the court cryede '*Crucifige!*' loude.
Thenne putte hym forth a pelour bifore Pilatus, and saide:
'This Jesu of oure Jewene temple japed and despised,   40
To for-don hit on a day, and in thre dayes after
Edefien hit eft newe—here he stant that saide hit—
And yut maken hit as moche in alle manere poyntes,
Bothe as longe and as large, alofte and o grounde,
And as wyde as hit evere was; this we witnesseth alle'.   45
 '*Crucifige!*' quod a cachepol, 'he can of wycche-crafte.'
'*Tolle, tolle!*' quod another, and tok of kene thornes
And bigan of a grene thorn a garlond to make
And sette hit sore on his heved, and sethe saide in envye,
'*Ave, rabbi,*' quod that ribaud, and redes shotte up to his yes;   50
And nayled hym with thre nayles, naked upon a rode
And, with a pole, poysen putten up to his lippes
And beden hym drynke, his deth to lette and his dayes lenghe,
And saiden, 'Yf he sotil be, hymsulve now he wol helpe;'
And 'Yf thow be Crist—and Crist, godes sone—   55
Come adoun of this rode and thenne shal we leve
That Lyf the loveth and wol nat late the deye'.

---

34. *XU* And forbete adown and bringe (*X* beynge) bale deth for evere

---

34f. 'O Death, I will be thy death' (*Hosea* 13: 14, sung as an antiphon on Holy Saturday).
  35. '. . . seated in the judgment seat' (*Matt.* 27: 19).
  36. 'To see what sort of fight Death would put up, and to judge the right of victory between them' (*beyre*, gen. pl., 'of both').
  39. *Matt.* 26: 61. The account of the Passion is taken chiefly from Matthew, with apocryphal additions, and no doubt some details from representations in the Mystery plays.
  47. 'Away with him' (*John* 19: 15).
  50. 'Hail, master, said that rogue, and thrust sharp reeds at his eyes.' Cf, *Matt.* 27: 29–30.

'*Consummatum est*', quod Crist, and comsed for to swone,
Pitousliche and pale, as prisoun that deyeth.
The lord of lyf and of liht tho leyde his eyes togederes;   60
The daye for drede therof withdrouh, and derke bicam the sonne;
The wal of the temple to-cleef evene al to peces,
The hard roch al to-rof, and riht derk nyht hit semede;
The erthe to-quasche and quok as hit quyk were
And dede men for that dene cam oute of depe graves   65
And tolde why the tempest so longe tyme durede.
'For a bitter bataile', the ded bodye saide,
'Lyf and Deth in this derkenesse here one for-doth another,
Ac shal no wyht wyte witterlich who shal have the maistry
Ar a Soneday, aboute the sonne-rysynge', and sank with that
     til erthe.   70
Somme saide he was godes sone that so fayre deyede,
     Vere filius dei erat iste,
And somme saide, 'He can of sorcerie; gode is that we assaie
Wher he be ded or nat ded, down or he be taken'.
     Two theves tho tholed deth that tyme
Uppon cros bisyde Crist, so was the comune lawe.   75
A cachepol cam and craked a-to her legges
And here arme after, of evereche of tho theves.
Ac was no boie so bold godes body to touche;
For he was knyht and kynges sone, Kynde for-yaf that tyme
That hadde no boie hardynesse hym to touche in deynge.   80
     Ac ther cam forth a blynde knyhte with a kene spere
     ygrounde,

68. another *U* : *X* her other   **74.** Two *U* : *X* Tho
76. *X* A cachepol of tho theves cam

71f. 'Truly this was the Son of God' (*Matt.* 27: 54).
79. *Kynde for-yaf*: 'Nature (God) granted'.
81. The story of Longeus (Longinus) is from the apocryphal *Gospel of Nicodemus*, a composite narrative deriving from about the 4th c. A.D., including also the story of Christ's descent into Hell, and attributed *c.* 1200 to the Nicodemus mentioned in *John* 19: 39 as Joseph of Arimathea's helper. Longinus also appears in the *Legenda Aurea*, a calendar of saints' lives, as being martyred in A.D. 58. His name may derive from the Greek word for 'lance', *longē*, in *John* 19: 34.

Hihte *Longies*, as the lettre telleth, and longe hadde lore his sihte;
Bifore Pilatus and othere peple in the place he hoved.
Maugre his mony teth, he was mad that tyme
Jouste with Jesus, this blynde Jewe *Longies*;   85
For alle were they unhardy, that hoved ther or stode,
To touche hym other to trinen hym other to taken hym down
    and grave hym,
Bote this blynde bacheler, that bar hym thorw the herte.
The blod sprang down by the sper and unspered the knyghte yes;
Tho ful the knyhte uppon knees and criede Jesu mercy—   90
'Ageyn my will hit was', quod he, 'that I yow wounde made!'
He syhed and saide, 'Sore hit me for-thenketh
Of the dede that I have do; I do me in youre grace.
Bothe my lond and my licame at youre likynge taketh hit,
And have mercy on me, rightful Jesu!' and riht with that he
    wepte.   95
    Thenne gan Faith fouly the false Jewes to dispise,
Calde hem caytyves, acorsed for evere,
'For this was a vyl vilanye, vengeaunce yow bifall
That made the blynde bete the dede—this was a boyes dede!
Corsede caytives! knyghtheed was hit nevere   100
To bete a body ybounde, with eny briht wepene.
The gre yut hath he geten, for al his grete woundes,
For youre chaumpioun chivaler, chief knyht of yow alle,
Yelde hym recreaunt rennyng, riht at Jesu wille.
For be this derkenesse ydo, Deth worth yvenkised,   105
And ye, lordeyns, han lost, for Lyf shal have maistrie,
And youre franchise that fre was yfallen is into thraldom,

---

87. trinen *U* : *X* turnen   **104.** *XU* creaunt
106. *X* lordeyne

---

84. 'Despite his protests he was then forced . . .' Longeus was asked to do
what none else would do, to deliver the last blow (though Jesus was already
dead), his blindness being his defence.

104. '(Death) acknowledges himself defeated in the running of the course
(the jousting).'

105. 'When this darkness is passed, Death shall be vanquished.' The darkness
is that of line 61. Services in these three days were often held in darkness, *in
tenebris*.

And alle youre childerne cherles, cheve shall thei nevere,
Ne have lordschipe in londe, ne no londe tulye,
And as bareyne be, and by usure libbe,   110
The which is lif that oure lord in all lawes defendeth.
Now ben youre gode dayes ydon, as Daniel of yow telleth,
When Crist thorw croos overcam, youre kyngdom sholde to-
        cleve.
    Cum venerit sanctus sanctorum, cessabit unctio vestra'.
    What for fere of this ferly and of the false Jewes
I withdrow in that derkenesse to *descendit ad inferna*,   115
And there I saw sothly, *secundum scripturas*,
Out of the west, as it were, a wenche, as me thouhte,
Cam walkynge in the way, to hell-ward she lokede.
Mercy hihte that mayde, a mylde thynge with-alle,
And a ful benyngne buyrde, and buxum of speche.   120
Here suster, as hit semede, cam softly walkynge
Evene oute of the eest, and westward she thouhte,
A comely creature and a clene, Treuthe she hihte;
For the vertue that her folewede, afered was she nevere.
When this maydenes metten, Mercy and Treuthe,   125
Ayther asked other of this grete wonder,
Of the dene and the derkenesse and how the day rowed,

---

108. thei *omitted in XU*

---

108. 'And all your children shall be bond-men, they shall never prosper.'
113f. 'When the Holy of Holies shall come, your anointing shall cease'
(cf. *Daniel* 9: 24–7).
116. '. . . according to the Scriptures.' The scriptural source for the debate
of the Four Daughters of God, which follows, is *Psalm* 85: 10: 'Mercy and
truth are met together; righteousness and peace have kissed each other.' The
debate was elaborately developed in the Middle Ages (see Owst, *Literature and
Pulpit*, pp. 90–92) as a means of explaining and justifying the doctrine of the
Atonement, within an allegorical framework. Langland's placing of it at this
point in the Christian narrative, however, is due to nothing more than his own
superb sense of drama.
117. *Out of the west.* The four daughters come from the four poles (see 122,
167, 170), perhaps in allusion to *Isaiah* 43: 6, and the two pairs from opposite
poles. There can be none of the usual symbolic significance in this (see 1.14n,
2.112n), though there is appropriateness in having Truth and Righteousness
come from the colder quarters of the north and east.

And which a lihte and a leem lay bifore helle.
 'I have ferly of this fare, in faith,' seide Treuthe,
'And am wendynge to wyte what this wonder meneth'.   130
   'Have no merveyle ther-of', quod Mercy, 'murthe hit bitokneth.
A mayde that hoteth Marie, a moder withouten felynge
Of eny kynde creature, conceyved thorw speche
And grace of the holy gost, wax grete with childe,
Withouten wommane wem into this world brouhte hym;   135
And that my tale is trewe, I take god to witnesse.
Sethe this barn was ybore ben thritty wynter ypassed,
Deyede and deth tholede this day aboute mydday;
And that is the cause of this clips that over-closeth now the
       sonne,
In menynge that man shal fro merkenesse be ydrawe,   140
The while this lihte and this lowe shal Lucifer ablende.
For patriarkes and prophetes han preched her-of ofte,
That was tynt thorw tre, tre shal hit wynne,
And that deth down brouhte, deth shal releve'.
   'That thow tellest', quod Treuthe, 'is bote a tale of Waltrot!   145
For Adam and Eve, and Abraham with othere,
Patriarkes and prophetes that in peyne liggen,
Leve hit nevere that yone liht hem alofte brynge
Ne have hem out of helle—holde thy tonge, Mercy,
Hit is bote truyfle that thow tellest; I, Treuthe, wot the
       sothe,   150
That thyng that ones is in helle out cometh hit nevere.
Job the parfit patriarke repreveth thy sawes:
       Quia in inferno nulla est redempcio'.

143-4. 'What was lost through the tree of Knowledge should be won back
through the Cross, and those that death cast down should be lifted up again
by (Christ's) death.' The lines echo the hymn, *Pange, lingua, gloriosi* ('Sing, my
tongue, the glorious battle', *A & M* 97), sung in the Veneration of the Cross
on Good Friday.
   145. *a tale of Waltrot:* an idle, foolish story. For a suggested etymology, see
Skeat's note.
   152f. 'There is no release from hell' (cf. *Job* 7: 9, 'He that goeth down to
the grave shall come up no more').

Thenne Mercy ful myldely mouthed this wordes:
'Thorw experiense', quod she, 'I hope they shal ben saved;
For venym for-doth venym, ther feche I evydence   155
That Adam and Eve have shullen bote.
For of alle fretynge venymes the vilest is the scorpioun;
May no medecyne amende the place there he styngeth,
Til he, ded, ydo therto, and thenne he destruyeth
The ferste venemouste thorw vertu of hymsulve.   160
And so shal this deth for-do, I dar my lyf legge,
Al that Deth and the devel dede formest to Eve.
And riht as the gylour thorw gyle bygiled man formest,
So shal grace, that bigan al, maken a gode ende
And bigile the gilour, and that is a gode sleythe: 165
    Ars ut artem falleret'.
'Now suffre we', saide Treuthe, 'I se, as me thynketh,
Out of the nype of the north, nat ful fer hennes,
Rihtwisnesse come rennynge. Reste we the while,
For she wot more then we—she was ar we bothe'.
'That is soth', saide Mercy, 'and I se here bi southe   170
Where cometh Pees pleiynge, in pacience yclothed;
Love hath coveyted here longe—leve I non othere
Bote Love have ysente her som lettre, what this liht bymeneth
That over-hoveth helle thus; she us shal telle'.
    Whenne Pees, in pacience yclothed, aproched her ayther
        other,
                                                            175
Rihtwisnesse reverenced Pees in here rich clothyng
And preyede Pees to tellen to what place she sholde,

---

155. 'For one poison expels another—from that I draw my evidence ...'
159–60. 'Till it be dead, and then, applied to the sore place, it dispels the first poison through the self-same power.' The notion is a familiar one in medieval natural histories which, by their allegorically evaluative rather than descriptive nature, are always available as repositories of 'examples' and similes. See 10.42n and, for a popular book on the bestiaries, T. H. White, *The Book of Beasts* (London, 1954).
163–5. This word-play (*permutatio*) is a favourite one in Middle English. Cf. 381, below.
165f. 'Art to deceive art' (from the hymn, *Pange, lingua, gloriosi*, 143n above).
166. 'Now let us be quiet.'
176. *Rihtwisnesse* is Justice, *Pees* the spirit of reconciliation.

And here gay garnementes, wham she gladie thouhte?
'My wil is to wende', quod Pees, 'and welcomen hem alle
That many day myhte I nat se, for merkenesse of synne.   180
Adam and Eve and other mo in helle,
Moises and many moo, mercy shal synge,
And I shal daunce ther-to—do thow so, suster!
For Jesus joustede wel, joy bigynneth dawe.
    Ad vesperum demorabitur fletus, et ad matutinum leticia.
Love, that is my lemman, such lettres he me sente   185
That Mercy, my suster, and I mankynde shal save,
And that god hath forgyve and graunted to alle mankynde,
Mercy and me to maynprisen hem alle;
And that Crist hath converted the kynde of rihtwisnesse
Into pees and pyte, of his puyr grace.   190
Loo, here the patente!' quod Pees, '*in pace in idipsum*—
And that this dede shal duyre—*dormiam et requiescam*'.
  'Ravest thou?' quod Rihtwisnesse, 'or thou art riht dronke!
Levest thow that yone lihte unlouke myhte helle
And save mannes soule? suster, wene hit nevere!   195
At the bigynnynge of the world, god gaf the dom hymsulve
That Adam and Eve and al his issue
Sholde deye down-riht and dwellen in payne evere
Yf that thei touchen that tre and of the fruyt eten.
Adam afturward, agenes his defense,   200
Freet of the fruyt and forsoke, as hit were,
The love of oure lord and his lore bothe,
And folewede that the fend tauhte and his flesch will,
Ageynes resoun and rihtwisnesse; recorde hit with treuthe
That her peyne is perpetuel—no preyer may hem helpe.   205
Forthy let hem chewe as they chose, and chyde we nat, sustres,

---

198. dwellen *U* : *X* down   **206.** let *omitted in XU*

---

178. 'And whom she was intending to make glad, with her gay clothes.'
  184f. 'Weeping may endure for a night, but joy cometh in the morning' (*Psalm* 30: 5).
  191–2. 'Look, here is the warrant of release: "In peace I will both lay me down"—and, to prove that the deed of gift is permanently binding—"and rest secure" ' (*Psalm* 4: 8). This psalm was sung in Matins on Holy Saturday.
  200. '. . . contrary to the prohibition laid upon him.'
  F*

For hit is boteles bale, the byte that they eten'.

'And I shal preye', quod Pees, 'here payne mot have ende,
And that her wo into wele mot wende at the laste.
For hadde they wist of no wo, wele hadde thay nat knowen;   210
For no wiht wot what wele is, that nevere wo soffrede,
Ne what is hot hunger, that hadde nevere defaute.
Who couthe kyndeliche whit colour discreve,
Yf all the world were whit, or swan-whit all thynges?
Yf no nyhte ne were, no man, I leve,   215
Sholde ywyte witterly what day is to mene;
Ne hadde god ysoffred of som other then hymsulve,
He hadde nat wist witterly where deth were sour or swete.
For sholde nevere right riche man, that lyveth in rest and in
       hele,
Ywyte what wo is, ne were the deth of kynde.   220
So god, that bigan al, of his gode wille
Bycam man of a mayde, mankynde to save,
And soffred to be sold to se the sorwe of deynge,
The which unknytteth alle care and comsyng is of reste.
For til moreyne mete with us, I may hit wel avowe,   225
Ne wot no wyht, as I wene, what is ynow to mene.
    Forthy god of his godenesse the furste man Adam
Sette hym in solace furste and in sovereyne murthe;
And sethe he soffrede hym to synne, sorwe to fele,
To wyte what wele was ther-thorw, kyndeliche to knowe.   230
And after, god auntred hymsulve and tok Adames kynde,
To wyte what he hath soffred in thre sundry places,

---

207. 'For the bite that they took is a disaster for which there is no remedy.'
212. 'Nor can he know what sharp hunger is, if he was never short of
food.'
217–18. 'God could never have known for certain what death was like if
he had not been prepared to suffer at the hands of others than himself.' This
is an interesting extension of the argument for 'experience'.
220. '... were it not part of his nature that he should die.'
224. A vivid proleptic or post-redemptive view of death. Cf. *Macbeth* II.
ii. 38.
225–6. 'Till we have experienced plague (and famine) ... we do not know
the meaning of "enough".'

Bothe in hevene and in erthe—and now to helle he thenketh,
To wyte what al wo is, that wot of alle joye.
    Omnia probate; quod bonum est tenete.
So hit shal fare bi this folke: here folye and here synne   235
Shal lere hem what love is, and lisse withouten ende.
For wot no wiht what werre is, ther as pees regneth,
Ne what is witterliche wele, til wel-a-way hym teche'.
    Thenne was ther a wihte with two brode yes,
Boke hihte that beau-pere, a bolde man of speche.   240
'By godes body', quod this Book, 'I wole bere witnesse,
Tho that this barn was ybore, ther blased a sterre,
That alle the wyse of the world in o wit acordede
That such a barn was ybore in Bethleem the citee
That mannes soule sholde save and synne distruye.   245
And all the elementis', quod the Boke, 'here-of bereth
    witnesse.
That he was god that al wrouhte, the welkene furste shewede:
Tho that weren in hevene token *stella comata*
And tenden hit as a torche to reverensen his burthe;
The lihte folewede the lord into the lowe erthe.   250
The water witnesseth that he was god, for he wente on hym drye:
Peter the apostel parceyved his gate
And, as he wente on the water, wel hym knewe, and saide,
    "*Domine, jube me venire ad te super aquas*".
And lo, how the sonne gan louke here lihte in heresulve
When she saw hym soffre, that sonne and se made!   255
Lo, how the erthe, for hevynesse that he wolde soffre,
Quakid as a quyk thyng, and also to-quasch the roches!
Loo, helle myhte nat holde, bote opened, tho god tholede,

234f. 'Prove all things; hold fast that which is good' (1 *Thess.* 5: 21).
238. 'Nor what true happiness is, till he has learnt to cry "Alas!" '
241. The debate is wound up with Scripture's evidence of the divinity of Jesus Christ, based, as he says (246), on the witness of the elements: air (247), water (251), fire (254) and earth (256).
242. ther blased *U* : *X* that blased as
248-9. 'The angels in heaven took a blazing star (comet) and kindled it like a torch in reverence of his birth.'
253f. 'Lord, bid me come unto thee on the water' (*Matt.* 14: 28).

And lette out Symondes sones to sen hym honge on rode.
> *Non visurum se mortem.*

And now shal Lucifer leve hit, thogh hym loth thynke;   260
For Jesus as a geaunt with a gyn cometh yonde
To breke and to bete adoun all that ben agaynes hym
And to have out alle of hem that hym liketh.
And yut I, Boke, wol be brente, bote he aryse to lyve
And comforte alle his kyn and out of care brynge   265
And alle the Jewene joye unjoynen and unlouken,
And bote they reverense this resurexioun, be ylost lyf and
> soule!'

'Soffre we', sayde Treuthe, 'I here and se bothe
A spirit speketh to helle and bit to unspere the gates.
> *Attollite portas.*'

A vois loude in that liht to Lucifer saide: 270
'*Principes* of this place, prest undo this gates,
For here he cometh with croune, the kynge of all glorie!'
> Thenne syhed Satoun and saide to helle,
'Suche a lyht agenes oure leve Lazar hit fette;
Care and combraunce is come to us all.   275
Yf this kyng come in, mankynde wol he fecche

---

260. hit *U* : *X* lihte

259. In the *Gospel of Nicodemus* the two sons of Simeon are raised from the dead at the moment of Christ's death (see the ME verse translation of Nicodemus, ed. W. H. Hulme, EETS, ES 100, 1907, line 1093), and it is they who describe the harrowing of hell. Simeon is the 'just and devout man' of *Luke* 2:25, to whom it was revealed 'that he should not see death' (259f.) before he had seen Christ.

264. 'And I, even I, the Book, will gladly be burnt if he does not rise again to life.'

269f. 'Lift up your heads, O ye gates; (even lift them up, ye everlasting doors, and the King of glory shall come in)' (*Psalm* 24:9, also sung on Holy Saturday). The narrative of Christ's descent into Hell to redeem the souls of the righteous is from Nicodemus. Langland's treatment may be compared with (and may have been influenced by) the powerful dramatization of the event in the Mystery-cycles (especially the York play), where it is called the 'Harrowing' (i.e. harrying) of Hell.

274. 'It was a light like this that heralded the fetching away of Lazarus, without so much as a "By your leave".'

And lede hit ther Lazar is, and lihtliche me bynde.
Patriarkes and prophetes han parled her-of longe,
That such a lord and a lihte shal lede hem alle hennes.
Ac arise up, Ragamoffyn, and areche me alle the barres   280
That Belial thy beel-syre beet with thy dame,
And I shal lette this lord and his liht stoppe.
Ar we thorw brihtnesse be blent, go barre we the gates.
Cheke and cheyne we and uch a chine stoppe,
That no liht lepe in at louer ne at loupe.   285
Astarot, hot out, and have out oure knaves,
Coltyng and al his kyn, the catel to save.
Brimston boylaunt brennyng out-cast hit
Al hot on here hedes that entrith ney the walles.
Setteth bowes of brake and brasene gonnes   290
And sheteth out shot ynow his sheltrom to blende.
Set Mahond at the mangonel and mulle-stones throweth,
And with crokes and with kalketrappes acloye we hem uchone!'
    'Lustneth', quod Lucifer, 'for I this lord knowe,
Bothe this lord and this lihte, ys longe ygo I knewe hym.   295

---

283. blent *U* : *X* brente   **287.** catel *P* : *XU* car
292. *XU* mangrel
293. *first* with *omitted in XU*; acloye *P* : *XU* and cloye

---

280. *Ragamoffyn:* a fanciful name for a demon. This passage (280–93), with its lively detail, is an addition in C, of a rather unexpected kind.

284-5. 'Let us check his course, and chain our doors and stop up every chink, so that no light can get in at louver nor loop-hole.' A louver was a lantern-like turret in the roof of a hall to let smoke out and light in.

286. Ashtaroth, another demon, originally the Phoenician moon-goddess. Hell, as in Milton, is peopled with pagan deities.

287. *Coltyng:* another demon (? perhaps from *colt*, with its association with wantonness and lechery).

290. *bowes of brake:* cross-bows with a winding mechanism to give tension.

292-3. 'Set Mahomet at the catapult, to hurl mill-stones, and let us harass them with hooked staves and caltrops' (spiked iron balls used to maim horses in battle). Christ has no *sheltrom*, but Satan is carried away by the prospect of battle.

294. Lucifer is distinguished from Satan in these scenes, probably for dramatic purposes, Lucifer representing the fallen angel, Satan the totally corrupted spirit of evil, in accordance with an exegetic tradition established by St. Jerome in his Commentary on *Isaiah* 14: 12.

May no deth this lord dere, ne no develes quentyse,
And where he wole, is his way—ac war hym of the perelles:
Yf he reve me of my rihte, he robbeth me of his maistrie.
For bi riht and by resoun, the renkes that ben here
Body and soule beth myne, bothe gode and ille.   300
For hymsulve said hit, that sire is of hevene,
That Adam and Eve and al his issue
Sholde deye with dole and here dwelle evere
Yf thei touched a tre or tok ther-of an appul.
Thus this lord of liht such a lawe made,   305
And sethe he is a lele lord, I leve that he wol nat
Reven us of oure riht, sethe resoun hem dampnede.   •
And sethe we han ben sesed sevene thousand wynter,
And nevere was ther-ageyne, and now wolde bigynne,
Thenne were he unwrast of his worde, that witnesse is of
    treuthe'.   310
    'That is soth', saide Satoun, 'bote I me sore doute,
For thow gete hem with gyle and his gardyn breke,
Ageyne his love and his leve on his londe yedest,
Not in forme of a fende bote in forme of an addre
And entisedest Eve to eten by here one—   315
    Ve soli!—
And byhihtest here and hym aftur to knowe,
As two godes, with god, bothe gode and ille.
Thus with treson and with tricherie thow troyledest hem bothe
And dust hem breke here buxumnesse thorw fals bihestes,

297-8. 'And it is his custom to go just where he wants—but he'd better beware of the risks: if he robs me of what is mine by right, he does so by mere force.'

308-10. 'And since we have had them as our legal property for seven thousand years, and no-one ever complained, and now they suddenly start raising objections, he would be going back on his word, he who is the very embodiment of truth.' 'Seven thousand' is conventionally arbitrary; the usual figure is nearer four (and Archbishop Usher's definitive calculation, 4004 years, from Creation to Christ's birth).

315f. 'Woe to him that is alone (when he falleth)' (*Eccles.* 4: 10).

316-17. 'And promised them both that like two gods they would afterwards have knowledge, with God, of good and evil.'

And so haddest hem out, and hiddere at the laste.   320
Hit is nat graythly ygete, ther gyle is the rote.
   And god wol nat be gyled', quod Gobelyne, 'ne by-japed.
We han no trewe title to hem, for thy tresoun hit maketh.
   Forthy I drede me', quod the devel, 'laste treuthe wol hem
      fecche.
And as thowe bigyledest godes ymages in goynge of an addre,   325
So hath god bigiled us alle in goynge of a weye.
   For god hath go', quod Gobelyn, 'in gome liknesse
This thritty wynter, as I wene, and wente aboute and prechede.
I have assayled hym with synne, and som tyme I askede
Where he were god or godes sone? He gaf me short answere.   330
Thus hath he trolled forth like a tydy man this two and thritty
      wynter;
And whenne I saw that hit was so, I sotilede how I myhte
Lette hem that lovede hym nat, laste they wolde hym martre.
I wolde have lenghed his lyf, for I leved, yf he deyede,
That if his soule hider cam, hit sholde shende us alle.   335
For the body, whiles hit on bones yede, aboute was hit evere
To lere men to be lele, and uch man to lovye other;
The which lyf and lawe, be hit longe y-used,
Hit shal undo us develes and down bryngen us all.
   And now I se where his soule cometh sylinge hiderward   340
With glorie and with gret lihte—god hit is, I wot wel.
I rede we flee', quod the fende, 'faste all hennes;
For us were bettere nat to be, then abyde in his sihte.
For thy lesinges, Lucifer, we losten furst oure joye,
And out of hevene hidere thy pryde made us falle;   345
For we leved on thy lesynges, ther losten we oure blysse.
And now, for a later lesynge that thow lowe til Eve,

---

337. be *omitted in* X
341. gret *omitted in* X   346–7. ther . . . lesynge *omitted in XU*

---

322. *Gobelyne*: another name for Satan.
332–3. The reference is to the dream that Satan sent to Pilate's wife, warning her to persuade her husband not to condemn Christ. This legend grew from *Matt.* 27: 19; it was extensively developed in the Mystery-cycles.
336. 'This man, while he went about in human form, was always busy . . .'

We han ylost oure lordschipe a londe and in helle.

> *Nunc princeps huius mundi ejicietur foras'*.

Sethe that Satan myssaide thus foule

Lucifer for his lesynges, leve I non other   350

Bote oure lord at the laste lyares here rebuke

And wyte hem al the wrechednesse that wrouhte is her on erthe.

Beth ywar, ye wyse clerkes and witty men of lawe,

That ye belyen nat this lewed men, for at the laste David

Witnesseth in his writynges what is lyares mede: 355

> *Odisti omnes qui operantur iniquitatem, et perdes omnes qui*
> *loquuntur mendacium.*

(A litel I over-leep for lesynges sake,

That I ne sygge as I saw, suynde my teme!)

For efte that lihte bade unlouke, and Lucifer answerede:

'What lord artow?' quod Lucifer. A voys aloude saide:

'The lord of myhte and of mayne, that made alle thynges.   360

Dukes of this demme place, anon undo this gates,

That Crist may come in, the kynges sone of hevene'.

And with that breth, helle breek, with alle Belialles barres;

For eny wey or warde, wyde open the gates.

Patriarkes and profetes, *populus in tenebris*,   365

Songen with seynt Johan '*Ecce agnus dei!*'

Lucifer loke ne myhte, so liht hym ablende;

And tho that oure lord lovede forth with that liht flowen.

---

358. and Lucifer answerede *omitted in XU*

348f. 'Now shall the prince of this world be cast out' (*John* 12: 31).

349–57. A typical little C-text digression.

355f. 'Thou hatest all workers of iniquity. Thou shalt destroy them that speak leasing' (*Psalm* 5: 5–6).

356–7. 'I digressed a little for the sake of saying something about lying, neglecting to pursue my main theme of saying what I saw.'

359–60. See *Psalm* 24: 8.

364. 'For all that any man or guard could do, the gates burst wide open.'

365. 'The people that walked in darkness (have seen a great light)' (*Isaiah* 9: 2, cf. *Matt.* 4: 16): the most significant of all prophecies of Advent, and with special application to the harrowing of Hell.

366. 'Behold the Lamb of God' (*John* 1: 36), John the Baptist's address to Jesus.

'Lo me here', quod oure lord, 'lyf and soule bothe,
For alle synful soules to save oure bothe rihte.   370
Myne they were and of me, I may the beter hem clayme.
Althouh resoun recordede, and rihte of mysulve,
That if they ete the appul, alle sholde deye,
I bihihte hem nat here, helle, for evere.
For the dedly synne that they dede, thi deseite hit made;   375
With gyle thow hem gete, agaynes all resoun.
For in my palays paradys, in persone of an addere,
Falsliche thou fettest there that me biful to loke,
Byglosedest hem and bigiledest hem and my gardyne breke,
Ageynes my love and my leve. The olde lawe techeth   380
That gylours be bigiled and in here gyle falle,
And who-so hit out a mannes eye or elles his fore-teth,
Or eny manere membre maymeth other herteth,
The same sore shal he have that eny so smyteth.
    Dentem pro dente, et oculum pro oculo.
So lyf shal lyf lete, ther lyf hath lyf anyented,   385
So that lyf quyte luf, the olde lawe hit asketh.
Ergo, soule shal soule quyte, and synne to synne wende,
And al that men mys-dede, I, man, to amenden hit;
And that deth for-dede, my deth to releve,
And bothe quykie and quyte that queynte was thorw synne,   390
And gyle be bigyled, thorw grace, at the laste.
    Ars ut artem falleret.

---

378. thou *omitted in XU*   381. be *omitted in XU*; in *om. in X*
385. lete U : X lede; X anended   391. be *omitted in XU*

369–70. 'Here I am, in body and spirit together, to claim our right to both (body and spirit) on behalf of all sinful souls.'

375. *made*: caused, brought about.

378. 'There you took away by deceit that which it was my job to look after.'

384f. 'Tooth for tooth, and eye for eye' (*Ex.* 21: 24; *Matt.* 5: 38).

385–8. 'So a living man must lose his life wherever that man has destroyed a life, so that one life may pay for another, as the Old Law demands. And so, in this case, one soul must pay for another, one sin [the Crucifixion] go to balance another [the Fall], and I, a man, make amends for man's misdoing.'

391f. See 165f., above.

So leve hit nat, Lucifer, ageynes the lawe I feche
Here eny synful soule sovereynliche by maistrie,
Bote thorw riht and thorw resoun raunsome here myn lege.
  Non veni solvere legem, sed adimplere.
So that with gyle was gete, thorw grace is now ywonne.   395
And as Adam and alle thorwe a tre deyede,
Adam and alle thorw a tre shal turne to lyve.
And now bygynneth thy gyle agayne on the to turne
And my grace to growe ay wyddere and wyddere.
The bitternesse that thow hast browe, now brouk hit thysulve; 400
That art doctour of deth, drynke that thow madest!
  For I that am lord of lyf, love is my drynke,
And for that drynke todaye I deyede, as hit semede.
Ac I wol drynke of no dische, ne of deep clergyse,
Bote of comune coppes, alle Cristene soules;   405
Ac thy drynke worth deth, and depe helle thy bolle.
I fauht so, me fursteth yut, for mannes soule sake.
  Sicio.
May no pyement ne pomade ne presiouse drynkes
Moiste me to the fulle ne my furste slakke
Til the ventage falle in the vale of Josophat,   410
And drynke riht rype must, *resurreccio mortuorum.*
And thenne shal I come as kyng, with croune and with angeles,
And have out of helle alle mennes soules.

394f. 'I am not come to destroy the law, but to fulfil' (*Matt.* 5: 17). Hence the scrupulous bargaining in terms of the Old Law, though that law is transcended in its fulfilment.

400-1. 'Now yourself enjoy the bitter drink that you have brewed; you, the physician that administered death, must now drink your own medicine.'

402-13. From the image of the drink of death, with its allusion to the bitter drink offered to Jesus on the cross, grows this magnificent elaboration of the image of the drink of love and life, of Christ thirsting for man's love.

404-5. 'I do not seek my drink from the fine bowls of profound learning, but from the homely cups of all Christian souls.'

407f. 'I thirst' (*John* 19: 28).

410-11. 'Till the time of vintage in the vale of Jehoshaphat [the future scene of the resurrection of mankind, from *Joel* 3: 2, 12–13], when I shall drink the ripe new wine [*must*] of the resurrection of the dead.'

Fendes and fendekynes byfore me shal stande
And be at my biddynge, at blisse or at payne.   415
Ac to be merciable to man thenne, my kynde asketh,
For we beth brethrene of o blod, ac nat in baptisme alle.
Ac alle that beth myn hole bretherene, in blod and in baptisme,
Shal nevere in helle eft come, be he ones oute.
    Tibi soli peccavi, et malum contra te feci, &c.
Hit is nat used on erthe to hangen eny felones   420
Ofter then ones, thogh they were tretours.
And yf the kynge of the kyngdom come in the tyme
Ther a thief tholie sholde deth other jewyse,
Lawe wolde he yove hym lyf, and he loked on hym.
And I, that am kynge over kynges, shal come such a tyme   425
Ther that dom to the deth dampneth alle wikkede;
And if lawe wol I loke on hem, hit lith in my grace
Where they deye or dey nat, dede they nevere so ille.
Be hit enythyng abouhte, the boldenesse of here synne,
I may do mercy of my rihtwysnesse and alle myn wordes trewe.   430
    For holy writ wol that I be wreke of hem that wrouhte ille,
As *nullum malum impunitum, et nullum bonum irremuneratum.*
And so of alle wykkede I wol here take venjaunce.
And yut my kynde, in my kene ire, shal constrayne my will—

430. I *U* : *X* Or   **434.** in *U* : *X* and

---

417. *nat in baptisme:* referring to those who liv.d under the old law.
419f. 'Against thee, thee only, have I sinned, and done this evil in thy sight'
(*Psalm* 51 : 4). Therefore Christ's forgiveness cancels the debt.
420–4. A criminal was not hanged again if the first hanging failed, especially
if the king were at hand to grant a personal pardon. A famous instance at
Leicester in 1363 probably prompted Langland's use of the secular analogy.
424. 'The law would require that he should grant him a reprieve, if he was
there to see him.'
429. 'If the greatest of their sins be already fully paid for' (i.e. by my sacrifice).
It is as if Christ were evolving, through his own compassionate meditation,
the doctrine of salvation through grace, turning the Last Judgment into a day
of mercy not of wrath.
432. '(He leaves) no evil unpunished, and no good unrewarded' (from the
De Contemptu Mundi of Innocent III, a famous treatise of ascetic repudiation
of the world, by the most powerful of all medieval popes, d. 1216).
434. 'And yet, in the fierceness of my wrath, my merciful nature shall
contradict my will.'

Domine, ne in furore tuo arguas me, neque in ira tua
        corripias me—
To be merciable to monye of my halve-bretherene.   435
For blod may se blod bothe a-furst and a-cale,
Ac blod may nat se blod blede, bote hym rewe.'—
        Audivi archana verba, que non licet homini loqui.—
'Ac my rihtwysnesse and rihte shal regnen in helle,
And mercy and mankynde bifore me in hevene.
For I were an unkynde kyng, bote I my kyn helpe,   440
And namliche at such a nede, that nedes helpe asketh.
        Non intres in judicium cum servo tuo, domine.
    Thus by lawe', quod oure lord, 'lede I wol fro hennes
Tho that I lovye and leved in my comynge.
Ac for the lesynge that thow low, Lucifer, til Eve,
Thow shalt abyye bittere', quod god, and bonde hym with
        chaynes.   445
Astarot and alle othere hidden hem in hernes,
They dorste nat loke on oure lord, the leste of hem alle,
Bote leten hym lede forth which hym luste and leve which hym
        likede.
    Many hundret of angels harpeden tho and songen,
        Culpat caro, purgat caro, regnat deus dei caro.
Thenne piped Pees of poetes a note: 450

434f. 'O Lord, rebuke me not in thy wrath: neither chasten me in thy hot
displeasure' (*Psalm* 38: 1).

436–7. 'A man may see his kin thirsty and cold, but he may not see them
bleed without taking pity.'

437. 'I heard unspeakable words, which it is not lawful for a man to utter'
(2 *Cor.* 12: 4). Langland transfers Paul's words, of the man caught up into
paradise, to himself, indicating the limits to which his vision of Christ's
redemptive mercy can be taken. Dante likewise falls back speechless at the end
of the *Paradiso* (xxxiii. 142).

441. 'And especially at such a time of need, when men must needs cry for help.'

441f. 'Enter not into judgment with thy servant, O Lord' (*Psalm* 143: 2).

445. 'You shall pay for it sorely.'

449f. 'The flesh sins, the flesh atones for sin, the flesh of God reigns as God.'
From the hymn *Æterne rex altissime* ('O Lord most high, eternal King', *A & M*
144), sung on Ascension day.

'*Clarior est solito post maxima nebula Phebus:*
Post inimicitias clarior est amor.
Aftur sharpest shoures', quod Pees, 'most shene is the sonne;
Is no wedere warmere then aftur watry cloudes,
Ne no love levere, ne no levere frendes,   455
Then aftur werre and wrake, when love and pees ben maistres.
Was nevere werre in this world, ne wykkeder envye,
That Love, and hym luste, to lauhynge brouhte,
And Pees thorw pacience alle perelles stopede'.
    'Trewes', quod Treuthe, 'thow tellest us soth, by Jesus!   460
Cluppe we in covenaunt and uch of us kusse othere!'
    'And lat no peple', quod Pees,' parceyve that we chydde,
For inposible is no thynge to hym that is almyhty'.
    'Thowe saiste soth', saide Rihtwisnesse, and reverentliche
        she custe
Pees, and Pees here *per secula seculorum.*   465
    Misericordia et veritas obviaverunt sibi; justicia et pax osculate
        sunt.
Treuthe trompede tho, and song '*Te deum laudamus*',
And thenne lutede Love in a loude note,
    '*Ecce quam bonum et quam jocundum est habitare fratres in*
        unum!'

Til the day dawed thes damoyseles caroled,
That men rang to the resureccioun, and riht with that I wakede,

464. she *P* : *X* here

451–2. 'The sun is wont to be brighter after the darkest clouds; and love
stronger after strife.' No source is known for these lines, but they embroider
one of the most familiar of medieval 'topics'.
461. 'Let us embrace in token of agreement.'
465. '. . . world without end.'
465f. See 116n, above.
467f. 'Behold, how good and how pleasing it is for brethren to dwell
together in unity' (*Psalm* 133 : 1).
469. Langland awakens to the ringing of bells on Easter morning, a return
to time which is also an assertion of the timelessness of the vision. Vision and
reality are at last united in a manner strikingly contrary to the earlier, weary
cry of 10.89–90.

And calde Kitte my wyf and Calote my douhter: 470
'Arise, and go reverense godes resureccioun,
And crepe to the cros on knees and kusse hit for a jewel
And rihtfullokest a relyk, noon richere on erthe.
For godes blessed body hit bar for oure bote,
And hit a-fereth the fende, for such is the myhte,   475
May no grisly gost glyde ther hit shaddeweth!'

At the Easter Mass, the poet falls asleep, and in his dream Conscience explains to him how Christ's life encompassed in itself Dowel, Dobet and Dobest, the last represented in his resurrection and the promise of redemption. The promise of grace descends as the paraclete upon Piers Plowman (Peter, the rock on which the Church is founded), and the founding of the Church is portrayed allegorically in ploughing terms—the plough is drawn by the four evangelists, the seeds are the cardinal virtues, and the barn for the matured corn is Unity or Holy Church. Conscience calls the people to a celebratory feast of the Eucharist, but there are signs already that cupidinous self is about to reassert itself, even within Holy Church.

The dreamer wakes and meets Need, who argues that Necessity knows no law of conscience or virtue and that people can only be expected to think of themselves first. In a final vision, the dreamer sees the coming of Antichrist.

16. The Coming of Antichrist (XXIII. 175–386, end)

Whenne Nede hadde undernome me thus, anon I ful aslepe,
And mette ful merveylousely that in mannes forme
Auntecrist cam thenne, and al the crop of treuthe

1. me omitted in XU

470. See 3.2 and note. This is Langland's only reference to his daughter Calote (Colette).
472. 'Creeping to the cross', and kissing it, were enjoined as devotional and penitential exercises, especially for Good Friday.
3. The name of Antichrist is derived from the Epistles of St. John (1 John 2.22; 2 John 7), where it is applied to those who deny the divinity of Christ. The concept was enriched by association with the demoniacal beasts of apocalyptic writing (Dan. 7; Rev. 13) and with Paul's 'son of perdition' (1 Thess. 2: 3), and out of this emerged the medieval belief in Antichrist as a kind of 'incarnation' of Satan, human, and yet the embodiment of evil. His coming

Turned hit tyd up-so-down, and over-tulde the rote,
And made fals sprynge and sprede and spede menne nedes,   5
In uch a contrey ther he cam, kutte awey treuthe
And garte gyle growe there, as he a god were.
   Freres folewed that fende, for he yaf hem copes,
And religious reverensed hym and rongen here belles
And al the covent cam to welcome the tyraunt,   10
And alle hise as wel as hym, save onelich foles,
The whiche fooles were wel gladere to deye
Then to lyve lengere, sethe leautee was so rebuked
And a fals fende Auntecrist over all folke regnede.
And that were mylde men and holy, that no meschief dradden,   15
Defyede all falsnesse and folke that hit usede,
And what kyng that hem confortede, knowynge here gyle,
Thei corsede, and here consail, were hit clerke or lewed.
   Auntecrist hadde thus sone hondredes at his baner
And Pryde hit bar baldly aboute,   20
With a lord that lyveth after likyng of body,
That cam agen Consience, that kepar was and gyour
Over kynde cristene and cardinale vertues.
   'I consail', quod Consience tho, 'cometh with me, ye foles,
In to Unite holi-churche, and halde we us there   25

---

5. spede *U* : *X* speke   **12.** The whiche fooles *omitted in XU*

---

was to inaugurate the tyranny of the Last Days, which in turn would precede
the Second Coming of Christ. The name Antichrist was thus often applied, in
reference to the prophecy, to any particularly wicked king or pope, though
the term was also used in the more abstract way, as here.
  5. 'And made falsehood grow and spread, so to satisfy men's desires (of the
false things of the world)'.
  11. 'And (to welcome) all Antichrist's followers, as well as him, except only
for fools' (i.e. ironically, the innocent faithful).
  15. 'Those (fools) were gentle, holy men, who feared no dangers.'
  20. Pride bears the banner, as the chief of the seven Deadly Sins. Langland's
vision of the coming of Antichrist takes the traditional form of a *psychomachia*,
or battle of the vices and virtues, with the vices besieging the fortress of Unity,
the Church.
  21. This *lord* plays the role of 'Pride of Life', familiar in morality plays, the
man dedicated to the pleasures of this world.
  24. *foles:* referring to the usage in line 11, above.

And crye we to Kynde that he come and defende us
Foles fro this fendes lymes, for Peres love the Plouhman;
And crye we on al the comune that thei come to Unite
And ther abyde and bikere ageyn Beliales childrene.'

Kynde Consience tho herde, and cam oute of the planetes   30
And sente forth his forreours, feveres and fluxes,
Cowhes and cardiacles, crampes and toth-aches,
Reumes and radegoundes and roynouse scabbes,
Byles and boches and brennynge aguwes;
Frenesyes and foule eveles, forageres of Kynde,   35
Hadde ypriked and preyede polles of peple;
Largeliche a legioun lees the lyf sone.

There was 'Harow!' and 'Help! here cometh Kynde,
With Deth that is dredful, to undon us alle!'
The lord that lyvede aftur lust tho aloud cryede   40
Aftur Conforte, a knyhte, come and beer his baner.
'Alarme! alarme!' quod that lord, 'uch lyf kepe his owene!'
Thenne mette thise men, ar munstrales myhte pype
And ar heroudes of armes hadden descreved lordes.

Elde the hore, he was in the vawwarde,   45
And bar the baner bifore Deth—bi riht he hit claymede.
Kynde cam aftur hym, with many kyne sores,
As pokkes and pestilences, and moche peple shente;
So Kynde thorw corupcions kulde ful mony.
Deth cam dryvyng aftur and al to duste paschte   50
Kynges and knyhtes, caysers and popes.
Lered ne lewed he lefte no man stande;

---

30. *oute of the planetes:* because the incidence of disease, in nature, was controlled by planetary influence. Nature's unexpected allies in the fight against Sin are Disease, Age and Death, since these reminders of mortality most surely bring man to his senses. But coercion is a desperate expedient, and no substitute for spiritual conviction, as Piers Plowman found earlier when he called in Hunger to discipline the people (Passus IX).

33–6. 'Colds and running sores and filthy scabs, boils and tumours and burning fevers, fits of madness and horrible illnesses—all these outriders of Nature had stabbed and afflicted the whole population.'

42. 'To arms! to arms! Every man for himself!'

44. 'Before the heralds had a chance to introduce the combatants by name and blazon', i.e. this battle is in earnest, not a chivalric exercise.

That he hitte evene, nevere stured aftur.
Many a lovly lady and here lemmanes knyhtes
Swowened and swelte for sorwe of dethes duntes.   55
   Consience of his cortesye tho Kynde he bisouhte
To sese and soffre, and se wher they wolde
Leve pryde priveyliche and be parfyt cristene.
And Kynde sesede tho, to se the peple amende.
   Fortune gan flateren thenne to fewe that were alyve   60
And bihihte hem long lyf, and Lecherye he sente
Amonges alle manere men, wedded and unwedded,
And gaderet a greet ost, alle agayn Consience.
This Lecherye leyde on with lauhyng chere
And with prive speche and paynted wordes,   65
And armed hym on ydelnesse and on hey berynge.
He bar a bowe on his hond, and many brode arwes,
Weren fythered with fayre biheste and many a fals treuthe,
And with untidy tales he tened ful ofte
Consience and his companye, of holy-churche the techares.   70
   Thenne cam Covetyse and caste how he myhte
Overcome Consience and cardinal vertues,
And armed hym in avarice and hungriliche lyvede.
His wepne was al wyles to wynnen and to hyden;
With glosynges and be gabbynges he gyled the peple.   75
Symonye hym suede to assaile Consience
And presed on the pope, and prelates thei made,
To holde with Auntecrist, here temperaltee to save;
And cam to the kynges consail as a kene baron
And knokked Consience in court bifore hem alle   80
And gert Gode-Faith fle and Fals to abyde
And baldeliche bar adoun, with many a brihte noble,

53. X hihte; nevere P : XU that evere

---

53. 'Those that he hit squarely never made another move.'
59. 'And Nature then relaxed its efforts, and waited to see whether people would behave better.' The failure of the people to respond to Nature's promptings is an allegory of the pattern that moralists saw in the Black Death and its aftermath.
64. 'This Lechery, he pressed into the attack with a smiling face.'
68. 'Feathered with fine promises and many false betrothals.'

Moche of the wyt and wisdom of Westministre-halle.
He jogged til a justice and justede in his ere
And over-tulde al his treuthe with 'Tak-this-on-amendement';   85
And in to the arches in haste he yede anon aftur
And turnede Syvyle into Symonye, and sethe he tok the official
And for a menever mantel he made leele matrimonye
Departen ar dethe come, and a devors shupte.
  'Allas!' quod Conscience tho, and cryede, 'Wolde Crist of his
     grace   90
That Coveytyse were cristene, that is so kene to fihte,
And bolde and abydynge, the while his bagge lasteth'.
  And thenne lowh Lyf, and lette dagge his clothes,
And armed hym in haste in harlotes wordes,
And helde Holinesse a jape, and Hendenesse a wastour,   95
And leet Leautee a cherl, and Lyare a freman;
Consience and conseil he counted hit folye.
Thus relyed Lyf for a litel fortune
And priketh forth with Pruyde—prayseth he no vertue
Ne careth nat how Kynde slowh, and shal come at the laste   100
And culle all erthely creature, save Consience one.
  Lyf lepte asyde and lauhte hym a lemman:
'Hele and I', quod he, 'and heynesse of herte
Shal do the nat drede nother Deth ne Elde,
And to foryete yowthe and yeve nat of synne'.   105

98. fortune *U* : *X* folye

---

83. *Westministre-halle:* where the law-courts were.
84–5. The image is that of a mock-joust, with the judge's ideas of truth and justice being overturned by the offer of a bribe to put things right.
86. *the arches:* the ecclesiastical court held at the church of St. Mary le Bow, in London, which was built on arches.
87–9. 'And made Civil law a matter of simony, and then gave a bribe to the court official, and, in return for the gift of a fur mantle, brought about the dissolution of a true marriage, and fixed up a divorce.' *Departen ar dethe come* alludes to the words of the marriage-service.
93. '... and had his clothes cut with jagged slits at the edge.' This extravagant fashion was much in vogue at the time.
96. 'And accounted loyalty a form of bondage, and lying the only true freedom.'

This likede Lyf, and his lemman Fortune,
And geten in here glorie a gadlyng at the laste,
One that moche wo wrouhte, Sleuthe was his name.
Sleuthe was wonder yerne, and sone was of age,
And wedded one Wanhope, a wenche of the stuyves;   110
Here syre was a sysour, that nevere swor treuthe,
One Tomme Two-tonge, ateynt at uch enqueste.
This Sleuthe was sley of werre, and a slynge made,
And throw drede of dispayr a doysayne myle aboute.

    For care Conscience tho cryede upon Elde   115
And bad hym fonde to fihte and afere Wanhope.
And Elde hente gode hope and hastiliche shrof hym
And wayved away Wanhope, and with Lyf he fihteth;
And Lyf fley for fere to Fisyk aftur helpe
And bisouhte hym of socour, and of here salve hadde,   120
And gaf hym golde, gode won, that gladde here hertes,
And they gyven hym agayne a glasene hove.
Lyf levede that lechecraft lette sholde Elde
And dryve awey Deth with dyas and drogges.

    And Elde auntered hym on Lyf, and at the laste he hitte   125
A fisician with a forred hod, that he ful in a palesye,
And ther deyede that doctour ar thre dayes aftur.
'Now I see', saide Lyf, 'that surgerie ne fysyke
May nat a myte avayle to medlen agen Elde'.
And in hope of his hele, gode herte he hente   130
And rode so to Revel, a ryche place and a merye,
(The compeny of Comfort men clepede hit som tyme),

---

108. The submission of Life to the attractions of worldly Fortune produces
a slothfulness in the works of the spirit which then issues in *Wanhope*, despair
of grace and amendment.

121-2. 'And gave him gold, in great plenty, which is a thing that gladdens
doctor's hearts, and they in return gave him a glass hood.' A 'glass hood' is a
proverbial metaphor for an imaginary protection, a 'cure' which is in fact worse
than useless.

125. 'Old Age ventured an attack on Life.' The abstraction 'Life' then
momentarily materializes as the 'life' of a physician.

130-2. Enjoying the pleasures of life puts away for a while thoughts of
growing old.

And Elde aftur hym, and over myn heved yede,
And made me balled bifore and bar on the crowne;
So harde he yede over myn heved, hit wol be sene evere!   135
    'Syre evele-taught Elde', quod I, 'unhende go with the!
Sennes whanne was the way over menne hevedes?
Haddest thow be hende,' quod I, 'thow wost have asked leve'.
    'Ye, leve, lordeyne!' quod he, and leide on me with age,
And hitte me under the ere—unnethe may I here.   140
He boffeted me aboute the mouthe and beet out my wang-teeth,
And gyved me in gowtes—I may nat go at large.
And of the wo that I was ynne, my wyf hadde reuthe,
And wisched wel witterly that I were in hevene,
For the lyme that she loved me fore, and leef was to fele   145
(A nyhtes, nameliche, when we naked were),
I ne myhte in none manere maken hit at here wille,
So Elde and she hit hadde for-bete.
    And as I sat in this sorwe, I saw how Kynde passede,
And Deth drow neyynge me, for drede gan I quaken   150
And cryede to Kynde out of care me brynge:
'Lo, how Elde the hore hath me byseye;
Awreke me, yif youre wille be, for I wolde be hennes'.
    'Yf thow wolde be wreke, wende in to Unite
And halde the there evere til I sende for the,   155
And loke thow conne som craft ar thow come thennes'.
    'Consaileth me, Kynde', quod I, 'what craft be beste to lere?'
    'Lerne to love', quod Kynde, 'and leef alle othere'.
    'How shal I come to catel so, to clothe me and to fede?'
    'And thow love lelly, lacke shal the nevere   160
Wede ne worldly mete while thy lif lasteth'.
And I bi conseil of Kynde comsed to rome

---

136. taught *U* : *X* ythoughte

---

133. 'Life' now materializes, in a slightly comical, almost accidental manner,
in the person of the dreamer, stricken by old age and grown bald. The vision
of the world running down to destruction is thus given a personal focus.
    158. A desperately abbreviated emergency transcript of the poem's argument.
    159. The dreamer is uneasily conscious of what Need was saying earlier:
love is all very well, but surely a certain enlightened self-interest is proper?

Thorw Contricion and Confessioun til I cam to Unite;
And ther was Conscience constable, cristene to save,
And biseged sothly with sevene grete geauntes   165
That with Auntecrist helden harde ageyn Consience.
   Sleuthe with his slynge an hard sawt he made.
Proude prestes cam with hym, passyng an hundred,
In paltokes and pikede shoes and pissares longe knyves
Comen agen Consience; with Covetyse they helden.   170
'By the Marie', quod a mansed prest, was of the marche of
    Ireland,
'I counte no more Consience, bi so I cache sulver,
Then I do to drynke a drauht of gode ale!'
And so sayde syxty of the same contreye,
And shoten ageynes hym with shotte, many a shef of othes,   175
And brode-hokede arwes—goddes herte, and his nayles—
And hadden almost Unite and holy-churche adowne.
   Consience cryede 'Helpe, Clergie, or I falle
Thorw imparfit prestes and prelates of holy-churche!'
Freres herde hym crye and comen hym to helpe,   180
Ac for they couthe nat wel here crafte, Consience for-sok hem.
Nede neyhede tho ner and Consience he tolde
That they cam for covetyse to have cure of soules:
'And for thei aren pore, paraunter, for patrimonye hem faileth,
Thei wol flatere, to fare wel, folke that ben riche.   185
And sethen thei chosen chele and cheytyf poverte,

---

175. with *omitted in X*   **177.** *XU* holynesse
181. Ac *P : X* And   **186.** *XU* cheytyftee

---

  163. Contrition and Confession are the first two stages of the act and sacrament of Penance, the third being Satisfaction or Amendment.

  165. The seven Deadly Sins.

  169. 'Wearing jackets and peaked shoes, and carrying long knives like common men.' Priests were not allowed to carry weapons; there is a suggestion of lechery as well. For *pissare* as a generic term for 'common man', see 1 *Kings* 14: 10.

  172. *by so:* 'provided that'.

  176. Oaths by God's heart, or the nails of the Cross, are like weapons used against the Church and God. Cf. Chaucer's *Pardoner's Tale*, *CT* VI. 474, 651.

  186-7. 'And since they chose a cold life and wretched poverty, let them eat as they chose, and don't "burden" them with any living, or cure of souls.'

Late hem chewe as thei chose, and charge hem with no cure!
For lomere he lyeth that lyflode mot begge
Then he that laboreth for lyflode and leneth hit beggares.
And senne freres forsoke the felicite of erthe,   190
Lat hem be as beggares, or lyve by angeles fode!'
     Consience of this consail tho comesede for to lawhe,
And corteysliche he confortede hem and calde hem in, alle freres,
And saide, 'Syres, sothly welcome be ye alle
To Unite and holi-churche, ac o thyng I yow preye—   195
Holdeth yow in Unite and haveth non envye
To lered ne to lewed, but lyveth aftur youre reule.
I wol be youre borwh, ye shal have breed and clothes
And other necessaries ynowe; yow shal no thyng lakke,
With that ye leve logyk and lerneth for to lovye.   200
For love lefte they lordschipe, bothe londe and scole,
Frere Fraunceys and Domynyk, for love to be holy.
     And yf ye coveiteth cure, Kynde wol yow telle
That in mesure god made alle manere thynges
And sette hit at a serteyne and at a syker nombre   205
And nempned hem names and nombred the sterres.
     Qui numerat multitudinem stellarum.
Kynges and knyghtes, that kepten and defenden,
Han officerys under hem and uch of hem a certeyne.
And yf thei wage men to werre, thei wryten hem in nombre;
Wol no tresorer taken hem wages, travayle they nevere so sore,   210
Bote they ben nempned in the nombre of hem that been
     ywaged.

190. *XU* felice   **204.** manere *omitted in* X

Need takes a cynical view of the friars' voluntary profession of poverty.
Conscience is more charitable, and gives them a chance.
     200. *with that:* 'provided that'. Friars were frequently attacked for logic-chopping and over-ingenious interpretation of the Scriptures. See 1.58n, 7.9n.
     201–2. 'It was love that made brothers Francis and Dominic [founders of the two main orders of friars] give up important positions, as landed and educated men, in their desire to live holy lives.'
     206f. 'He telleth the number of the stars' (*Psalm* 147:4). Not to be numbered is to be lost from God's sight (see 220, below).

Alle othere in bataile been yholde brybours,
Pilours and pike-harneys, in uche a parsch acorsed.
Monkes and monyales and alle men of religioun,
Here order and here reule wol to have a certeyne nombre.   215
Of lewed and of lered the lawe wol and asketh
A certeyne for a certeyne—save onliche of freres!
Forthy,' quod Consience, 'bi Crist, Kynde Wit me telleth
Hit is wikked to wage yow, ye wexeth out of nombre!
Heven hath evene nombre, and helle ys withouten nombre;   220
Forthy I wolde witterly that ye were in registre
And youre nombre under notarie sygne, and nother mo ne
    lasse!'
  Envye herde this, and heete freres go to scole
And lerne logyk and lawe and eke contemplacioun,
And preche men of Plato and proven hit by Seneca   225
That alle thynges under hevene ouhte to be in comune.
  He lyeth, as I leve, that to the lewed so precheth,
For god made to men a lawe and Moyses hit tauhte:
    Non concupisces rem proximi tui.
And evele is this yholde in parsches of Yngelonde,

220. *line omitted in X*

212–13. 'All others who take part in battle are considered robbers, the kind of men who pillage the dead and despoil them of their armour, men condemned by all.'

215. 'Their order and their rule require them to keep to a fixed number.' Religious houses ordinarily had a fixed 'establishment', so that proper discipline and supervision could be maintained.

216–17. 'With both the clergy and the laity, the law demands a certain number for a certain job—friars are the only exception.'

226. Friars preached the virtues of communalty of possession as an extension of their doctrine of voluntary poverty, but to Langland it looks like a way of poaching on people who earn their living honestly.

228f. 'Thou shalt not covet any thing that is thy neighbour's' (*Ex.* 20: 17).

229–36. 'And this law is ill-kept throughout England, for where parsons and parish-priests should be shriving the people—they are called "curates" because their job is to know the people's faults and heal them—and enjoining penance on all their parishioners, and bidding them be properly contrite in confession, instead of this, the people for shame run off to the friars, just as swindlers borrow money to take their cases to court, and then ask their friends to let them off payment, or for a longer extension.'

For persones and parsche-prestes, that sholde the peple shryve—   230
And they ben curatours cald, to knowe and to hele,
Alle that been here parschienes, penaunses enjoynen,
And be aschamed in her shryft; ac shame maketh hem wende
And fle to the freres, as fals folke to Westmynstre,
That borweth and bereth hit theddere and thenne biddeth
      frendes   235
Yerne of foryevenesse or lengere yeres leve.
Ac while he is in Westmynstre, he wol be bifore
And maken hym merye with other menne godes.
And so hit fareth with moche folke that the freres shryven:
As sisours and secutours they shall yeve the freres   240
A parcel to preye for hem, and make hem merye
With the remenaunt that othere men biswonke,
And soffren the dede in dette to the day of dome.
   Envye herefore hatede Consience,
And freres to filosophye he fond hem to scole,   245
The while Covetyse and Unkyndenesse Consience assailede.
In Unite holi-churche Consience heeld hym
And made Pees porter to pynne the gates.
Of all tale-tellares and titerares an ydel,
Ypocrisye and they an hard sawt they yeven.   250
Ypocrisye at the gate harde gan fyhte
And wounded wel wykkedly many a wys techare
That with Consience acordede and cardinal vertues.
Consience calde a leche, that couthe wel shryve,
To salve tho that syke were and thorw synne ywounded.   255
Shrift schupte scharpe salve and made men do penaunses
For here mysdedes that thei wrouht hadde,
And that Peres pardon were ypayd, *redde quod debes.*

---

233. hem *omitted in* X   **239.** the U : X to

   240–3. 'Such as jurymen and executors, who give the friars some small sum
to pray for the soul of the dead man, and then enjoy themselves with the rest
of the hard-earned money, leaving the dead man to pay his debts at Doomsday.'
   258. 'And made sure that Piers' pardon was paid for—"Pay back what you
owe".' Restitution, literal or otherwise (i.e. 'making good' the sin), is essential
to complete the act of penance. See 4.132n.

Some liked nat this leche and lettres they sente,
Yf eny surgien were in the sege that softer couthe plastre.   260
Sire Lyf-to-lyve-in-lecherye lay there and groned;
For fastyng of a Fryday he feerde as he wolde deye.
'Ther is a surgien in the sege that softe can handele,
And more of fysyke bi fer, and fayrer he plastereth;
One frere Flatrere is fisicien and surgien'.   265
Quod Contricion to Consience, 'Do hym come to Unite,
For here is many man hert thorw Ypocrisye'.
'We han no nede', quod Consience; 'I wot no bettere leche
Than person other parsche-prest, penytauncer or bischope,
Save Peres the Ploghman, that hath power over alle   270
And indulgence may do, but yf dette lette hit.
I may wel soffre', sayde Consience, 'sennes ye desiren,
That frere Flaterare be fet and fisyke yow seke'.

The frere her-of herde and hyede faste
To a lord for a lettre, leve to have to curen   275
As a curatour he were, and kam with his lettre
Baldly to the bishope and his breef hadde,
In contreys ther he cam, confessiones to here;
And cam ther Consience was, and knokked at the gate.
Pees unpynned hyt, was porter of Unite,   280
And in haste askede what his wille were?
'In fayth,' quod this frere, 'for profyt and for helthe,
Carpe I wolde with Contricioun and therfore I cam heddere'.
'He is syke', saide Pees, 'and so ar many other;
Ypocrisye hath herte hem—ful hard is yf thei kevere.'   285
'I am a surgien', saide the frere, 'and salves can make;
Consience knoweth me wel and what I can bothe'.
'I preye the', quod Pees tho, 'ar thow passe forthere,
What hattest thow? I praye the, hele nat thy name',
'Certes', saide his felawe, 'sire *Penetrans-domos*'.   290

---

271. 'And who may grant grace unless the debt of sin (not having been paid by penance) prevents him.'

290. *Penetrans-domos*: 'For of this sort are they which *creep into houses*, and lead captive silly women laden with sins, led away with divers lusts' (2 *Tim.* 3:6).

G

'Ye, go thy gate', quod Pees, 'bi god, for al thi fisyke,
Bote thow conne eny craft, thou comest nat here-ynne!
I knewe such one ones, nat eyhte wynter passed,
Cam ynne thus ycoped at a court ther I dwelte,
And was my lordes leche and my ladyes bothe,   295
And at the laste this lymytour, tho my lord was oute,
He salved so oure wymmen til some were with childe!'
    Hende-speche heet Pees tho opene the gates:
'Lat in the frere and his felawe and make hem fayre chiere.
He may se and here her, so may bifalle,   300
That Lyf thorw his lore shal leve Covetyse
And he adrad of Deth and withdrawe hym from Pruyde
And acorde with Consience and kusse here ayther other'.
    Thus thorw Hende-speche entred the frere
And cam to Consience and corteyslich hym grette.   305
'Thow art welcome', quod Consience, 'can thow hele syke?
Here is Contricioun', quod Consience, 'my cosyn, ywounded;
Conforte hym', quod Consience, 'and tak kepe to his sores.
The plasteres of the persoun, and poudres, ben to sore,
And lat hem lygge over-longe, and loth is to chaungen;   310
Fro lente to lente he lat his plastres byte'.
    'That is over-long', quod this lymitour, 'I leve I schal amenden
        hit';
And goth and gropeth Contricion and gaf hym a plastre
Of a pryve payement and 'I shal preye for yow,
And for hem that ye aren helde to, al my lyf-tyme,   315
And make yow my Ladye in masse and in matynes
Of freres of oure fraternite, for a litel sulver'.
Thus he goth and gedereth, and gloseth ther he shryveth,
Til Contricioun hadde clene foryete to crye and to wepe
And wake for his wikkede werkes, as he was woned bifore.   320
For confort of his confessour, Contricioun he lefte,
That is the sovereyne salve for alle kyne synnes.

---

313. *second* and *omitted in* XU

316-7. 'And, for the sake of a little money, make the friars of our brother-hood pray for you with the same zeal that they pray to Our Lady.'

Sleuth saw that, and so dede Pruyde,
And comen with a kene wil, Consience to assaile.
Consience cryede efte Clergie come help hym,   325
And bad Contricioun to come to helpe kepe the gate.
'He lyeth adreint', saide Pees, 'and so doth mony othere;
The frere with his fisyke this folke hath enchaunted
And doth men drynke dwale, that men drat no synne'.

  'By Crist', quod Consience tho, 'I wol bicome a pilgrime,   330
And wenden as wyde as the world regneth
To seke Peres the Ploghman, that Pruyde myhte destruye,
And that freres hadde a fyndynge, that for nede flateren,
And countrepledeth me, Consience. Now Kynde me avenge,
And sende me hap and hele til I have Peres Ploghman'.   335
And sethe he gradde aftur grace tyl I gan awake.

323. X Sleyth

332–4. 'To seek Piers Plowman, who alone can bring down Pride, and find some honest living for these friars, who now use flattery out of sheer necessity, and oppose me at every turn.'

336. This last episode—closely detailed, bitterly specific, dry, toneless, unheroic, almost comic—makes an extraordinary ending to a long Christian poem, as Langland focuses his vision of the world's ills with desperate clarity upon the undermining of the necessary act of penance by the friars' abuse of the sacrament. History brings us only to the edge of destruction, and each man's life teaches that salvation can only be sought and sought again in a search to which there is no end. To criticism of the poem's 'inconclusiveness', Skeat answers nobly: 'What other ending can there be? or rather, the end is not yet. We may be defeated, yet not cast down; we may be dying, and behold, we live. We are all still pilgrims upon earth.' So Conscience goes out once more in search of Piers Plowman, and the poem begins again, for its meaning is in the process, not the product.

Bibliography

(1) *Editions and Translations*

The Vision of William concerning Piers the Plowman, in Three Parallel Texts, ed. W. W. Skeat (Oxford, 1886), 2 vols., reprinted 1954, with additional bibliography by Dr. J. A. W. Bennett

Piers Plowman: The A Version. Will's Vision of Piers Plowman and Do-Well, ed. G. Kane (University of London, Athlone Press, 1960), Part 1 of *Piers Plowman: The Three Versions*, General Editor, G. Kane

Piers Plowman: a Selection, ed. C. Wilcockson (London, 1966)

William Langland. The Book Concerning Piers the Plowman, translated into modern English verse by D. and R. Attwater (London, Everyman, 1957)

Piers the Ploughman, translated into modern English prose by J. F. Goodridge (Penguin, 1959, repr. 1960)

(2) *Studies*

M. W. Bloomfield, *Piers Plowman as a Fourteenth Century Apocalypse* (New Brunswick, N.J., 1963)

R. W. Chambers, *Man's Unconquerable Mind* (London, 1939), pp. 88–171

E. T. Donaldson, *Piers Plowman: The C-Text and its Poet* (New Haven, 1949)

T. P. Dunning, *Piers Plowman: An Interpretation of the A-Text* (Dublin, 1937)

R. W. Frank, *Piers Plowman and the Scheme of Salvation* (New Haven, 1957)

G. Hort, *Piers Plowman and Contemporary Religious Thought* (London, n.d.)

G. Kane, *Middle English Literature: a Critical Study of the Romances, the Religious Lyrics and Piers Plowman* (London, 1951)

J. Lawlor, *Piers Plowman. An Essay in Criticism* (London, 1962)

D. W. Robertson and B. F. Huppé, *Piers Plowman and Scriptural Tradition* (Princeton, 1951)

E. Salter, *Piers Plowman: An Introduction* (Oxford, 1962)

(3) *Articles*

J. A. Burrow, 'The Audience of Piers Plowman', *Anglia*, LXXV (1957), 373–84

N. Coghill, 'The Character of Piers Plowman Considered from the B-Text', *M. Aev.*, II (1933), 108–35. 'The Pardon of Piers Plowman', *Proc. Brit. Acad.*, XXX (1944), 303–57

T. P. Dunning, 'The Structure of the B-Text of *Piers Plowman*', *R.E.S.*, N.S. VII (1956), 225–37

R. W. Frank, 'The Art of Reading Mediaeval Personification Allegory', *E.L.H.*, XX (1953), 237–50

G*

S. S. Hussey, 'Langland, Hilton and the Three Lives', *R.E.S.*, N.S. VII (1956), 132–50

J. Lawlor, 'The Imaginative Unity of *Piers Plowman*', *R.E.S.*, N.S. VIII (1957), 113–26

A. G. Mitchell, 'Lady Meed and the Art of *Piers Plowman*', Chambers Memorial Lecture (London, 1956)

H. W. Wells, 'The Construction of *Piers Plowman*', *P.M.L.A.*, XLIV (1929), 123–40. 'The Philosophy of *Piers Plowman*', *P.M.L.A.*, LIII (1938), 339–49

R. Woolf, 'Some Non-Mediaeval Qualities of *Piers Plowman*', *Essays in Criticism*, XII (1962), 111–25

E. Zeeman (Salter), 'Piers Plowman and the Pilgrimage to Truth', *Essays and Studies*, N.S. XI (1958), 1–16

(4) *Background Reading*

E. Auerbach, *Mimesis*, tr. W. R. Trask (New York, 1957). 'Figura', in *Scenes from the Drama of European Literature* (New York, 1959), pp. 11–76

D. Bethurum (ed.), *Critical Approaches to Mediaeval Literature*, Selected Papers from the English Institute, 1958–9 (New York, 1960)

M. W. Bloomfield, 'Symbolism in Mediaeval Literature', *M.P.*, LVI (1958–59), 73–81

Lay Folk's Mass Book, ed. T. F. Simmons (E.E.T.S., O.S. 71, 1879)

M. McKisack, *The Fourteenth Century* (Oxford, 1959)

J. P. Oakden, *Alliterative Poetry in Middle English*, 2 vols. (Manchester, 1930–35)

G. R. Owst, *Literature and Pulpit in Mediaeval England* (Cambridge, 1933, repr. 1961)

W. A. Pantin, *The English Church in the Fourteenth Century* (Cambridge, 1955)

Glossary

This is a glossary of words which may give difficulty to the reader, and is designed solely for the needs of the text. It does not aim to repeat explanations already given in the notes. Alphabetical order is normal, except that initial *y* as past participle prefix is ignored.

a *prep.* in, on 10.19, 11.19, 14.51

abasched *pp.* ashamed 11.163

abate *inf.* cure, cool the fever of 2.147

abiteth *pres3sg.* bites at 13.32

ablende *inf.* blind 15.141; *pa.t.sg.* blinded 15.367

abouhte *pa.t.sg.* bought, paid for 9.123

ac *conj.* but 1.6, 1.62, 2.24, &c.

accidie *n.* fit of sleepiness 4.204

acombred *pp.* burdened, overcome, troubled 2.31, 2.199

adreint *pp.* drugged 16.327

afere *inf.* frighten away 16.116; **afereth** *pres3sg.* 15.475

aferes *n.pl.* affairs, business 4.50

afraynede *pa.t.sg.* asked 15.16

aftir *prep.* after; in the direction of 1.14

a-furst *adj.* parched with thirst 8.43

a-fyngred *adj.* starving with hunger 8.43, 8.50

ageyn, ageynes, agen, agenes *prep.* against 3.74, 5.32, 5.131, &c.

alloweth *pres3sg.* approves 13.82; **allowed** *pp.* praised 9.55

alose *inf.* praise 14.56

als *prep.* as 12.66

an *prep.* on 13.106

and *conj.* if 6.11, 9.53, 11.160, &c.

anhengede *pa.t.sg.* hanged 2.64

ankeres *n.pl.* anchorites 1.30

anon, anoon *adv.* straightway 2.115, 6.103, 10.18, &c.

apayed *pp.* pleased 11.64

apayre *inf.* harm, injure 5.92

apeward *n.* ape-keeper 5.165

apose *inf.* ask 11.93; **aposed** *pa.t.pl.* questioned 2.45

ar *conj.* ere, before 5.19, 5.148, 7.11, &c.

areche *v.imp.* reach, pass 15.280

aresenede, areso(u)nede *pa.t.sg.* argued with, reasoned with 10.1, 10.67, 10.117

ariste *pres.pl.* arise 9.90

as *conj.* as if 1.66

assaye *inf.* try 4.144

assoylen *inf.* absolve 1.68

asterte *inf.* escape, avoid 10.83

atamede *pa.t.sg.* opened 14.23

ateynt *pp.* accused 16.112

a-to *adv.* in two 15.76

auntred *pa.t.sg.* ventured 15.231

auntres *n.pl.* adventurous knights 15.14

averous *adj.* avaricious 2.189

Averous *n.* Avarice 7.86

awreke *v.imp.* revenge 16.153

axen *inf.* ask 5.62

ayres *n.pl.* heirs 7.86

ayther *pron.* each, either, both 4.47, 12.62, 15.126, &c.

baburlippid *adj.* thick-lipped 4.96

baches *n.pl.* valleys 5.40

balayshed *pp.* whipped 4.55

baldly, baldeliche *adv.* boldly 16.20, 16.82, 16.277

bale *n.* misery 9.129, 10.13, 15.34

banne *inf.* curse 2.58; **banneth** *pres3sg.* curses, forbids 6.102

bar *pa.t.sg.* pierced 15.88

barn *n.* child 14.39, 14.41, 14.43;
　barnes *pl.* sons 3.70
bayard *n.* horse 14.25
be *prep.* by 3.42, 4.173, 5.55, &c.
be, ybe *see* **ben**
beau-pere *n.* reverend father 15.240
beden *pa.t.pl.* offered, bade, com-
　manded 11.27, 15.53
bedredne *adj.* bed-ridden 6.117
beel-syre *n.* grandfather 15.281
been *see* **ben**
beknowe *see* **biknowe**
belyen *pres.subj.pl.* slander 15.354;
　bylowe *pp.* 6.121
ben, been *inf.* be 3.15, 4.166, &c.;
　pres.pl. are 2.6, 2.81, 2.176, &c.;
　beth *pres3sg.* shall be 14.39; **beth**
　imp. be 2.173; **be, ybe** *pp.* 4.28,
　4.112, 5.70, &c.
bere *inf.* low 10.22
bernis *n.pl.* barns 9.74
berw *n.* hill 5.108
bet *comp.adj. & adv.* better 3.96,
　5.121
beth *see* **ben**
biddares, bidders *n.pl.* beggars
　1.41, 6.1
biddeth *pres3sg.* begs 6.3, 12.86;
　biddyng *presp.* 12.66
biful *pa.t.sg.* befell, happened 7.8;
　me biful I happened 1.7
bigerdeles *n.pl.* money-bags 7.85
biheste *n.* promise 13.123
bihihte *pa.t.sg.* promised 15.374,
　16.61
bikere *pres.pl.* fight 16.29
biknowe, beknowe, byknowe *v.*
　acknowledge 3.92, 4.104; *pp.* 9.118
bileve *n.* belief 13.51
bit, byt *pres3sg.* commands 11.77,
　15.269
bitelbrowed *adj.* with overhanging
　brows 4.96
bitit *pres3sg.* betides 10.84
blaun-manger *n.* chicken-stew
　11.100

blenche *inf.* turn aside 5.108
blende *inf.* blind 15.291; **blente**
　pa.t.sg. 5.16; **blent** *pp.* 15.283
bochere *n.* butcher 4.166; *pl.* 1.88
boie *n.* lad, fellow 15.80
bolle *n.* bowl 15.406
bonde-men *n.pl.* farm labourers 1.86
borde *n.* side of a boat 7.40
bordiours, bordyors *n.pl.* jesters
　6.67, 6.76
borwh *n.* guarantor 16.198;
　borewes *pl.* sureties, sponsors 2.74
bote *see* **but**
bote *n.* remedy, help, salvation
　15.156, 15.474
botles *adj.* barefoot 15.9
bouketh *pres3sg.* cleanse, scour 12.48
breef *n.* written authority 16.277
brennyng *presp.* burning 15.288
bretful *adv.* to the brim 1.42
bretil *adj.* frail 7.47
breuh-wyf *n.* ale-wife, barmaid
　4.141
brugge *n.* bridge 5.94
bulle *n.* papal edict 6.1, 6.100
but, bote *conj.* but; unless 1.64,
　5.163, 6.2, &c.; **but yf** unless
　2.184, 3.63, 5.103, &c.
burgeys *n.pl.* burgesses, citizens 1.86
burne *n.* man 11.163; *pl.* 13.11
buxum *adj.* gentle, courteous 15.120
buxumnesse *n.* obedience 5.120;
　promise of obedience 15.319
buyrde *n.* maiden 15.120
bycam *pa.t.sg.* became; **where**
　bycam what became of 11.150
byde *v.imp.* pray 5.121
byfalleth *pres3sg.* belongs 2.48
byglosedest *pa.t.sg.* deceived by
　talk 15.379
byjapede *pa.t.sg.* tricked, cheated
　2.63
bykenne *v.* commend 7.58
byknowe *see* **biknowe**
byleyven *inf.* believe 12.73

bylive, bylyve *n.* living, food 3.29, 12.52

bylongeth *pres3sg.* it belongs to, befits 3.66

bylowe *see* **belyen**

bylyve *see* **bylive**

bymene *inf.* signify, mean 2.56; **bymeneth** *pres3sg.* 2.1, 15.173; **bymente** *pa.t.sg.* 15.16

bynome *pa.t.sg.* took, seized 9.116

byquath *pa.t.sg.* bequeathed 11.12

byseye *pp.* treated 16.152

byt *see* **bit**

byteche *v.* commend 11.183

bythenke *v.* think up 4.5

by-tymes *adv.* betimes, in time 5.172

cachepol *n.* officer 15.46, 15.76

camaca *n.* rich silk 12.16

can *see* **gan**

can *pres3sg.* knows 15.46, 15.72; **conne** *pres.subj.sg.* know, learn 16.156; **conneth** *pres.pl.* know how 1.35; **couthe** *pa.t.sg.* knew, could 5.39, 5.72. 7.6, &c.; **couthest, kouthest** *pa.t.2sg.* could 7.74, 13.2; could (you) 5.59

canon *n.* canon law 11.85

carde *inf.* card (wool) 6.20

cardiacles *n.pl.* heart-attacks 16.32

carful *adj.* full of care, distressed 8.42; **careful** *adj. as n.* distressed (man) 14.18

carneles *n.pl.* battlements 5.116

carpe *inf.* talk, speak, chatter 10.50; *imp.* 11.128; **carpen** *pres.pl.* 8.52; **carpede** *pa.t.sg.* 11.109

carpynge *n.* speech 12.55

carse *n.* cress 8.14

caste *inf.* plan, plot 8.16, 8.18; **cast** *pres3sg.* 6.91; **caste** *pa.t.sg.* 16.71

catel *n.* wealth, property 6.30, 6.121, 9.74, &c.

caudel *n.* mess 4.199

caysers *n.pl.* emperors 16.51

caytyves, caytives *n.pl.* wretches

15.97, 15.100

certes *adv.* certainly, indeed 3.22, 7.25, 10.68, &c.

chafferen *pres.pl.* trade 9.87; **ychaffared** *pp.* 3.94

chaffare *n.* merchandise, goods 4.167

chapmen *n.pl.* merchants, traders 4.133, 4.167, 9.87

chargeth *pres3sg.* blames 12.5; **charged** *pp.* burdened 6.13

chees *pa.t.sg.* chose 9.110

chide *pres.pl.* complain, quarrel, argue 9.87; **chyt** *pres3sg.* 2.177, 12.5; **chydde** *pa.t.sg.* 4.45

clemb *pa.t.sg.* 13.108

clepede *pa.t.sg.* called 4.47, 16.132; **cleped** *pp.* summoned 8.18

clips *n.* eclipse 15.139

cloute *n.* patch 6.20

yclyketed *pp.* locked 5.147

cockes *n.pl.* cockles 6.35

cokeres *n.pl.* men making haycocks 3.13

cokewolde *n.* cuckold 4.32

colhoppes *n.pl.* collops, rissoles 11.68

combraunce *n.* trouble, burden, hindrance 9.105, 15.275

comen *pa.t.pl.* came 1.71

comesede *see* **comsed**

comissarie *n.* commissary, bishop's legal representative 12.78

commen *see* **comune**

compenable *adj.* companionable 12.58

comsed, comesede *pa.t.sg.* began 7.20, 10.86, 13.108, &c.

comsyng *n.* beginning 15.224

comune *n.* commons, common folk 11.11, 11.169, 12.76, 16.28; **commen** *adj.* common 9.28

conjeyed, ycongeyed *pa.t.sg., pp.* dismissed, got rid of 11.176, 12.83

conne, conneth *see* **can**

connynge *n.* knowledge 10.105, 11.18; **konnynges** *pl.* forms of knowledge 11.132

constorie *n.* consistory, ecclesiastical court 12.78

continaunce *n.* face, facial gesture 4.63, 11.120

contrarie *n.* opposite 2.122

contraryed *pa.t.pl.* contradicted 1.59

copis *n.pl.* copes, cloaks 1.54, 1.59

cornel *n.* kernel 9.7, 9.10

cors *n.* process 10.17

cors *n.* corpse 11.11

cor-seint *n.* holy person 5.58

costes *n.pl.* regions 7.12

cote *n.* cottage, hovel 3.2, 6.91; *pl.* 6.12, 6.23

coterelles *n.pl.* peasants 6.37

coupe *n.* guilt 4.138

couthe, couthest *see* **can**

covent *n.* convent 4.28

coveytyse, coveytise *n.* covetousness, greed 1.59, 9.101, 9.105, &c.

cowed *pa.t.sg.* coughed 4.199

cowhes *n.pl.* coughs 16.32

crache *v.* scratch 4.38

craftes *n.pl.* forms of knowledge 11.132

croft *n.* field 3.17, 5.100

culle(n) *inf.* kill 2.62, 9.101, 16.101

curatour *n.* priest with charge of souls 16.276; *pl.* 11.16

cure *n.* charge of souls 16.183, 16.203

curen *inf.* have 'cure' of souls 16.275

daffe *n.* fool, idiot 2.139, 10.107

dawe *inf.* dawn 15.184; **dawed** *pa.t.sg.* 15.468

decretistre *n.* legal expert 11.85

dede *pa.t.sg. & pl.* did 15.162, 15.428; made, caused to 2.103

dedeynous *adj.* disdainful, proud 7.81

defaute *n.* lack, want 6.40, 8.43

defendeth *pres3sg.* forbids 15.111

defy, defyen *inf.* digest 1.97, 4.226

dele *inf.* give (to) 2.197, 8.71; **deleth** *pres3sg.* 8.69

delitable *adj.* delightful 2.32

demme *adj.* dim, dark 15.361

dene *n.* noise 15.65, 15.127

dere *inf.* harm 15.296

der(e)worthe *adj.* precious 2.83, 9.125

dernely *adv.* secretly 10.35

descreve *see* **discreve**

despeneth *pres3sg.* is spent 9.95

devyne *inf.* explain, interpret 11.98

devynours *see* **dyvynour**

deyneth *pres3sg.* deigns 8.61

deys *n.* dais 11.66

dighte *pa.t.sg.* took, laid hands on 2.27

discreve, descreve *inf.* describe 4.94, 15.213

disseyved *pa.t.sg.* deceived 13.123

distruye *inf.* destroy 15.245; **distrueth** *pres3sg.* 9.94

do *v.* do; put 15.93; **do** *pp.* done 4.7, 15.93

dobelares *n.pl.* platters 11.91

dole *n.* suffering 15.303

dompynges *n.pl.* diving-birds 10.40

dotede *adj.* foolish 2.139

doute *pres.pl.* fear 7.126

drad *see* **drat**

draf *n.* pig-swill 8.9

drat, drad *pres3sg.* dreads, fears 9.12, 12.27, 16.329

dremeles *n.* dream 11.17

drevele *inf.* drivel, slobber 8.9

driveth *pres.pl.* drive; **driveth forth** pass away 1.92

dronklewe *adj.* given to drink 7.81

druie *adj.* dry; **drynke druie** drain the pot 6.85

druerie *n.* love-token, treasure 2.83

duntes *n.pl.* blows 16.55

durede *see* **duyren**

dust *pa.t.sg.* didst, caused to 15.319

duyre(n) *inf.* last, endure 3.25, 11.58; **dureth, duyreth** *pres3sg.* 8.90, 9.82; **durede, duyred** *pa.t.sg.* 2.107, 15.66

dwale *n.* opiate 16.329

dyas *n.pl.* medicines 16.124

dykers *n.pl.* ditchers 1.91

dykke *n.* ditch 10.107

dysores *n.gen.sg.* minstrel's 11.171

dyvynour *n.* learned divine 11.85; **devynours** *pl.* 11.123

edwitede *pa.t.sg.* reproached 4.208

eft, efte *adv.* again 5.148, 9.21, 10.4, &c.

Elde *n.* Old age 13.106, 13.108, 13.111, &c.

ellerne *n.* elder-tree 2.64

elles *adv.* else, otherwise 2.174, 5.150, 6.39, &c.

emcristene *n.* fellow-Christian 7.79

emforth *prep.* in proportion to 11.142

enbaumed *pa.t.sg.* anointed 14.25; *pp.* 14.41

engendrure *n.* procreation 10.16

enlevene *adj.* eleven 9.35

enqueste *n.* court of inquiry 16.112

ensaumple *n.* example 2.195; *pl.* 2.169

entermetynge *n.* meddling, interfering 10.97

erber *n.* enclosed garden, arbour 13.5

evene *adj.* equal 13.90; exact 16.220; *adv.* directly 2.122

evereche *pron.* each one 15.77

fair *see* **fayr**

fallas *n.* deceit 8.22

falle *pp.* befallen 1.63

fare *n.* proceeding, goings-on, business 15.16, 15.129

fauntes *n.pl.* children 6.110

fay *adj.* doomed to die 11.2

fayleth *pres3sg.* is lacking 2.187

fayn *adv.* fain, gladly 13.103

fayr, fayre, fair *adv.* courteously 2.54, 10.119; plainly 2.2, 7.32

faytest *pres2sg.* beg falsely 3.30; **fayteth** *pres3sg.* 6.40; **fayten** *pres.pl.* 6.110; **fayteden** *pa.t.pl.* 1.43

faytour *n.* false beggar 6.4; *pl.* 8.54

feerde *see* **ferde**

feet *n.* deed, works 2.183

fel, felle *adj.* fierce, harsh, severe 4.50, 13.35

fele *adj., pron.* many 4.16, 6.31, 6.35, &c.

felle *see* **fel**

felonliche *adv.* like a thief 9.98

felynge *n.* touch, contact 15.132

fenestre *n.* window 15.13

fer *adj.* far 9.97; *adv.* far 15.167, 16.264; long ago 12.70

ferddede *pa.t.pl.* gathered together 10.20

ferde, feerde *pa.t.sg.* behaved, proceeded 10.101, 16.262

fere *n.* companion, mate 10.36

ferly *n.* marvel, wonder 12.11, 13.56, 15.114, &c.; *pl.* 1.63

fet *pp.* fetched 16.273

fley, fleyh, fly *pa.t.sg.* fled, flew 2.119, 13.121, 14.12, 16.119; **flowe(n)** *pa.t.pl.* 14.35, 15.368

flux *n.* running flow, issue 4.59

folde *n.* earth 2.153

fond(e) *see* **fynde**

fonde *inf.* try 16.116; **fond** *imp.* 11.144; **fondeth** *pres3sg.* 13.43

fondynges *n.pl.* temptations 7.42

fonge *inf.* take, receive 5.83, 6.31

forbere *inf.* leave off, discard 2.99

forbete *inf.* beat down 15.34

forbisene *n.* illustrative story, exemplum 7.32

for-bit *pres3sg.* eats away 13.39

for-do(n) *inf.* destroy, undo 15.28, 15.41, 15.161; **for-doth** *pres3sg.* 15.68; **for-dede** *pa.t.sg.* 15.389

for-fret *pres3sg.* eats away at 13.33

for-glotten *pres.pl.* swallow up 8.66

formest *superl.adv.* first 15.162, 15.163

forreours *n.pl.* foragers, outriders 16.31

forst *n.* frost 9.53

for-thenketh *pres3sg. impers.* repents, regrets 15.92

forthy *adv.* therefore 2.32, 2.156, 2.172, &c.

foryete *inf.* forget 16.105; *pp.* forgotten 16.319

franchise *n.* freedom 15.107

frayned(e) *pa.t.sg. & pl.* asked 2.54, 5.51, 7.3

fre *adj.* generous 8.57

freek *see* **freke**

freel *adj.* frail, fickle 7.48

freet *pa.t.sg.* ate 15.201

freke, freek *n.* man 11.2, 11.81; *pl.* 4.50

fremde *adj.* unrelated, stranger 9.16

frentike *adj.* mad, silly 8.6

fretynge *adj.* destructive 15.157

ful *pa.t.sg.* fell 2.120, 7.39, 15.90, 16.126; **fullen** *pa.t.pl.* fell 2.126

fulle *inf.* fill 4.177

furste *n.* thirst 15.409

fursteth *pres3sg.* thirsts 15.407

fuyr *n.* fire 6.122, 11.165

fynde *inf.* find, provide, provide for 3.76; **fynd, fynt** *pres3sg.* 12.30, 12.33; **fond, fonde** *pa.t.sg. & pl.* 1.19, 1.56, 3.36, &c.; founded 2.60

ga *v.imp.* go 1.94

gabbynges *n.pl.* lies 16.75

gadlyng *n.* vagabond 16.107

galpe *inf.* yawn 11.97

gan, gonne *v.* began to, (*as aux.*) did 2.170, 4.77, 5.4, &c.; **can** *v.aux.* did 11.2

garnement *n.* garment 6.59

garte, gert *pa.t.sg.* caused to, made 16.7, 16.81

gate *n.* way 16.291; manner of going 15.252

gentel(e) *adj.* noble 8.23, 9.122, 9.132

gert *see* **garte**

gete *pa.t.sg.* got 15.312, 15.376; **gete, ygete, geten** *pp.* 15.102, 15.321, 15.395; **geten** *pa.t.pl.* begot 16.107

geven *see* **yeve**

gileth *see* **gyle**

gistes *n.pl.* stories 8.23

yglobbed *pp.* gulped down 4.184

gloseth *pres3sg.* interprets falsely 16.318; **glosede** *pa.t.pl.* 1.58

glosynges *n.pl.* deceitful talk 16.75

gnedy *adj.* miserly 11.86

go *pp.* gone 4.111, 15.327

god, gode *n.* goods, wealth 8.77, 9.111

gome *n.* man 5.60, 10.70, 12.22, &c.; *gen.sg.* 15.327; **gomes** *pl.* 12.61

gonne *see* **gan**

gossip *n.* friend, neighbour 4.144

gost *n.* spirit 4.73, 5.32

gothelen, gothly *inf.* rumble 4.185, 11.97

gradde *pa.t.sg.* cried aloud 16.336

graythly *adv.* properly 15.321

gre *n.* prize 15.102

greut *n.* earth 9.130, 10.48

gropeth *pres3sg.* examines by touch 16.313

ygrounde *pp.* whetted, sharpened 15.81

grys *n.pl.* little pigs 1.94

gulte *pa.t.pl.* sinned 5.32

gultes *n.pl.* sins 8.62

gurles *n.pl.* children 2.29, 12.17

gyle *inf.* deceive 12.22; **gileth** *pres3sg.* 6.5

gyle *n.* guile, deceit 9.100

gyn *n.* 'engine', weapon 15.261

gynnen *pres.pl.* begin 11.97

gyour *n.* guide 16.22

gyved *pa.t.sg.* shackled 16.142

halie *inf.* drag, haul 7.93

halsed *pa.t.sg.* besought 2.70

halsyng *n.* embracing 4.85

halt *pres3sg.* holds, detains 12.81, 12.87

han *pres.pl.* have 1.63, 2.132, 3.70, &c.

hansull *n.* gift; **to hansull** as a gift 4.162

hap *n.* good fortune 16.335

hardy *adj.* brave, bold 9.117

harlotes *n.pl.* ribalds, profligate rogues 8.28; *gen.sg.* 16.94

harlotrye *n.* ribaldry, profligacy 8.28

harow *interj.* alas 16.38

hatte *see* **hoteth**

haylsede *pa.t.sg.* greeted 7.10

hayward *n.* 'hedge-warden', a man whose job was to prevent cattle straying from the common ground 3.16, 4.155

heddere *see* **hider**

heep, hep *n.* crowd 1.51, 4.133, 4.161

heet(e) *see* **hoteth**

heihte *see* **hoteth**

helde *pp.* bound, closely related 16.315

hele *n.* health 3.7, 6.42, 6.45, &c.

hele *v.imp.* conceal 16.289; **helede** *pa.t.pl.* 10.35; **yheled** *pp.* covered, roofed 5.118

helle-pouke *n.* devil of hell 11.164

hem *pron.3pl.acc.* them 1.25, 1.27, 1.30, &c.

hende *adj.* polite 16.138, 16.298

hendely, hendly *adv.* courteously 7.10, 13.132

hendenesse *n.* courtesy, kindness, gentleness 8.13, 13.13, 16.95

hendly *see* **hendely**

hengen *pa.t.pl.* hanged 2.171

hennes *adv.* hence, ago 2.175, 3.35, 3.80, &c.

hente *pa.t.sg.* seized, took 5.33, 16.117, 16.130

hep *see* **heep**

herberwed *pp.* lodged 4.133

here *adj.poss.3pl.* their 1.30, 1.32, 1.42, &c.

hernes *n.pl.* corners 15.446

hert(e) *pp.* hurt 16.267, 16.285

hette *see* **hoteth**

heved *n.* head 4.100, 5.63, 5.162, &c.

hevene-riche, -ryche *n.gen.sg.* of the kingdom of heaven 1.29, 9.19

hevynesse *n.* sorrow 15.256

hey, heye, hye *adj.* high 2.64, 2.70, 2.155, &c.; **an hey** on high, strong 4.22; **heye, hye** *adv.* high 2.171, 4.136, &c.

heynesse *n.* loftiness, pride 16.103

hider(e) hiddere, heddere *adv.* hither 15.320, 15.335, 15.345, &c.

hihte *see* **hoteth**

hit *pa.t.sg.* threw in 4.165

hokede *adj.* hooked 1.51

hokkerye *n.* retail-dealing 4.131

holde *pp.* held, kept up 4.131

holdyng *n.* grasping ways 9.104

holpe, yholpe *pp.* helped 8.28, 14.15

hoor *see* **hore**

hope *v.* think, expect, believe 5.171, 7.19, 13.1, &c.; **hopeth** *pres3sg.* expects 9.59

hore, hoor *adj.* white-haired with age 4.91, 6.115, 16.45

hore *n.* whore 4.47

hosbondrye *n.* thrift 2.53

hosebonde *n.* husbandman, farmer 9.59

hostiler *n.* ostler 4.176

hot *v.imp.* shout 15.286

hoteth *pres3sg.* commands 8.67; is called 13.18, 15.132; **hatte** is called 5.101, 5.105, 5.121, &c.; **hihte, heihte** *pa.t.sg.* was called 13.4, 13.7, 13.8, &c.; **hihte, hyhte, heet(e), hette** commanded 2.17, 4.110, 5.128, &c.; **hote** *pp.* called 8.1

hous *n.pl.* houses, buildings 5.118

hoved *pa.t.sg.* was hanging about 15.83; *pa.t.pl.* 15.86

hulle *n.* hill 9.78; *pl.* 1.6

huppynge *presp.* hopping, skipping 14.14

huyre *n.* wages 5.75

hye *see* **hey**

hyhte *see* **hoteth**

iliche, ilych *see* **yliche**

ilke *adj.* same 5.126; *pron.* same one, very thing 2.79, 12.28

ingang *n.* entrance 5.163

inpugnede *pa.t.sg.* found fault with 11.131

inwit, inwyt *n.* inward knowledge, conscience 4.208, 6.57

jaced *pa.t.sg.* galloped 14.5

jangle *inf.* quarrel 11.92

Jewene *n.gen.pl.* of the Jews 15.40, 15.266

jewyse *n.* justice 15.423

jurdan *n.* chamber-pot (term of contempt) 11.92

juyste *adj.* swollen like a bottle 11.92

kayres *pres3sg.* goes 4.138

kaytif *n.* wretch 4.104

kembe *inf.* comb wool 6.20

kenne *inf.* teach, direct 2.78, 2.88; **kenneth** *pres3sg.* 2.141; **kenne** *pres.pl.* 8.91; **kenned, kende** *pa.t.sg.* 5.65, 13.17

kepe *n.* heed 10.17, 10.37, 11.176; **take kepe to** look after 14.29

kepeth *pres3sg.* cares, is interested 10.105

kevere *pres.pl.* recover 16.285; **kevered** *pp.* covered, sealed 6.78

knowlechede *pa.t.pl.* confessed 5.29

knyhtes-fees *n.pl.* knights' feudal lands 3.77

koke *inf.* make hay-cocks 3.13

konnynges *see* **connynge**

kouthest *see* **can**

kulde *pa.t.sg.* killed 16.49

kyn *see* **kyne**

kynde *adj.* proper, own, correct, natural 2.141, 7.69, 11.182

kynde *n.* nature, Nature 4.217, 9.7, 10.3, &c.; natural power 4.91; natural creature 10.23

kyndely, kyndeliche *adv.* naturally, instinctively 5.64; properly 15.213, 15.230; plainly, clearly 8.91

Kynde-Wit *n.* natural wisdom, common sense 5.65, 10.110, &c.

kyne, kyn, kynne, kynes *n.* kind(s) of 3.20, 5.72, 7.15, &c.

kyneriche, kyneryche *n.* kingdom 7.111, 9.29

kynne *see* **kyne**

lacche *inf.* obtain, get 2.101; **lauhte** *pa.t.sg.* seized 16.102; took (her leave) 2.205

lacke(n) *inf.* blame, find fault with, slander 11.79, 14.56

lacles *adj.* blameless 10.82

lad *pp.* led 11.15

lape *inf.* lap up 4.201

large *adj.* generous 8.73

lat(e) *see* **lete**

lauhte *see* **lacche**

lauhynge *see* **lawhe**

launceth, launseth *pres3sg.* springs, sends up 9.82, 13.10; *pres.pl.* spring 9.46

launde *n.* field, meadow 1.8, 7.64

launseth *see* **launceth**

lavendrie *n.* laundry 12.47

laveth *pres3sg.* washes 12.47

lawhe *inf.* laugh 12.19, 12.24, 16.192; **lawhen, lawheth** *pres.pl.* 12.17, 12.19; **lowh, louh** *pa.t.sg.* 13.3, 16.93; **lauhynge** *presp.* 8.85; **lauhynge, leyhing** *n.* laughing, laughter 4.181, 15.458

leautee *see* **leute**

lechen *inf.* heal 14.48

lede *n.* man 5.41, 10.82, 14.31; *pl.* 8.69, 8.73

leef *n.* page, words 11.104

leef *n.* leaf; **at a leef** at nothing 3.97

leef *see* **leve**

leel(e) *see* **lele**

leely *see* **lely**

leem *n.* glow, light 15.128

lees *pa.t.sg.* lost 5.13, 10.24, 16.37; **lore, ylore** *pp.* lost, abandoned 4.91, 9.44, 12.28, 15.82

leet *pp.* esteemed 8.34

lef *see* **leve**

lege *adj. as n.* lieges, true subjects 15.394

legge *inf.* lay 10.31, 15.33; wager 15.161

lek-sed *n.* leek-seed 9.51

lele, leel(e) *adj.* true, loyal, honest, faithful 3.103, 5.78, 5.119, &c.

lely, lelly, leely, lelelyche *adv.* truly 5.89, 11.154, 12.73, 14.47

lemman *n.* lover 15.185, 16.102; *pl.* 16.54

lened *pa.t.sg.* reclined, lay down 1.8, 7.64, 15.5

lene *v.imp.* give (to) 7.91; **leneth** *pres3sg.* 16.189; **lened** *pa.t.sg.* gave away to 12.28

lenghe *inf.* lengthen 15.53; **lenghed** *pp.* 15.334

lenten *n.* spring; **to lenten** at the approach of spring 15.5

lente-sedes *n.pl.* seeds sown in spring 9.51

lere *n.* face 2.3

lere *inf.* teach, learn 2.205, 6.104, 15.236, 16.157; *imp.* 2.135; **lereth** *pres3sg.* 11.94; **lered** *pa.t.sg.* 14.54; **ylered** *pp.* 7.10

lered *adj.* learned 8.36, 13.82

lesyng(e) *n.* lie, untruth 4.107, 15.347; *pl.* 11.104, 13.44, 15.344, &c.

lete, late *inf.* let 15.57; give up 9.75; **lat** *pres3sg.* lets, allows 5.156; **leten** *pres.pl.* give up, leave 8.24

letrure *see* **lettrure**

lette, letten *inf.* stop, hinder, prevent 8.60, 9.117, 11.166; keep out 2.155; remain, delay, tarry 2.204, 14.31; **letteth** *pres.pl.* hinder 11.181; **lette** *pa.t.sg.* stopped 13.115

lettre *n.* scripture 11.74, 15.82

lettrure, leture *n.* learning, education 11.181; scripture 8.26

leute, lewete, leautee *n.* truth, loyalty, faith 4.93, 11.133. 16.13

leve *pres.subj.* grant, permit 5.38

leve *n.* leave, permission 1.83, 4.227; leave, 'licence' 1.50; liberty 6.86

leve *v.* live 3.44

leve, lef, leef *adj.* dear 4.69, 5.81, 5.134, &c.; glad, willing 4.81; fond 16.145; **lever(e)** *comp.adj.* dearer 15.455; preferable 8.9; rather 4.27; **me were levere** I would rather 11.179; **levest** *superl.adj.* dearest, most precious 2.142, 3.85

leve *v.* believe 1.17, 10.70, 13.1, &c.; *inf.* 2.75, 14.56; *imp.* 6.113, 11.104, 13.58; **leef, lef** *imp.* 2.36, 2.195, 3.24, &c. **leved** *pa.t.pl.* 1.70

lewed(e) *adj.* ignorant, uneducated, lay, common 1.70, 2.135, 2.195, &c.

lewete *see* **leute**

leyhing *see* **lawhe**

libbe *inf.* live 15.110

licame *see* **lycame**

liche *see* **yliche**

ligge(n) *see* **lygge**

lihtlich(e) *adv.* quickly 9.82, 15.277

lihtloker *comp.adv.* more lightly 5.97

likede *v.impers.* pleased; **as hem likede** as it pleased them 1.58

likerous *adj.* luxurious, intoxicating 2.25

lisse *n.* joy 15.236

lithe *inf.* soothe, relieve 14.24

lithereth *pres.pl.* cast stones 13.48

lixt *see* **lyeth**

lobies *n.pl.* lubbers 1.53

logh *see* **louh**

loketh *pres.pl.* look, have sight 15.29; **lokede** *pa.t.sg.* looked; **hym lokede** he looked like 4.95

lollarne *n.gen.pl.* idlers' 6.80

lomere *comp.adv.* more often 16.188

lomes *n.pl.* tools 3.45

longe *inf.* remain, stay long 4.56; **longed** *pa.t.sg.* dwelt 7.7

longe *adj.* tall 1.53

lordeth *pres3sg.* lords it, swaggers 8.69

lordeyn(e)s *n.pl.* villains 13.48, 15.106

lore *n.* teaching 4.16, 6.44, 8.36, &c.

lore, ylore *see* **lees**

lorel *n.* vagabond, wretch 15.3; *pl.* 6.77

loth *adj.* loath, reluctant 1.53, 9.75; hard 11.138; **me thynketh loth** I am reluctant 11.79

louable *adj.* praiseworthy 3.103

louh(e), logh *adj.* low, humble, common 4.125, 5.78, 7.83, 9.44

louh *see* **lawhe**

louke *inf.* lock, close up 15.254

loure *inf.* frown 12.19; **louren** *pres.pl.* 12.19

louryng *n.* scowling 4.181

loute *inf.* bow, make obeisance, kneel, pray 8.87, 11.169; *imp.* 4.69; **louted** *pa.t.sg.* 8.85

lovelokest *superl.adj.* loveliest 2.107, 4.90

lovye *inf.* love 2.142

low(e) *see* **lyeth**

lowe *n.* light 15.141

loweth *pres3sg.* humbles 9.18

lowh *see* **lawhe**

luppen *inf.* leap, ascend 2.113; **lup** *pa.t.sg.* leapt 5.16

lust(e) *n.* desire, pleasure 2.111, 4.56, 16.40

lust(e) *v.impers.* pleases 6.86, 7.95, 8.76, &c.; *pa.t.sg.* 11.25, 15.458

luther, luyther *adj.* bad, wicked 2.195, 4.224, 6.121

lyard *n.* horse 14.19, 14.31

lycame, licame *n.* body 2.36, 11.58, 14.48, 15.94; **lycames** *gen.sg.* 4.74

lycour *n.* juice 9.80

lyeth *pres3sg.* tells lies 16.188; **lixt** *pres2sg.* liest 4.36; **low(e)** *pa.t.sg.* lied 15.347, 15.444

lyeth *see* **lygge**

lyf *n.* creature 11.19, 13.105

lyflode *n.* living, livelihood 3.42, 3.45, 6.40, &c.

lygge, ligge *inf.* lie, lie down 3.16, 6.83, 10.108, &c.; lie, stay on 16.310; **lyeth** *pres3sg.* applies, is relevant 3.89; **liggen** *pres.pl.* lie 15.147

ylyk *see* **yliche**

lykynde *adj.* agreeable 13.78

lykynge *n.* pleasure 8.12

lymes *n.pl.* limbs 3.8, 6.43; agents 16.27

lymytour *n.* friar authorised to beg 16.296

lynage *n.* lineage, relations 3.26

lynde *n.* linden, lime-tree 2.152, 7.64

lyn-sed *n.* linseed, flax 9.51

lyte *adj.* little 2.140

lythe(n) *inf.* listen to, hear 4.92, 7.65, 8.77

maistres *n.pl.* masters (of divinity) 1.60, 12.2

maistrie, maistry *n.* force, mastery 4.89, 15.69, 15.106

make *n.* mate 10.8, 10.11, 10.25

males *n.pl.* bags 4.134

mal ese *n.* suffering 11.84

mamelede *pa.t.sg.* prated 10.99

manere *n.* manor, castle 5.114

mansed *pp.* excommunicated 16.171

marche *n.* district 16.171

mareys *n.pl.* marshes 10.39

mase *n.* confused turmoil of people 2.6

maundement *n.* commandment 14.15

maynprisen *inf.* bail out, release from prison 15.188

mayre *n.* mayor 6.62

mebles *n.pl.* possessions 9.113, 11.168

mede *n.* reward 5.81, 5.84, 10.14, 15.355

medlen *inf.* interfere 16.129

meke *inf.* introduce humbly 5.129

mendena(u)nt *n.* mendicant, beggar 1.60, 11.3; *pl.* 6.119, 8.50

mene *adj.* common, poor, low 1.20, 1.85

menne, men *n.gen.pl.* men's 3.29, 5.101, 7.16, 11.172

meritorie *adj.* necessary 6.8

merke *adj.* dark 2.1

merkenesse *n.* darkness 15.140, 15.180

merye *adv.* pleasantly 10.88

meschief *n.* trouble, distress, affliction 1.65, 6.119; **meschiefes, mescheves** *pl.* 6.123, 9.39, 9.62, &c.

mesels *n.pl.* lepers 6.119

meseyse *n.* distress 11.159

met *see* **mette**

meteles *n.* dream 11.4

meteth *pres.pl.* measure 2.174

mette *v.impers.pa.t.sg.* dreamt 1.9, 1.85, 7.67, &c.; **met** *pp.* 10.88

mette *n.* table-companion 11.55; *pl.* 11.41

meven *inf.* move; speak, argue 2.123; **meved(e)** *pa.t.sg.* moved, stirred 10.51, 13.110

mevynge *presp.* wandering 6.50

mo, moo *adj., pron.* more 6.111, 9.32, 11.152, &c.

mod *n.* mood, spirit 10.51

molde *n.* earth, world 1.65, 2.42, 6.112, &c.; **under molde** on earth 14.37

monyal(e)s *n.pl.* nuns 3.76, 13.74

moo *see* **mo**

mores *n.pl.* moors 10.39

mornyng *n.* mourning, misery 9.64

ymorthred *pp.* murdered 9.102

mortrewes *n.pl.* mince-stews 11.47, 11.67, 11.100

morwenynge *n.* morning 10.19

moskeles *n.pl.* mussels 6.34

mot, mote *pres3sg.* may 15.208, 15.209; must 9.30, 14.40, 16.188; **mote** *pres.pl.* may 5.38; must 5.87; **mowe(n)** *pres.pl.* may 6.116, 9.52; must 9.47; **most** *pa.t.sg.* might 11.11

mote *inf.* argue a law-case 2.173

mowe(n) *see* **mot**

muche *adj.* big 7.68

myht(e), myghte *pa.t.sg.* might 1.39, 2.146, 2.150, &c.

myhtfull *adj.* powerful 2.170

mynte-while *n.* very short while 10.71

myres *n.pl.* swamps 10.39

mysliked *pa.t.sg.* was displeased 12.28

myspened *pp.* misspent 3.93

myssaide *pa.t.sg.* slandered, reproached 15.349

mywen *inf.* stack hay in heaps 3.14

nay *prep.* near 15.289

nedede *pa.t.sg.* was necessary to 12.9

nelde *n.* needle 2.154

nelle *pres.sg.* will not 2.123

nemne *inf.* name 2.21; **nempned(e)** *pa.t.sg.* named, nominated 4.164, 16.206; **nempned** *pp.* 16.211

nere *adv.* never 3.40

nere *pa.t.subj.* were not 2.115

ner-hande *adv.* nearly 11.1

nerre *comp.adv.* nearer 14.17

neyynge *presp.* drawing near 16.150

no *conj.* nor 4.64

no *pron.* none 6.63

noble *n.* gold coin 16.82

noon *pron.* no, none 7.115

nother, noythere *conj.* neither, nor 2.99, 2.177, 4.190, &c.

nouthe *adv.* now 4.69, 6.103, 10.46, &c.

noythere *see* **nother**

nuye *inf.* harm, hurt 5.102

nyme *inf.* take, seize 12.9, 13.85; *pres.pl.* 6.11; **nymeth** *pres3sg.* 10.112

nype *n.* sharp cold 15.167

o *prep.* in, on 11.19

o *adj.* one 13.20, 13.21, 13.28, &c.

obediencer *n.* monastic officer 3.91

of *adv.* off 4.47, 4.163

on *prep.* in 1.51

on *pron.* one 2.108

on(e) *adj.* one, unanimous 4.79; alone 2.169, 12.88, 15.315

ones *adv.* once 4.133, 9.117, 10.13, &c.

or *conj.* ere, before 2.70, 15.73

other *conj.* or 2.174, 4.107, 4.136, &c.

other-while(s) *adv.* at other times, now and then 3.50, 12.38, 12.81

over-hoveth *pres3sg.* hangs over 15.174

over-tulde *pa.t.sg.* overturned 16.4

ownere *adj.* own 13.76

palle *v.* beat 13.50

panes, pans *n.pl.* pence 6.31, 9.25, 9.106, &c.

parail *n.* apparel 7.116

paramours *n.pl.* lovers, mistresses 4.84

paraunter *adv.* perhaps 6.120, 9.104, 16.184

parceles *n.pl.* separate parts 14.51

parled *pp.* spoken 15.278

parschiens *n.pl.* parishioners 4.18

parten *pres.pl.* share, 1.79; **parteth** *pres. pl.* 8.65, 11.116

party(e) *n.* part, passage 11.157; **moste party** majority 2.7

paschte *pa.t.sg.* dashed, struck down 16.50

passeth *pres3sg.* oversteps, transgresses 2.98; *pres.pl.* surpass, go beyond 11.116

paye *n.* pleasure; **to paye** to his satisfaction 5.71, 5.74, 10.32

pelour *n.* accuser 15.39

pere *n.* equal 13.90

pere-jonettes *n.pl.* early pears 9.81

persaunt *adj.* piercing 2.154

persoun *n.* parson, priest 16.309; **persones** *pl.* 1.81

perye *n.* jewelry 8.10

pesecoddes *n.pl.* peascods 9.81

pilours *n.pl.* thieves 9.109

pistul *n.* epistle 12.6

pleyneth *pres.pl.* make complaint 4.18; **pleyned** *pa.t.pl.* 1.81

plighten *pa.t.pl.* agreed (to go) 1.47; **yplyht** *pp.* bound 4.106

plonte *n.* plant 2.149

yplyht *see* **plighten**

pokede *pa.t.sg.* pricked, urged on 2.129

pomade *n.* apple-juice 15.408

pors *v.imp.* purse up 9.25

portatif *adj.* light, easily carried 2.154

portinaunces *n.pl.* appurtenances 12.46

postles *n.pl.* apostles 6.58

potages *n.pl.* soups 11.47

potel *n.* half-gallon-potful 4.186

pouke *n.* devil 13.50

pous *n.* pulse 14.21

preisede *see* **preyse**

prente *see* **preynte**

prest *adv.* quickly 15.271

presteste *superl.adj.* promptest 5.76

preve(n) *inf.* prove, demonstrate, put into practice 8.39, 9.34, 11.99, &c.; **preveth** *pres3sg.* 11.88, 11.136; *pres.pl.* 9.37, 9.61; **proveden** *pa.t.pl.* 4.84

preynte, prente *pa.t.sg.* looked, nodded 15.19; winked, gave the nod 11.121

preyse *inf.* appraise, value 4.167; **preisede** *pa.t.pl.* 4.171

priketh *pres3sg.* rides 16.99; **prikynge** *presp.* 15.9

prisoun *n.* prisoner 15.59; **prisones** *pl.* 6.12, 12.39

prive, pryve *adj.* private, secret, intimate 16.65, 16.314; **priveeste** *superl.adj.* 13.98

priveliche *adv.* secretly, quietly 11.150, 13.101

properliche *adv.* suitably, in accord with his proper role 11.153

propre *adj.* fine 13.101

proveden *see* **preven**

pryve *see* **prive**

pryvete *n.* secret 10.102; **pryvatees** *pl.* 13.5

pur *prep.* for 7.11

putour *n.* lecher 4.70

putrie *n.* lechery 4.84

putten *pa.t.pl.* set; **putten hem in** set themselves to 1.27

puttes *n.pl.* pits, dungeons 6.12

puyr(e) *adj.* pure, sheer, very, absolute 6.125, 8.56, 8.65, &c.; *adv.* very 13.103

pyement *n.* spiced drink 15.408

pyk *n.* staff 5.61

pykares *n.pl.* pilferers 3.17

pyonie *n.* peony-seed 4.146

pytaunce *n.* dish, course at a meal 11.61

quentyse *n.* trickery 15.296

questes *n.pl.* inquiries 8.22

queynte *pp.* quenched, destroyed 15.390

quod *pa.t.sg.* said 2.12, 2.44, 2.72, &c.

quok *pa.t.sg.* quaked 15.64

quor *n.* choir 3.60

quyk(e) *adj.* alive, live 11.12, 15.64, 15.257

quykie *inf.* quicken, make alive 15.390

quyte *inf.* pay, pay for 11.12, 15.390

radde *see* **rede**

rape, rappe *v.imp.* hasten 3.102; **rappe adoun** hasten about 2.91; **rapede** *pa.t.sg.* 14.32

rape, raply *adv.* quickly 4.170, 14.3

rappe *see* **rape**

rat *pres3sg.* reads 9.70; **ret** *pres.pl.* read 9.112

rathe *adv.* soon, early 8.89; **rathest** *superl.adv.* soonest, above all 6.88, 9.83, 12.67

reaumes *see* **reume**

reche *v.imp.* care 6.41, 10.67; **recheth, reccheth** *pres3sg.* 10.109, 12.32, 15.2

recheles *adj.* free of care 15.2

rede *v.* advise, direct, tell 2.172, 3.102, 10.78, &c.; **redde, radde** *pa.t.sg.* 5.1, 11.52

regneth *pres3sg.* extends 16.331

regrater *n.* retail-dealer 4.130

reherce *v.imp.* repeat, recount, go over again 4.62; **rehersed** *pp.* 10.96

relyed *pa.t.sg.* rallied, took heart again 16.98

renkes *n.pl.* men 10.58, 10.63, 15.299

rennynge *presp.* running 15.168

repreveth *pres3sg.* proves wrong 15.152

resonede *pa.t.sg.* argued with 10.55

ret *see* **rat**

reule *n.* narrow space between bed and wall 6.19

reume *n.* realm, kingdom 3.74, 8.59; **reumes, reaumes** *pl.* 2.91, 7.104

reuthe *n.* pity 2.172, 4.210, 5.31, &c.

reve(n) *inf.* rob 13.122, 15.307

rewe *n.* row; **by rewe** in order 2.22

rodded *pp.* grown red 11.108

rode *n.* cross 15.51, 15.56, 15.259

ronde *n.* round, rasher 6.88

ropere *n.* rope-maker 4.174

roteyed *pp.* rutted 10.18

rotye *inf.* rot 13.60

rounned *pa.t.pl.* whispered 4.170

roweth *pres3sg.* dawns 2.114; **rowed** *pa.t.sg.* 15.127

rug *n.* back 6.84

russet *n.* coarse red cloth 12.15

rybaudes *n.pl.* sinners 5.31

rybaudrye *n.* ribaldry 1.45

yryfled *pp.* robbed 14.45

rypereve *n.* man in charge of reapers 3.15

sad *adj.* steadfast 3.90; true, righteous, just 7.31; sober, serious 7.117; **saddest** *superl.adj.* truest 7.49

salve *n.* soothing ointment 16.120

sauter *n.* psalter 8.25, 8.51

sawes *n.pl.* sayings 15.152

sawt *n.* assault 16.167, 16.250

scale *n.* shell 9.6

schrewes *see* **shrewe**

schupte *see* **shapeth**

scrippe *n.* pilgrim's bag 5.61

secte, sekte *n.* form, likeness, species 5.11, 5.18, 5.22

seel *n.* seal 1.77; **selys** *pl.* 1.67

sege *n.* place 16.260, 16.263

segg(e) *n.* man 9.11, 9.22, 10.69, &c.

segge *v., inf.* say 3.48, 9.93, 10.46; **seggeth** *pres.pl.* 10.114

seke *adj.* sick 16.273

sekte *see* **secte**

selcouthe *adj.* marvellous 10.49

selcouthes *n.pl.* marvels 10.46

selde *adv.* seldom 1.22, 12.71, 12.76, &c.

selys *see* **seel**

semblant *n.* appearance 7.117

semyvyf *adj.* half-dead 14.10

sennes, senne *prep., conj.* since 8.55, 16.137, 16.190, 16.272; *adv.* then, afterwards 4.143

serk *n.* shirt 2.99

serven *inf.* serve (in church) 3.12; **yserved** *pp.* satisfied 4.178

sese *inf.* cease 16.57

seth *(conj.)* *see* **sith**

sethe *(n.pl.)* *see* **sithe**

sethe, sethen *adv.* then, afterward 5.6, 5.11, 5.26, &c.; since then 12.71

sette *inf.* plant 5.67

settynge *n.* planting 1.23

sewe(n), suewen *inf.* follow, accompany 10.15, 10.52; look after, tend 5.68; **sueth** *pres.pl.* follow, accompany 1.46; **sue** *imp.* 9.27; **sewede, suede** *pa.t.sg.* 14.34, 16.76

sey, yseye *pp.* seen 10.114, 12.64

shapeth *pres3sg.* makes, determines 2.158; induces 6.2; **shop** *pa.t.sg.* made (to), prepared 10.118; **schupte** *pa.t.sg.* prescribed 16.256

sheltrom *n.* body of troops 15.291

shende *inf.* destroy 15.335; **shente** *pa.t.sg.* 16.48

shene *adj.* bright 15.453

sheteth *v.imp.pl.* shoot 15.291

shette *pa.t.pl.* shut 5.131

shollen *pres.pl.* shall 13.96

shon *n.pl.* shoes 3.18

shop *see* **shapeth**

shrewe *n.* rogue, villain, evil-doer 4.71, 4.209, 5.142, &c.; **schrewes** *pl.* 8.26

sib, syb, sybbe *adj.* related, kin 5.159, 5.161, 5.170, &c.

sighte *see* **syhed**

sikerere *comp.adv.* more securely 9.11

sikerly *adv.* truly, certainly 7.26

sithe *n.* time 7.23; **sithes, sythe(s), sethe** *pl.* times 1.98, 4.215, 7.31, 13.17

sith(e), sythe, seth *conj.*, *prep.* since 1.62, 1.82, 3.40, &c.

skil, skyle *n.* reason 11.136, 13.84; **skilles** *pl.* well-reasoned arguments 10.2

sle *inf.* slay 4.5

sleuthe, slewthe *n.* sloth, idleness 1.46, 6.99

sley *adj.* cunning 16.113

sleyliche *adv.* by cunning 4.5

sleythe *n.* trick 15.165; *pl.* 4.5

smauhte *pa.t.sg.* smelt 4.201

smerte *adv.* sharply, sorely 10.115

smyt *pres3sg.* strikes 10.115

so *conj.* as 10.59, 10.74, 14.18

sode *pp.* cooked 6.89

somdel, somdeel *adv.* somewhat, to some extent 5.71, 15.8

sond *n.* sand 10.7

sooth *see* **soth**

sorfeten *inf.* surfeit, live to excess 10.59

soth(e), sooth *n.:* truth 2.122, 3.92, 5.126, &c.; **for sothe** truly, indeed 4.135, 5.124

soth *adj.* true 6.2

sothly, sothliche *adv.* 2.47, 5.71, 5.90, &c.

sotil *adj.* clever 15.54

sotiled(e) *pa.t.sg.* schemed 15.332; skilfully made up 4.87

sotiltees *n.pl.* subtle plots 9.100

souche *inf.* devise, plot 9.100

souhteres *n.* shoemaker's wife 4.149

soutares *n.pl.* shoemakers 3.72

sovereynliche *adv.* above all, principally 10.74

spedde *pa.t.sg.* prospered, fared 9.131

spene *inf.* spend 3.28, 8.77, &c.

spille *inf.* die, be destroyed 8.43

spille-tyme *n.* time-waster 3.28

spores *n.pl.* spurs 15.10

stere *inf.* stir, move 14.9

steryng *n.* movement 7.36

stounde *n.* time, little while 7.64

stryk *v.imp.* stride 5.105

stuyves *n.pl.* stews, brothels 16.110

styhlede *pa.t.sg.* did the arranging 11.40

stynte *v.imp.* stop, tarry 5.104

sue, suede, sueth, suewen *see* **sewen**

sull(e) *inf.* sell 4.123, 4.164, 9.78; *imp.* 9.24

sulve *adj.* own 5.136; *pron.* self 13.96

sundry *adj.* separate 15.232

suppriour *n.* sub-prior 4.51

swelte *inf.* die 4.27; *pa.t.pl.* died 16.55

swonken *see* **swynke**

swowe *inf.* swoon 4.27

swynke *inf.* work 1.36, 1.53, 5.67, &c.; **swonken** *pa.t.pl.* 1.23

swythe *adv.* very 1.28; quickly 4.209

sybbe *see* **sib**

syhed, sighte *pa.t.sg.* sighed 13.16, 15.92, 15.273

syke *adj. as n.* sick man 14.16

syker *adj.* certain 16.205; **sykerest** *superl.adj.* safest 3.39

sykeren *inf.* promise faithfully 5.66

sylinge *presp.* sailing 15.340

synege *inf.* sin 4.143, 5.6, 9.100, &c.; **synegeth** *pres3sg.* 7.23, 7.25, 7.26

sysour *n.* juryman 16.111

sythe(s) *see* **sith(e)**

take *inf.* take; give 2.52; arrest (criminals) 2.96; **tok** *pa.t.sg.* gave 14.29; **ytake** *pp.* taken 9.8

teme *n.* theme, text 11.82

tene *n.* suffering 2.166, 9.114

tene *inf.* trouble, injure 11.160; **tened** *pa.t.sg.* vexed, annoyed 16.69

tene *adj.* ten 2.105

termyned *pp.* determined, given judgment on 2.93

teyen *inf.* tie, bind 2.92

than *adv.* then 4.41

that *rel.pron.* what, who that, he who 1.24, 1.39, 2.130, &c.

the *pron.2sg.acc.* thee 2.22, 2.24, 2.37, &c.

thenke *v.* think; intend 2.21

thenne, then *conj.* than 2.114, 2.144, 2.188, &c.

thennes *adv.* thence 2.70, 5.17, 16.156

ther(e) *adv.* where 2.114, 2.121, 2.131, &c.

thewes *n.pl.* habits, manners 4.39

this, thyse *adj., pron.* these 1.24, 2.196, 3.41, &c.

tho *adv.* then 2.54, 2.107, 2.112, &c.; when 10.94

tho *adj., pron.* those 1.18, 1.44, 1.45, &c.

tholye *inf.* suffer 14.60; **tholed(e)** *pa.t.sg.* 11.73, 11.84, 15.138; **tholed(en)** *pa.t.pl.* 9.65, 15.74

thorlede *pa.t.sg.* pierced 2.171

thorpes *n.pl.* villages 1.86

thorw *prep.* through 2.25, 2.31, 2.63, &c.

thridde *adj.* third 13.50

thromblede *pa.t.sg.* stumbled 4.195

thus-gates *adv.* thus 12.23

thyse *see* **this**

til *prep.* to 2.133, 4.86, 5.8, &c.

titerares *n.pl.* tattlers; **titerares an ydel** idle tale-mongers 16.249

to *conj.* till; **for to** until 5.95

to *adv.* too 12.71, 16.309

to *prep.* to; as; **to nonne** who is a nun 4.26

to-broke(n) *pp.* broken, maimed 6.39, 7.85

to-cleve *inf.* be cleft asunder 15.113; **to-cleef** *pa.t.sg.* was cleft asunder 15.62

tofte *n.* hill 2.12

togederes, togyderes *adv.* together 1.47, 2.38, 2.53, &c.

to-grynt *pres3sg.* grinds up 8.62

togyderes *see* **togederes**

tok *see* **take**

tokene *n.* password 5.126

to-quasche *pa.t.sg.* shook 15.64; **to-quasch** *pa.t.pl.* shattered in pieces 15.257

tore *adj.* torn 4.101

to-rof *pa.t.sg.* was split open 15.63

toted *pa.t.sg.* looked 13.53

travayle *n.* work 6.92

travayleth *pres3sg.* labours 11.126

treden *pa.t.pl.* mated 10.37

trewes *n.* truce, peace 15.460

triacle *n.* sweet remedy 2.147

trinen *inf.* touch 15.87

trolled *pp.* traipsed about 15.331

trowe *v.* believe 1.15, 2.145, 3.49, &c.

troyledest *pa.t.2sg.* deceived 15.318

truyfle *n.* trifle, nonsense 15.150

tulye *inf.* till 15.109

tulyers *n.pl.* tillers 1.90

tweye, tweyne *num.* two 4.107, 4.151

tyd *adv.* quickly 16.4

tydy *adj.* honest 15.331

ytynt *pp.* lost, wasted 3.93

uch *adj.* each, every 6.56, 10.5, 10.69, &c.

uchon *pron.* each one 4.20

Umbletee *n.* Humility 5.153

umbywhile *adv.* from time to time 4.183

underfonge *pp.* received 5.160

undernome *pp.* rebuked 16.1

under-shored *pp.* propped up 13.47

unhardy *adj.* cowardly 15.86

unhende *adj.* ill-mannered 16.136

unkunynge *adj.* ignorant 11.16

unlouke(n) *inf.* undo, destroy 15.266; spread 6.83

unnethe *adv.* hardly 16.140

unsaverly *adv.* with an unpleasant taste 11.49

unspere *inf.* unbar, open 15.269;

unspered *pa.t.sg.* 15.89

untidy *adj.* indecorous 16.69

upholderes, uphalderes *n.pl.* second-hand dealers 4.161, 9.78

uppe *prep.* upon 9.90

vanne-warde *n.* vanguard of an army 3.58

vouchen-saf *pres.pl.* guarantee 3.49

wage *inf.* engage, pay wages to 16.219; *pres.pl.* 16.209

waggede *pa.t.sg.* shook 13.109

wagyng *n.* rocking 7.34

walkeres *n.pl.* fullers (of cloth) 1.89

walnote *n.* walnut 9.5

wang-teeth *n.pl.* 'cheek-teeth', molars 16.141

wanne *adj.* pale 4.206

wanyeth *pres3sg.* wanes 7.44

war, ywar *adj.* aware, ready, made wary 4.46, 7.114, 8.63, &c.

warde *v.* guard 13.42

watschod *adj.* with wet feet 15.1

ywax *see* wexe

waye *inf.* weigh 4.108; weye *pp.* 2.175

wayke *adj.* weak 3.23

wayte *inf.* look for, seek 4.106; waytede *pa.t.sg.* 1.16

waytynge *n.* looking 4.75

wayved *pa.t.sg.* drove 16.118

webbe *n.* weaver 4.119

webbesteres *n.pl.* weaving-women 1.89

wedde *n.* pledge; to wedde as a wager 15.30; leyde to wedde mortgaged 3.73

wede, wedes *n.pl.* clothes 4.75, 10.61, 16.161

wederes *n.pl.* storms 9.50

weldeth *pres3sg.* possesses 8.10, 8.72

wele *n.* wealth, happiness 9.69, 9.96

welkene *n.* sky 15.247

wem *n.* stain, uncleanness 15.135

wende(n) *inf.* go 2.130, 2.132, &c.

wene *v.* think, believe 6.10, 10.32; *imp.* 15.195; weneth *pres3sg.* 12.21

wernare *n.* warren-keeper 4.150

werre *n.* war 15.237, 15.456, 15.457

wexe *v., inf.* grow 4.22, 9.42; ywax *pa.t.sg.* 4.209

wey(e), wye *n.* man, creature 4.3, 5.39, 9.121, &c.

weye *see* waye

wham *rel.pron.* whom 2.43, 5.50

wher(e) *conj.* whether 13.54, 13.57, 15.73

white *pres3sg.* grows white 12.49

whoder *adv.* whither 5.59

wiht(e), wyht(e) *n.* man, person, creature 6.56, 7.4, 7.6, &c.

wilde *adj. as n.* wild creatures 10.41

wille *n.* wish; at my wille as I wanted 4.11

wilneth *pres3sg.* wishes 2.85, 5.79; wilnede *pa.t.sg.* 15.4

wirdes *n.pl.* fortunes, destiny 9.69

wisse(n) *inf.* direct, guide, advise, instruct 5.59, 5.80, 7.6, &c.; wisseth *pres3sg.* 10.75, 11.20; wissede *pa.t.sg.* 2.71

wist(e) *see* wyte

with that *conj.* provided that 8.91

witte *see* wyte

witterly, wytterly, witterlich(e) *adv.* truly, for certain 1.11, 2.71, 3.37, &c.

wokes *n.pl.* weeks 13.134

woketh *pres3sg.* soaks, softens 12.49

wol *pres3sg.* will; wishes 15.427, 15.431; wollen, wolleth *pres.pl.* will 1.36, 13.60; wolde *pa.t.sg.* would wish 16.221; wolden *pa.t.pl.* wished 14.60

wolleward *adj.* wearing only a garment of rough wool 15.1

wombe *n.* belly 1.57, 4.226, 11.92

wonderwyse *adv.* in marvellous fashion 2.126

wone *n.* custom, habit 12.38

woned *pp.* accustomed 16.320

woneth, wonyeth *pres3sg.* dwells 2.59, 5.59, 5.79; *pres.pl.* 6.23; **woned(e)** *pa.t.sg.* 1.18, 3.1

wones *n.pl.* dwelling-places 1.18

ywonne *pp.* won, obtained 9.95

wonyeth *see* **woneth**

worchyng *presp.* working 1.21

wormes *n.pl.* snakes 10.9

worschipe *n.* honour, respect 3.75, 4.40

worthen *in₁.* become 8.24, 8.88; **worth** *pres.sg. & pl.* shall be, will be 2.185, 9.55, 12.43, 14.42

wose *n.* ooze, slime 9.89

wost, wot *see* **wyte**

wrake *n.* strife 15.456

wrathe(d) *pa.t.sg.* angered, grew angry 2.26, 4.46

wreke *pp.* revenged 15.431, 16.154

wrethe *n.* anger 4.65

wriht *n.* carpenter 10.32

wye *see* **weye**

wyht(e) *see* **wiht**

wyhte *adj.* strong, active 11.172

wynkyng *presp.* half-asleep, in a dream 1.11

wyste *see* **wyte**

wyte, ywyte *inf.* know 5.79, 7.124, 10.90, &c.; **wot** *pres.1 & 3sg.* 3.1, 5.126, 6.10, &c.; **wost** *pres2sg.* 7.71; **wot, wyteth** *pres.pl.* 2.122, 6.68, 9.21; **wiste, wyste** *pa.t.sg.* knew 3.37, 6.7, 7.4, &c.; **wist** *pp.* 15.210

wyte *v.* blame 15.352; **witte** *pa.t.sg.* 2.30, 4.11

wytterly *see* **witterly**

yaf *see* **yeve**

ye *int.* yea 13.81

yede *pa.t.sg.* went 1.41, 4.205, 11.151, &c.; **yedest** *pa.t.2sg.* 5.18; **yeden** *pa.t.pl.* 4.79, 7.112, 10.8, &c.

yeepliche *adv.* eagerly 12.45

yef *see* **yeve**

yelde *inf.* pay back 12.86

yerne *adj.* quick to grow 16.109

yerneth *pres3sg.* hastens 12.45

yes *n.pl.* eyes 4.194, 12.49, 13.49, &c.

yeve *inf.* give 6.56; **yeve nat of** care nothing for 16.105; **yef** *imp.* give 9.25, 9.26, 11.145; **yeveth** *pres3sg.* 6.8, 8.27, 11.20; **yaf** *pa.t.sg.* 2.15, 11.18, 16.8; **yeven, geven** *pa.t.pl.* 4.162, 16.250; **yeve** *pp.* 4.227

yliche, ylyche, iliche, ilych, liche, ylyk *adj.* like, alike 4.81, 5.5, 5.10, &c.; *adv.* alike, equally 13.22, 13.62

ympe *n.* grafted tree 13.6

ynow(e) *adj.* enough, in plenty 15.291, 16.199

yut *adv.* yet, still 2.166, 3.94, 4.54, &c.

ywis *adv.* indeed 10.92